Lana and Lilly Wachowski |

Contemporary Film Directors

Edited by Justus Nieland and Jennifer Fay

The Contemporary Film Directors series provides concise, well-written introductions to directors from around the world and from every level of the film industry. Its chief aims are to broaden our awareness of important artists, to give serious critical attention to their work, and to illustrate the variety and vitality of contemporary cinema. Contributors to the series include an array of internationally respected critics and academics. Each volume contains an incisive critical commentary, an informative interview with the director, and a detailed filmography.

A list of books in the series appears at the end of this book.

Lana and Lilly Wachowski

Cáel M. Keegan

UNIVERSITY
OF
ILLINOIS
PRESS
URBANA,
CHICAGO,
AND
SPRINGFIELD

© 2018 by the Board of Trustees
of the University of Illinois
All rights reserved
1 2 3 4 5 C P 5 4 3 2 1
∞ This book is printed on acid-free paper.
Printed and bound in Great Britain by
Marston Book Services Ltd, Oxfordshire

"Interview with Lana Wachowski" appears by permission of Lana Wachowski.
Frontispieces: Lana Wachowski (courtesy of Karin Winslow Wachowski); Lilly
Wachowski (courtesy of Lilly Wachowski).

Library of Congress Cataloging-in-Publication Data
Names: Keegan, Cael M., author.
Title: Lana and Lilly Wachowski / by Cael M. Keegan.
Description: [Urbana, Illinois] : [University of Illinois Press], [2018] | Series:
    Contemporary film directors | Includes bibliographical references,
    filmography, and index.
Identifiers: LCCN 2018022138| ISBN 9780252042126 (hardcover : alk. paper) |
    ISBN 9780252083839 (paperback : alk. paper)
Subjects: LCSH Wachowski, Lana, 1965– —Criticism and interpretation. |
    Wachowski, Lilly, 1967– —Criticism and interpretation.
Classification: LCC PN1998.3.W33 K44 2018 | DDC 791.4302/33092273 dc23
LC record available at https://lccn.loc.gov/2018022138)

ISBN 978-0-252-05087-9 (ebook)

Contents |

Acknowledgments ix

SENSING TRANSGENDER | 1

Trans Opt: Received 6

"You Can Believe What You Feel": *Bound* 8

Ecstatic Passages: *The Matrix* 23

Redpill 47

Adventures in Transreality: *The Animatrix* 48

Heroic Ends: *The Matrix Reloaded* and *The Matrix Revolutions* 55

Revolutionary Guises: *V for Vendetta* 65

Sensorial Assault 75

Fixed Races: *Speed Racer* 76

Escaping History: *Cloud Atlas* 87

Speculative Heights: *Jupiter Ascending* 100

Epilogue—Event Horizon: *Sense8* 106

INTERVIEW WITH LANA WACHOWSKI | 131

Filmography | 153

Bibliography | 161

Index | 177

Nothing could have happened without the cinema, and so this work is indebted to Lana and Lilly Wachowski's sensational artistic vision. I am equally grateful to Karin Winslow Wachowski and the Ravenswood Kinowerks staff, especially Dave Walsh, for their generous support of this project. I thank Meredith Freeberg for the delicious vegan lunch, and Xoe Wise for saving me when my phone crashed. Appreciation to Belinda McClory for helping me finally understand Switch. Heartfelt regards to the cast, crew, and production team of *Sense8* season two, with special thanks to Lana Wachowski, James McTeigue, Aimee Allegretti, and Ethan Stoller for their warmth in sharing their work.

Jennifer Fay and Justus Neiland were inviting and insightful editors whose suggestions and questions were crucial to the growth of this book. Danny Nasset was a superb guide who ensured this project found its final form. Cindy Wu and Girish Shambu gave gracious feedback at the proposal stage, and Alex Wescott provided expert bibliographic and indexing support. Kristine Krueger at the Margaret Herrick Library supplied archival materials, and a grant from the Center for Scholarly and Creative Excellence at Grand Valley State University (GVSU) provided key funding. Kevvo Gierman made the images beautiful. Gratitude to my interlocutors at the National Women Studies Association, Society for Cinema and Media Studies, American Studies Association, WisCon, the Trans° Temporalities Conference, the D.C. Queer Studies Symposium, Stanford University, the University of Turku, Sonoma State University, and especially the International Trans° Studies Conference, whose spirited engagement gave the ideas here life and shape.

This book was inspired by Susan Stryker's lecture "Disciplinary Kinship," delivered in 2013 at the Queer Method symposium at the

University of Pennsylvania, and would not exist without her intellectual example and caring mentorship. Early encouragers included Matthew Holota, Diana Elrod, Geoffrey Babbit, Kathryn Cowles, and Anna Creadick. Jason Laker and Caetlin Benson-Allot were indispensable sources of advice. My Queer Theory students were an enthusiastic sounding board, pushing me to an ever finer grasp of the material and my own thoughts. A wonderful cluster of colleagues and friends opened around the project, including Laura Horak, Eliza Steinbock, Roxanne Samer, micha cárdenas, C. Riley Snorton, Lotta Kähkönen, Alexis Lothian, Ramzi Fawaz, Chris Straayer, David Getsy, Don Romesburg, Cam Awkward-Rich, Sheila Cavanagh, Deborah Shaw, Trish Salah, Jack Halberstam, and Dana Polan, all of whom provided feedback and encouragement throughout the research and writing process. GVSU colleagues Patrick Johnson, Lindsay Ellis, Jae Basiliere, and Karen Zivi gave stalwart motivation. Guin Thompson and Durwin Talon came through in the clutch, lending me their laserdisc player (which is still in my office and may never be returned). The lovely Anne Statton put me up in Chicago more times than I can count and showed me around with native zeal. I think we ate the whole city. To Laura, Roxanne, and Matthew especially, thank you. You were my deepest readers and made sure I kept finding what it was I had to say.

To my wife, Marla Wick, I owe every word. This book is for her and for Violet—the ones who make it real.

Lana and Lilly Wachowski |

Sensing Transgender |

It is the day after the Orlando Pulse massacre, and Lana Wachowski is wearing black.

I am as well, but this is purely coincidence. Rushing with the jittery nerves of a young researcher to the *Sense8* shoot in Gary, Indiana, that June morning, I had not given much thought to the news or to the color of my T-shirt. When Wachowski arrives to begin the day's work, I see immediately that she has: her black shirt is emblazoned with a pink triangle accompanied by what I learn are the words "Who's next?" in Cyrillic. When I inquire about the language, Karin Winslow Wachowski (Lana's wife) explains to me that Lana and her sister, Lilly, wore these shirts during their press tour for *Jupiter Ascending*. Knowing they would be screening the film in Russia, the siblings and longtime codirectors used the shirts and matching armbands to protest the anti–gay propaganda law instated there in 2013. Today, in the wake of the forty-nine murders at Pulse,[1] "Who's next?" carries a renewed and terrible resonance. Quietly observing the crew's unfolding preparations, the previous day's news slowly catches my heels. I struggle to make sense of this scene in the face of such disaster for others.

As the sun begins to arc high, we throng into a ruined Gothic Revival church, its ceiling caved in by fire. From behind my dust mask and hardhat, I watch Wachowski work for hours with the cast, crew, and codirector James McTeigue in beating, early summer heat. More than anything, I am struck by the remarkably *touching* nature of her process: She touches everyone—blocking the cast members, physically guiding her Steadicam operator from behind while looking past his shoulder into the camera. She stands side by side with an actor for nearly an hour, asking for a short set of lines again and again until the necessary emotion pours out. She even touches me in a brief hug. I notice how by simply wearing the shirt, Wachowski has wordlessly brought the violence of the massacre into the shoot as an acknowledgment and a challenge: these are the stakes of being queer, trans, and of color in America; *this is what we are imagining against*. In response, the shoot feels full of a fierce sorrow, a desiring strain toward something else. The next day, as I drive back to Michigan, tears will unexpectedly roll down my face.

In a 2012 interview with the *Village Voice*, Lana Wachowski reflects: "Growing up, fantasy was the world as the world would never be, and science fiction was the world—filled with problems and ideas—as it *could* be. We were always drawn more to science fiction than to fantasy. . . . But for [Lilly and me], science fiction has always been an experimental genre." At the very bottom of the same interview, she touches again on this utopian theme: "I believe inherent in any artist's work is an optimistic truth. That the very creation of art is in itself an act of optimism" (Abrams). Across these statements, Wachowski expresses a faith in the subjunctive quality of art to lead us elsewhere:[2] if by art we come to sense differently, we might then arrive at another world. This is the thesis and animating philosophy behind all of the Wachowskis' cinema. It is also a conviction uniquely attuned with transgender experience. Transgender phenomenology is rooted in the desire to make perceivable a feeling of gender that others have not (yet) witnessed. In his enthralling exploration of transsexual self-narration, *Second Skins*, Jay Prosser grounds transgender subjectivity in a felt imaginary that seeks "to recover what was not." Sensing something others miss, the trans imaginary summons its own literalization, "its externalization, its substantiation, in material flesh" (84–86). We could say that "trans" describes an inherently subjunctive relation to what is considered real, to what can be commonly sensed. To survive, transgender people have had to craft imaginaries that sustain our desire to become, our belief that we might come into perception differently. *The world, and me, as we could be.*

Transgender studies grows out of this same desiring resistance to dictated form. In her foundational 1992 essay, "The *Empire* Strikes Back: A Posttranssexual Manifesto," Sandy Stone called for a new transgender movement that would cast off the linear medical model imposed on transsexual identity, reconstituting trans not as a gender but rather as a *genre* "whose potential for productive disruption of structured sexualities and spectra of desire has yet to be explored" (231). An entire field concatenated in the quarter century following Stone's call, shifting the focus of inquiry from transgender objects to "trans" as an analytic for "linking the questions of space and movement . . . to other critical crossings of categorical territories" (Stryker, Currah, and Moore 12).[3] Today transgender studies describes *trans°* not as an identification, but as a force characterized by unpredictable flows across discrete forms, a "paratactic" that enacts the prepositional "with, through, of, in, and across" animating vitality itself (Hayward and Weinstein 196). Like science fiction, trans° is about how *what could happen* haunts the present, asking us to consider where elements in reality might lead if permitted to reach (Shaviro, *No Speed Limit* 2). The sticky fingers of the fronded asterisk (°) are the speculative lines of transgender's felt imaginary, sensing outward with faith to realize new contacts. Trans° thus marks the "capacity to transform one reality into another" (Stryker, Foreword x)—how transgender phenomenology necessitates a ceaseless navigation between the tangible and intangible, perception and sense, the real and the imaginary.

Toward what might a trans° cinema reach? Cinema, of course, is a technology that orders our senses. As the phenomenological turn in film theory illustrates, cinema filters our pre-discursive affects so that they might become collectively, cognitively grasped.[4] Much like gender, cinematic technology thoroughly permeates our idea of the real, such that we cannot access "the world" except through its language. Cinematic schemas arrange our shared expectations of what might happen at any moment—our *common sense*.[5] We occupy a cinematic reality,[6] cinematic bodies. Early on, transgender studies noted the similarities between transsexual and cinematic material processes. In an essay published in 2000, Susan Stryker writes:

> The transsexual body . . . presents critical opportunities similar to those offered by the camera. Just as the camera offers a means for externalizing and examining a particular way of constructing time and space, the transsexual body—in the process of its transition from one sex to another—renders visible the culturally specific mechanisms of achieving gendered embodiment. It becomes paradigmatic of the gendering process, functioning, in Sandy Stone's words, as "a meaning machine for the production of ideal type." ("Transsexuality" 592)

As Stryker points out, medical transition is indeed similar to cinematic technique. As in editing or montage, surgical transition rearranges the flesh to tell a coherent story about gender. Yet the relation she notes between cinema and trans is a *reciprocal* one: Cinema is also "like" transgender phenomenology. Cinema, like trans° ideation, is a medium for expressing unrealized bodies. Both animate what is latent, distilling from the world forms that have been present all along, if imperceptibly. Both seem to reveal something new, even as they disclose only what idealities and objects preexist them. Cinema is, obviously, durational—the medium perhaps most capable of representing our sensorial life *as it feels to happen*. Like experience, cinema must move temporally forward. Its technicity is inherently speculative, opening a horizon in the text's unfolding that is much like gender transition itself.[7] The *couldness* of both cinema and trans° is a faith that other affects might come into perception. At the outset, we never know what will emerge. Inside the transitional space of cinema/cinematic space of transition, *we become subjunctive*—feeling in the dark toward what might happen, marking how we've become by touching back on our prior selves.

A popular trans° cinema would thus have speculative designs on cinematic reality. We could envision such a cinema as a desiring confrontation with what might be commonly perceived—a sensing at the far edges of preexisting cinematic forms, arising from within a trans° imaginary. Such a popular cinema would appear to not *yet* exist. Operating within the marginalized realm of independent queer/LGBT cinema, trans-authored films have rarely received widespread distribution, viewership, or critical attention. Or so we might presume. When

Lana and Lilly Wachowski came out as transgender women, they retroactively altered the history of transgender cultural production, disclosing how trans-authored work is *already located* at the very center of our cultural imaginary.[8] There is little theoretical context for such a revelation. Until recently, studies of transgender and cinema have largely been of transgender *in* cinema, the literature overdetermined by a focus on representation, casting, and performance.[9] To make sense of the Wachowskis' work as popular cinema produced *by* transgender creators requires alternative praxes, through which we might revisit objects to "tell new stories about things many of us thought we already knew" (Stryker, "(De)Subjugated" 13). Such "revisitations" (Keegan, "Revisitation") are an inherent part of trans° meaning-making, crucial to how trans lives demand recognition in "new" genders and sexes that are not new—how trans people make ourselves perceivable in reverse. Lilly Wachowski invites such a return when she states, "There's a critical eye being cast back on Lana's and my work through the lens of our transness, and this is a cool thing, because it's an excellent reminder that art is never static" ("Lilly Wachowski Shares").

To read trans° in the Wachowskis' cinema would therefore be to meet transgender *as it is practiced*,[10] deploying the heuristics by which trans subjects bring what has only been sensed into shared recognition. Below I argue that the Wachowskis' cinema establishes a common cinematic language for sensing beyond gender's dictated forms, and therefore "the real," that can be periodized to the turn of the twenty-first century. Mutually constitutive with the historical formation of transgender as a phenomenological form and a politics, their cinema can be understood as an aesthetic record of how mass cultural forms are interlaced with the "genealogy of trans cultural production" (Steinbock, "Towards" 401). I thus employ the asterisk in trans° to denote the potential of this convergence where cinema, theory, history, politics, and autoethnography collide to concatenate a trans° *imaginary of the senses* that has appeared, unnoticed, at the heart of our cinematic reality. Oriented by the same desiring tense that drives the Wachowskis' cinematic vision, I seek to turn trans° studies toward the sensorial field as activated by film theory, leaping this limit to produce a cross-pollinating discussion of the directors as inventors of a popular trans° cinema. In what follows, I trace how their work has established trans° as a millennial and speculative mode for imagining against and beyond dominant representations of gender, race, space, and time, discussing how their films invent a trans° aesthetic that strains against the colonial foundations of modernity. The asterisk marks the subjunctive roving across and through vitality I follow in their cinema, leaping from affects toward new perceptions.

"Sensing transgender" is thus both call and response, a delayed yet faithful exchange (the response is belated) that relates how over their two decades of filmmaking, the Wachowskis have offered us a trans°cinematic engagement with the world. An aesthetic, a method, and an intervention, *sensing transgender* names how the Wachowskis' cinema animates trans° as a sensing beyond the representational edges of popular media forms. Their work offers a sustained confrontation with the sensorial borders that demarcate cinematic reality, illustrating how involuntary forms of common sense fix the perceptible field ("perception" being a derivation of "to seize" or "take entirely"). The aesthetic I seek to describe therefore treats cinema *as if it were gender itself*—disrupting, rearranging, and evolving the cinematic sensorium in the same manner that trans° disrupts, rearranges, and evolves discrete genders and sexes. Sensing transgender does not search the Wachowskis' cinema for transgender identity alone, but instead reads trans° in its moments of speculative expansion—where it confronts what makes sense. My transgender life and body cannot be extracted from such a process, from how the cinema I work upon here has helped me come to my (own) senses. To *sense transgender* is therefore not merely to sense *for* transgender, but to sense *as* transgender: a desiring feeling for what might otherwise go unrealized. Drawn from my own affective engagement with the Wachowskis' cinema, my retrospective method here traces a mutually constitutive process by which I and the work have *become trans°* together, over time.[11] Having learned how to arrive in reverse, I turn to my sensorial archive to recover what was not (yet) perceived.

Trans Opt: Received

Messages are sometimes received later.

There are those that come as an accretion of brushes with something impalpable over time. The message isn't in any one *then*, but is a happening that has been happening all along. Say we revisit the same object repeatedly. Perhaps because we do not know how to pay attention to ourselves, we think, "Ah, this again"—forgetting all the while that in each encounter we are not the same. We cannot help these conditions, of course. Our affects live inside time. History, culture, and information are working upon us in ways we cannot tell. "Our senses are evolving" (*Sense8*). After many encounters, in what can seem like a flash of intuition, the object may appear differently. A sense that has been blocked from our own perception at last impinges (Massumi 30–32). We come to a new sense of the situation in which we are situated. These excavated sensations might subsequently aid us in finding a way we couldn't find until then. We learn how to believe what we feel, receiving a message we could not at first seek. An option is received.

Such retrospective practices are as fundamental to film analysis as they are to trans° phenomenology. I am not going to claim that *Bound* (1996) and *The Matrix* (1999) made me transgender, as possible as that ever may have been. I am going to argue that somewhere between these films arriving, their invitation to sense differently, and myself in this moment, trans° happened, keeps happening, in the relation between myself and the world. If we are not yet sure what "transgender" cinema is, or who is permitted to make such definitions, then perhaps this is as decisive a claim as any: a trans° cinema would support such happenings. Appearing as they did in the period of transgender's categorical imagination (Valentine), *Bound* and *The Matrix* offer sensorial encounters that we might today recognize as the start of a distinctly trans° popular cinema. That these films are, presumably, the earliest studio-produced, feature-length works by transgender directors demands historicization.[12] However, by inviting us to revisit their art through this new frame, the Wachowskis have also opened a different engagement with their archive, requiring of us the same speculative leap their work uniquely encourages. In their coming-out statements to the press, both Lana and Lilly Wachowski suggest that transgender self-actualization has been co-constitutive with their own cinematic imaginations—their own desires for "(an)other world(s)" (Baim; "Lana Wachowski Receives"). Unrecognized without the necessary conditions, *Bound* and *The Matrix* now make transgender sensationally, historically perceivable. They show us how when trans° arrived, it was cinematic.

"You Can Believe What You Feel": *Bound*

The Wachowskis' official film career begins with *Bound*, a neo-noir thriller financed by producer Dino De Laurentiis after he was impressed with their script for *Assassins*.[13] While it is the first major motion picture to be written and directed by transgender women, *Bound* was not and still is not considered an important film of the New Queer Cinema wave, garnering only one line in B. Ruby Rich's 2013 reassessment of the movement (*New Queer Cinema* 113). The film continues to be critically ignored in contrast to the breakout texts of the period, such as *My Own Private Idaho* (1991), *Poison* (1991), *The Watermelon Woman* (1997), and *Boys Don't Cry* (1999), which have become classics of twentieth-century queer cinema. The reasons for *Bound*'s comparatively flat reception and lack of institutionalization as "queer" by film critics and theorists are complex. In contrast to many experimental New Queer Cinema films, *Bound* is heavily inspired by classic noir and its genre conventions, which the directors intentionally invert to deliver a queer-yet-happy Hollywood ending.[14] *Bound* also enjoyed industry financing, which disqualified it from consideration under Rich's 1992 definition of the New Queer wave as an independently funded movement (Kalin et al.). But perhaps most importantly, in 1996 the Wachowskis were not recognized as queer and transgender filmmakers. Credited on *Bound* as "The Wachowski Brothers," they were not yet recognizable contributors to the archive of queer and trans cinema.[15] Rather than the groundbreaking film it was and continues to be, *Bound* was received as a highly "stylized" (K. Kessler 14) exercise in the noir genre, its lesbian content legitimized as realistic due to technical direction from "native informant" Susie Bright (Noble 35). Lana Wachowski raised the issue of *Bound*'s historical delegitimization while accepting the 2014 Equality Illinois Freedom Award, asking, "How come no one ever mentions *Bound*? I'm curious about that."

Wachowski's call to revisit *Bound*'s historical significance after her public coming out requires a retrospective analysis that shifts our awareness of what might be "already inside" (White 197) the producers and therefore the text. There is a glaring need to revisit the Wachowskis' cinema—especially *Bound*—as work created by queer transgender women who have been marginalized from New Queer Cinema history and its critical contexts. This has been due as much to the initial definition of the movement as it is to B. Ruby Rich's recently expressed presumption that "trans is the new queer" (*New Queer Cinema* 271) and the ongoing, stubborn misrecognition of the Wachowskis as straight male directors. There has been little if any attention to the Wachowskis' role as groundbreaking artists who have created some of the world's first transgender-authored mainstream film and television. This lack has persisted well past Lana's public coming out in 2012; she and Lilly are still cited as "The Wachowski Brothers" in film scholarship appearing as recently as 2014 (Hobson; McDowell; Whissel). Such studies, which tend to examine the ongoing impact of the Wachowskis' visual innovation, are incomplete in their oversight of the sisters as both queer and transgender cultural producers. A reassessment of their work and its crucial position in the history of queer and transgender image-making is therefore part of a larger project—one in which film scholars might use trans° studies methods to "desubjugate trans forms of knowing" (Steinbock, "Towards" 401), revealing trans cultural production from within the body of formal, priorly established knowledges (Stryker, "(De) Subjugated"). In the case of the Wachowskis, such an endeavor must begin with a return to their debut film, *Bound*.

To revisit *Bound* two decades after its release is to be shocked by what is one of the most radical depictions of queer women's sexuality ever to emerge from Hollywood. Not written and directed by "two brothers from Hollywood" as the film was billed at the Frameline Film Festival ("20th Anniversary" 15), *Bound* is suffused with subcultural lesbian integrity signs that at its release were unreadable to mainstream audiences. *Bound*'s accomplished deployments of both camp and the visual iconography of lesbian erotics mystified queer scholars who could not "come to terms" (K. Kessler 13) with their "embarrassing attachment" (Noble 30) to a lesbian film made by what appeared to be a pair of straight men. *Bound* confounded queer film critics precisely because what it offers viewers (the feel and look of authentic lesbian sex) and its perceived authorship were constructed by prior film criticism to be at cross-purposes: in a cultural moment when lesbian directors were presumed to be "more capable" (Berenstein 131) of depicting lesbian sex than others, *Bound* and the Wachowskis themselves were consistently rendered in contemporaneous film scholarship as either exceptional (how is this film *doing this*?) or unreadable (who *are* these directors?). *Bound*'s reception thus was, and continues today to be, limited by essentialist and cissexist frameworks for what counts as a "lesbian film."

Obviously informed by *Double Indemnity* (1944) and *Treasure of the Sierra Madre* (1948), *Bound* explores gender, class, and desire as constructed by cinematic genre, capitalizing on the inherent undecidability of noir (Dyer 90) in a remarkably queer exploration of its lead characters' mutual desire for freedom. Occurring almost entirely in three apartments (two of them adjoining), the film's closed domestic setting and low-key, chiaroscuro luster suffuse it with a sensation of entrapment and barely suppressed eroticism. Its look is fittingly described in the laserdisc commentary by Bright as "wet." Like Violet's painted lips and Corky's leather jacket, its surfaces are glossed and dewy, communicating the expectation and humidity that come with close quarters. Multiple fluids—water, blood, liquor, paint—play important symbolic and narrative roles in the film, while its subdued palette of grays, blacks, purples, and muted reds leaves our eyes wanting. *Bound*'s sexually magnetic sense of anticipation, its wetness, is Corky and Violet's shared desire to bind through senses and across surfaces, a desire that the film's walls foreclose. This longing for movement, for a way "out" through a shared wish to change reality (Oliver and Trigo 192), will press against and eventually burst the text's architectural container, spilling the two women into an uncharted future.

Thematically, *Bound* is perhaps most interested in how one thing might pass for another, how under the force of assumption or control, suppressed sensation and meaning can hide in plain sight—only to leap into vital expression under the right conditions. The film therefore capitalizes on noir's inherent assertion that separations between seeming opposites (straight/gay, feminine/masculine) are in themselves unreliable fictions (Fay and Nieland 154). In what sometimes seems like a meta-commentary on the Wachowskis' own identities, the film constantly asks audiences to sense beyond appearances and question dominant modes of visualization. Surrounded by men who see only what they already believe (Oliver and Trigo 191), both Corky and Violet are repeatedly misrecognized: Corky as a man, Violet as straight. These misreadings—one gendered, the other sexualized—place trans° and queer modes of knowing otherwise about gender and sexuality in conversation. Resisting the modern insistence on singular and incompatible L/G/B/T identity positions, the film demonstrates how trans and queer subjectivities are interdependent, interlaced around foundational questions of identification and desire. Appearing in the moment when the first recession of AIDS signaled a new future for queer life, *Bound* explores triangulated points of feminist solidarity across lesbian, queer, and trans° modes of utopian imagination that have subsequently eroded in the identity wars of the twenty-first century.[16] It thus returns us to a historical point at which "queer" and "trans" emerged through one another in a mutually constitutive process of aesthetic elaboration and political demand. This mutuality, which *Bound* references in its title, is a mapping of the potential for an as yet unrealized, collective trans°feminist imaginary.

In *Bound*'s opening shot, a sort of birth begins—a fitting sequence for the first moments of a first film. Initiating us into the vertical organization of the film's space, the camera sweeps behind and then over the film's title, *BOUND*, which is blocked out on a carpeted floor in ominously shadowed capital letters. The frame then wipes into blackness, dropping us into a downward shot that slowly traces a long umbilicus. Designed to disorient the viewer,[17] the "unfixed" scene (Hanson 3) withholds our directional relation to the surrounding architecture, which remains defamiliarized (fig. 1). We are not yet sure whose senses we are inside. Slowly the camera glides past hat boxes and pairs of pumps, and we realize that we are upside down in a closet—a wealthy woman's closet—in which we are suspended, inverted, off the ground. The umbilicus is a pull chain in extreme close-up.[18] A woman's voice repeats, "I have this image of you inside of me, like a part of me. . . . I want out. . . . Like a part of me," and these words echo like memory. Lying far below us on the white carpet, a small and fetal figure emerges, revealed from underneath the inverted rows of hanging clothes. This is Corky (Gina Gershon), our hero. Or, rather, she is one of our heroes. Violet (Jennifer Tilly) is the other.

We have begun in a moment of temporal suspension that will lead into extended flashback, only to flash forward and then surpass this point again later in the film. We are hearing Violet's voice as she is recalled inside Corky's memory. Violet's abusive husband, Caesar (Joe Pantoliano), has beaten Corky, tied her up, and tossed her into Violet's closet after realizing that the two of them are having an affair and are planning to steal $2 million of the Mafia's money from him. Corky is literally bound

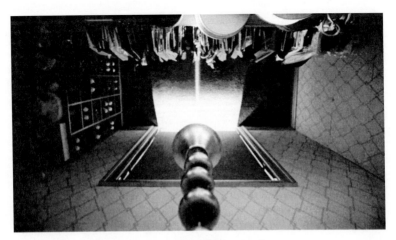

Figure 1: Ambiguous interiors: doing time in
Violet's closet.

and gagged inside this closet—the camera is careful to pan across her roped wrists and ankles—an immediate nod to the film's title. The word "bound" references the illicit sexuality associated with BDSM (cited by the film's visual interest in leather) but also the ways we are bound to others through affects and social forces beyond our control. Like the characters in the film, we too are bound to categories, spaces, and relations that are difficult to exit. Over the course of the film, Corky and Violet will become bound to each other by a shared sense of possibility outside of what is considered life for women. *Bound* thus reverses the fatalism of classic noir: our heroes are bound to each other and to the future (Oliver and Trigo 203) rather than to the past. By binding to each other through a shared utopian resistance to the logics of gender and sexuality, they will sever ties to the family, to labor, and to the law. They will steal the Mafia's money, kill Caesar, and escape—alive and together.

A closet, of course, is not a neutral space to begin a film about lesbians. Queer theory has established the closet as a repressive architecture, fundamental to modern epistemology, that expresses its power through silence (Sedgwick). In narratives of LGBQ identity, the closet is therefore traditionally a space where things are suppressed (Brown). However, *Bound*'s opening closet is exaggeratedly deep, its contents disclosed to us in a languid tracking shot that suggests its interior might also serve as a reservoir for new meaning. While a closet references the familiar coming-out trope of LGBQ narrativity, a closet is also gendered—representing the snare of assigned sex and its required public performance through clothing. Before we ever meet her, we know Violet is playing the femme fatale role that her wardrobe promises. This architecturally loaded moment in Violet's closet thus gestures simultaneously at sexual repression and the burden of assuming a gender (Salamon). The camera lowers us into an interstice where queer and trans° modes of critique are enfolded. We see Corky *in* Violet's closet, her obvious butchness enclosed within Violet's high-femme attire—an oblique allusion to the "trapped in the wrong body" trope that structures dominant narratives of trans identity. We hear Violet repeating her desire for escape and her feeling of Corky inside her. It is as if Violet's desire to get "out"—of the Mafia and its business, of her marriage and its heterosexual labor, of the building where Caesar has her ensconced—has created the sensorial space of the film itself, into which we are now being drawn.

Violet's desire has led Corky to end up exactly where Violet imagined her: "Inside of me." The echoed line repeats an earlier moment that we will recognize when it arrives later in the film's looped temporality. After they have sex for the second time, Violet tells Corky, "I have this image of you inside of me, like a part of me," a line evoking the same-sex structure of lesbian erotics but also the feeling of gender dysphoria, in which subjective gender is carried as a psychically internalized image—sensed but impossible to see.[19] In this crucially positioned line, *Bound* illustrates how both trans° and queer aesthetics are interlaced modes of feeling and desiring gender—the gender of others or the gender of the self—that are not entirely distinct. Violet's line might be whispered to a same-sex lover or to that correctly gendered self that the trans subject sustains internally. In a trans° reading of *Bound*, Violet's line "This image of you, inside of me" connects fantasy with both pleasure and emergence, describing how trans subjects might sense ourselves across the process of gender transition.

This queerly trans° scenario in the closet is the temporally and spatially central moment in *Bound*. Everything happens either in flashback before this point in the closet or immediately afterward. Narrative time is bent inside Violet's closet, layered much like the shelves of clothing, stacked upon itself like fabric. We have entered a box that symbolizes heteronormative control of sexuality but also a form of "pleated time" (Carter) that mimics the folded-back temporality of gender transition, in which memory is experienced across differentially gendered versions of the self. The geometry of this moment resembles a set of Russian nesting dolls: Corky is inside Violet's closet, and Violet's voice is inside Corky, but inside Violet's internalized voice is the desire for Corky, which Violet felt before she had ever seen Corky in their building's elevator. Inside Corky's memory, Violet voices her dissatisfaction with her life and world—*I want out*. Inside Corky, Violet is dysphoric, longing and waiting for escape from the meaning of her gender, which is domestication and heterosexual labor. Corky, we will learn, is Violet's transition. Time lies coiled like a spring, waiting to expand and transport them both beyond the limits of the film's horizon.

If its opening shot aestheticizes the space of the closet as a fundamentally shared architecture of queer and trans oppression, then *Bound*'s following sequences propose the cultivation of shared desire as a way to sense beyond that space's meaning. In the closet we hear Violet's echoed fantasy of escape. In the ensuing flashback, Corky arrives to make it real (Oliver and Trigo 194), becoming the axis through which this fantasy might materially manifest. As we jump backward in time, we enter the moment when Violet and Corky first meet in the building's elevator, yet another boxed space. Violet's sunglasses initially frame Corky as an image—the part of her that is both missing and anticipated. When she removes the lenses and meets Corky's flat stare, she performs a femme invitation that collapses the space between them and shows how it might be traversed through desire. What was a scene demonstrating class and gendered difference becomes the beginning of something else: Violet, herself named for the color of light at the very edge of the visible spectrum (Wiess 2), models a different way of looking that asks Corky to sense what is not apparent. Thus begins Violet's seduction of Corky, which is an expansion of the space of the film toward an impossible future. When Violet brings coffee to Corky as she renovates the apartment next door, Violet says, "My pleasure," in pointed response to Corky's thanks. *Bound* is about Violet's capacity for fantasy, her capacity to imagine pleasures that should not exist. Corky manifests through Violet's desire for something that was not yet tangible but still sensed as an incipience—an approaching possibility of more. Violet's fantasy about *getting out*, about finding herself in another place, is therefore the transitory affect that drives the film's entire plot.

The basis of eroticism between Violet and Corky is not only their mutual desire for each other but also their shared desire for an outside to gender-as-architecture. When Violet first approaches Corky with her plan to steal from Caesar, they discover that each has spent an equivalent amount of time in captivity: Corky has been incarcerated for five years; Violet has been married to Caesar for the same five years. Separated by distance and their class positions, they have nonetheless had the same spatial experience inside patriarchal time. The prison, the Mafia, and the building where Violet is trapped all share the same carceral shape; they are "all part of the business." What gets the two hot is not just the body, then, but the new potential for embodiment that committing a crime might produce. When they first begin plotting their caper, Corky says to Violet that crime is "like sex"—the pleasure of exiting the structure of the law, which is also the structure of gender, is erotic. How the camera performs in *Bound*, how it floats over and passes above the opening titles as well as the characters and sets, produces a constant suggestion that an outside to the law of gender exists. The hottest possibility imaginable, the *new life* Violet yearns for, does indeed arrive. By end of the film, Corky and Violet will achieve this outside, which emerges in the form of a utopian trans°feminist flight.

If a trans° aesthetic traverses unanticipated passages or bindings across times and spaces, then *Bound*'s camera movement illustrates this transitive promise. In a 1998 interview with Nat Whilk and Jayson Whitehead for *Gadfly*, Lana and Lilly Wachowski discussed the inspiration for *Bound*'s many overhead shots:

> GADFLY: Another thing I noticed when I was watching the film was that a lot of the camera shots start very high and are shot down at the characters. Was there a special reason for that?
> LANA: Uh, we think it looks cool? (laughs) You know, when we started the movie, we had the idea that the opening shot was going to be this down-shot of a closet where you really wouldn't know where you were exactly and you'd be trailing along this pull chain which would be giant in the foreground, and we wanted foreground and background, and we wanted the closet to seem like it was a hundred feet deep. And that sort of overhead feeling carried over into the rest of the movie.

LILLY: It's about the boxes people make of their lives as well, and we wanted actually to be able to see that stuff.

GADFLY: Was that the philosophy of the movie? You know, you mentioned all those great directors of the past. They all had a philosophy. What was your philosophy?

LANA: We think that not only gay people or queer people live in closets. Everybody does. We all tend to put ourselves into these boxes, these traps. And so what we tried to do is we tried to define as many of the characters through the sort of trap that they were making out of their lives. Getting out of the closet was meant to take on a bigger meaning than just the typical gay meaning.

The closet that *Bound* begins in, then, should not be read only as a "homosexual lesson" (Wallace 375) but also as a comment on how the structure of identity encloses us, how it creates new closets (Butler, "Imitation" 309). The danger of closed forms is an early and repeating theme in the Wachowskis' work. One of Lana's earliest published writings was a 1991 issue for Epic Comics titled "Closets." *Bound*'s shared walls, traveling sounds, and depictions of marital and janitorial labor give us the sensation of capture and indicate the ubiquitous violence it conceals. The overhead camera shots, moving high above an architecture in which the characters are horizontally trapped, suggest an exterior to the gendered paradigms—heterosexual marriage, organized crime, incarceration and parole—that confine Violet and Corky. This vantage suggests a way to sense beyond the limited perceptions unfolding below us, a perspective that Corky and Violet gain as they are romantically drawn together in utopian desire. In a particularly overt example, the camera pans over them as they speak to each other on the phone from opposite sides of the same wall,[20] pressing their hands together as if to push through its materiality. "I know," Corky says to Violet in an admission of their unnamed affinity. "It's why I'm still here." What is this power of affect to alter form, this moving beyond the entrapment of gender and its constrictions, other than trans°?

Reading desire in *Bound* returns us to the psychoanalytic convolutions of contemporaneous lesbian spectatorship theories, which often involved the speculation of a symbolic trans° position generated by viewing film through the camera's male gaze.[21] If in classical film theory lesbian desire can only appear as either (1) wanting to be a man or

(2) wanting to be the other woman (Traub 117–18), then this dualistic structure inadvertently renders the "wanting to be" affect of trans subjectivity inherently suspect. Theorizations of lesbian viewing pleasure that attempt to shore up the same-sex homology of lesbian identification as not "wanting to be" anything but rather merely "wanting a woman" render cross-gender ideation as only ever the suspicious result of phallocentricism. Trans° therefore haunts lesbian film theory, if only as an imposed obstacle to a purely lesbian encounter with the image. The very conditions of film studies at the time of *Bound*'s release thus demanded its trans° aesthetics be overlooked in favor of a reading for "real" lesbian sex. This required scholars and viewers to reduce Violet's affect to an expression of sexual desire alone rather than a more capacious sense that gender might feel and signify otherwise. Violet wants Corky and therefore desires to become cognizable as what Corky might want, but she also wants what Corky's gender offers: newness, transit, mobility.

Bound thus draws the trans° presence haunting lesbian signification into perception by pluralizing female genders so that each woman's gender becomes the point of fantasy and potentiality for the other. The film thus alerts us to the foundational instability between sexual orientation and gender identity: do I sexually desire that body, or do I want *to be* that body?[22] Corky and Violet—one butch, one femme—do not obviously share a gender or sexuality. Violet refuses to be marked as a lesbian (she rejects the identificatory emblem of Corky's labrys tattoo), while Corky is only tenuously recognized as a woman, often slipping over the edge of the frame (Wallace 384) as if—like Caesar—the film itself struggles to picture her. Does the femme desiring the butch constitute same-sex desire or the desire to occupy a different gender? Extraordinarily, *Bound* does not force us to disambiguate or hierarchize lesbian and trans° modes of desire. Instead, it reveals how a queered lesbian erotics might simultaneously offer points for trans° ideation. Desire between Violet and Corky is at once same-sex desire and the desire for a different gender's fugitive, expansive possibilities.

When Violet first seduces Corky, she convinces Corky of her desire by asking her to stop looking and feel another way. Gazing into Corky's eyes, she says, "You can't believe what you see, but you can believe what you feel," and places Corky's hand between her legs, where she is ostensibly wet, sexually open. The shot twins them in facing profile (fig. 2), mirroring how the line works in double register—an indication not only of sexual arousal but also a longing to be recognized *by feel*. Violet's femme body is materially sincere in its desire for Corky as erotic object. Despite her heterosexual practice, she cannot lie: she feels wet to the touch, anticipating the feel of Corky. When Corky later questions Violet's allegiance by pointing out her marriage, Violet rejects Corky's implication that she cannot actually be a dyke, redefining her sex with Caesar as "work." Violet's identity is not determined by her look, she insists, but by her desire—which she invites Corky to sense and believe in. Violet's desire thus conscripts Corky; Violet even tops Corky in the film's gorgeously crafted sex scene.[23] The film thus presents a reversal of traditional noir in that the femme fatale does not suffer for her wanting. Instead, her longing for something else creates the sense, the fluidity or flex, through which Corky enters. Violet wants queerly, she plots, and she gets away with it. Violet's desire structures the narrative, opening paths for the camera to travel and Corky to feel along.

Believing the "feel" of Violet asks us to inhabit Corky's touch but also Violet's feeling—her senses, which are other than her appearance communicates. Violets wants Corky to sense that she is appearing as something in practice—a submissive wife, a heterosexual woman—that she does not feel subjectively. Her desire to be felt rather than merely

Figure 2: Permission to enter: believing Violet's feel.

seen is both a physically queer urge and an affective demand that cites the trans experience of passing in an assigned gender. *Bound* imparts the feel of gender dysphoria by nesting it inside a lesbian erotic, allying queer and trans° desires in their shared vision of an escape from misrecognition and entrapment. If the "transgender look" is formally constructed as one "divided within itself" (Halberstam, *Queer Time* 88), then *Bound*'s lesbian-trans-queer *feel* is one in which wanting and wanting *to be* mutually constitute one another as desiring positions. The film references this utopian mesh of desires repeatedly in shots that ask us to feel two feels at once. Immediately after promising "You can believe what you feel," Violet places Corky's finger in her mouth, an opening that asks her to abandon sight and feel Violet's inside, even as Violet feels Corky entering her. Later, in the 180-degree shot that tracks their first sex, Violet manually penetrates Corky in turn, simultaneously placing her fingers in Corky's mouth—a doubling of the opening/entering motif from their first physical contact. The doubled feel transforms how Corky looks. She turns over on the mattress and says, "I can see again." Visuality has been restored, but with a difference: if Violet can feel how Corky looks at her (the objectification as straight that Violet refuses), then Corky learns to see how Violet feels (Violet's gender performance does not disclose her affect). This queer oscillation across lesbian and trans° modes of sensation asks us to believe in gendered desire's realness, even as it demands that we look beyond gender's outward display.

The rich surfaces of desire exchanged between Violet and Corky increase their capacity for utopian imagination, leading to a passageway out—an escape from both patriarchal control and eventually from the space of film. They plot their crime together, and it works. In the final few minutes, Corky struggles out of the closet and cuts her bindings, leading Caesar into a trap. Violet then kills him, shooting him repeatedly in the chest. They hide the body, and the Mafia assumes Caesar stole the money. Neither Corky nor Violet are caught. They don't die, and they stay together. This alone makes *Bound* one of the most radical lesbian films ever to emerge from Hollywood. Violet and Corky's queer conspiracy pushes against noir form, asserting a communal future the genre would traditionally deny. The film's accelerating future tense aligns the women in a manner that is greater than any difference between them: *I will, you will, we will*, they tell each other. Sensing differently together, both Corky and Violet know that overcoming oppression means dreaming the future could be otherwise, subjunctively "imagining the present injustice as already past" (Oliver and Trigo 204).

However, the proposed color of futurity as *Bound* progresses is, literally and undeniably, white. Throughout the second half of the film, multiple white fades move us forward (Wallace 379) in the timeline so that as Violet and Corky gain their escape, the film lightens in an intensifying manner that posits whiteness as an ability status subtending their physical movement into the opening future. The penultimate sequences of the film propose this white temporality as a potential emancipation from the film's suffocating environment: Violet guns Caesar down in a lake of white paint poured from the tubs where Corky has hidden the money. A white dissolve then transports us into the next scene, where an apartment (we're not sure which one) stands vacant and repainted the same white. A tracking shot walks us through the light-drenched, deserted apartment and into the closet where the film ostensibly began—now empty and freshly painted, awaiting a new tenant. The camera lingers on the white space inside the closet for a moment before cutting to the final exterior sequence, where Violet and Corky will appear in the light together for the first time. Implicit whiteness thus threatens to become the narrative spillway for Corky's and Violet's line of flight,[24] the unspoken identity they might both occupy despite their differing genders and class positions.

Below in the street, Violet and Corky are about to make their escape. Violet is wearing her sunglasses from their initial meeting in the elevator, reminding us of the invitation in her first look at Corky. As they approach each other, Corky is dollied toward Violet in an effect that stresses the sexual magnetism and utopian orientation they share. The space between them is finally, permanently collapsed. No more boxes. Muted colors have peaked into brilliance. A brand-new cherry red truck purchased with the stolen Mafia money waits at the curb for their getaway. The light, however, reveals something new that changes what we, like Corky, might see: Jennifer Tilly's Asian/First Nations heritage, until now lingering just below the film's visual address, suddenly leaps closer to perception (fig. 3). The film's progressive whiteness, which has subsumed Caesar's autocratic body, thus makes possible an accompanying mode of discovery: *Bound* is not necessarily the story of "two

Figure 3: The queer/trans* femme and the racial trace: Violet is unfixed.

white dykes" (Noble 31). Violet's racial trace stalls the film's accelerating whiteness, returning us to her earlier line: "You can't believe what you see." Much like her closet, Violet cannot be visually fixed.[25]

Bound's liberatory promise thus delivers us to the trembling edge of racialization, where Violet shimmers as an image (Steinbock, "Shimmering Images"), bound in liminality—not an "utter impossibility" (Noble 34), but a set of tremulous potentials (queer/trans*/raced/femme) that lies submerged at the very heart of the film. If Violet remains unfixed—not coming to rest as white, as lesbian, or as cisgender—then so too is the future she desired into reality, which the film's last moments turn backward to conjure from the dark.

Inside the idling truck, Corky leans over to Violet in the passenger seat and asks, rhetorically, "You know what the difference is between you and me, Violet?"

"No," says Violet.

Corky pauses, then revokes her question. "Me neither." She slides on a new pair of sunglasses, mirroring Violet's image as Tom Jones's 1971 hit song "She's a Lady" begins to play. If both differently gendered and raced women share a criminalized wish to escape from patriarchy, the film suggests, then there is indeed no crucial difference between them. This "no difference" is not equivalent to the white and cissexed sameness that many responses to *Bound* assert as its happy ending.[26] Corky and Violet do not need to be the same to share their unnamed, mutually fugitive urge. Rather, the scene permits their identities and desires to become both the same and different simultaneously (Oliver and Trigo 200). Whatever the difference might be between them, it goes unstated and unresolved, carried forward as an open possibility that gestures toward a mutual life outside the norms of sex, race, and gender. In a tight shot, their fingers interlace over a black and white blanket—an image citing both racial imbrication and the enfoldedness of lesbian, queer, and trans° utopian ideations (fig. 4).

In this last moment, the film reveals yet another obscured potential: Violet's fingernails, having passed for black through much of the film, are exposed instead to be a deep aubergine, a reminder that "the set of what appears is never perfectly closed" (Keeling, *Witch's Flight* 143). A final crane shot sweeps upward over the truck's dash, capturing the headiness of Violet and Corky's passionate kiss. Reciprocal cuts place us behind the truck as it squeals into motion, then facing it in reverse as it races directly at the camera in a static shot. The image cuts into blackness at the last instant. The end credits begin to pop up as Jones continues to croon.

Even as the film's queer and feminist contexts provide an ironic deconstruction of Paul Anka's sexist lyrics (What exactly *is* a lady, any-

Figure 4: Thick with the future: enfolded utopian relations.

way?), Jones's voice grants us a nostalgic return to the historical period immediately after Stonewall, when gay and black radical politics were not yet divorced, still linked in a shared vision for potential liberation. The song's chorus repeats, returning over and over to the same interstice of identification-as/desire-for where trans°, queer, and lesbian meet: "She's a lady . . . and the lady is mine." At its conclusion, *Bound* implies an interlocking utopian alliance between trans, queer, and lesbian women across race, auguring a trans°feminist destiny in which getting *to be* a lady ("she's a lady") and wanting *to have* a lady ("and the lady is mine") are reconciled as desires. These urges, the film asserts, are not opposed but are politically interdependent in their radical and feminist sense of an escape from gender as we know it. The two women's desire has, in its very unfixedness, opened up an unknown destiny that will not be like the past (Oliver and Trigo 204). *Bound's* final black frame turns against and swallows the film's last image, insisting on a future without asserting whiteness as that future's condition. Violet and Corky speed into the horizon of the film's dark cut, cruising for the utopia (Muñoz, *Cruising Utopia*) they dreamed up together, just over the edge of their world.

Ecstatic Passages: *The Matrix*

If *Bound* is the Wachowskis' most undervalued work, then *The Matrix* guarantees their indelible and continuing impact on film and media history. Its critical success and unfolding virality across global popular culture has fundamentally impacted the common themes, look, and techniques of mainstream film and television. Digital imaging innovations developed for *The Matrix* franchise (bullet time and virtual camera) have subsequently became industrialized by Hollywood (Rehak 27), permanently altering cinematic representations of time, space, and embodiment. Nearly twenty years after its release, film studies scholarship continues to revisit *The Matrix* series to extend already-rich discussions of its craftsmanship and its depiction of race (Hobson; Nama; Whissel), but the film franchise has also been widely analyzed for its exploration of postmodernity; its religious undertones; its transmedia platforming across movies, video games, and comics; and its representation of the virtual realities associated with the rise of internet culture.[27] Multiple studies situate *The Matrix* at a turning point, as a film that visually defined the advent of the twenty-first century, introducing a new multicultural utopianism and illustrating the approaching convergence of film production with video gaming and the internet with daily life (J. Clover, *Matrix*; Jenkins, *Convergence Culture*; Nakamura, *Cybertypes*). However, scholarship on *The Matrix* series and its immense cultural and aesthetic repercussions remains incomplete without a consideration of its production by transgender writers and directors.

The Matrix is the most influential media text yet created by transgender cultural producers. As a product of the millennial period, the film reflects the historical emergence of trans° as an analytic possessing a specific political and phenomenological relationship to dominant reality (Boucher 2)—a deconstructive stance toward the perceivable world that now permeates much of speculative cinema. As Lana expressed in the Wachowskis' appearance at DePaul University in 2014, when writing *The Matrix* she and Lilly were asking "how you interrogate reality and what reality is, and that led us into the entire philosophical spectrum of what the Matrix ended up being" ("Lilly Wachowski and Lana Wachowski"). Thematically similar to *Bound* in its concerns with imprisonment and misrecognition, *The Matrix* makes thrilling leaps in aesthetic design that bring the relativity of identity and embodiment, the traversal of defined space and time, and the futurist sensations of verticality and speed into new and spectacular perspective. While *Bound* explores the mutually constitutive relation between lesbian, queer, and trans identity positions, *The Matrix* disambiguates trans° from these other modes, delivering a fully articulated cinematic aestheticization of the trans° sensorium. To assert that *The Matrix* invents twenty-first-century trans° aesthetics is not to dismiss the multifarious interpretations of the film, but to highlight how trans° is an inextricable component of the conditions it thematizes: late capitalism, postmodernity, biopolitics, virtuality, and the proliferation of sensorial realities. Transgender is a phenomenon inherently bound up in these twenty-first-century developments not merely as an effect but simultaneously as a driver of how they are aestheticized and culturally understood.

The retrospective reading I seek here places *The Matrix* in conversation with *Boys Don't Cry*, the film commonly credited with the invention of a transgender cinematic gaze. Directed by lesbian filmmaker Kimberley Peirce and released the same year as *The Matrix*, *Boys Don't Cry* fictionalizes the real life of Brandon Teena (Hilary Swank), a trans youth who was murdered in Nebraska in 1993 after being publicly outed by the local newspaper. Canonized in the scholarship of queer film studies, *Boys* is considered a defining text of the New Queer Cinema era and the ur-text of late-twentieth-century transgender representation. J. Jack Halberstam has theorized the film as pioneering the "transgender look" (*Queer Time* 86), which he argues replicates the divided consciousness of the dysphoric transgender subject for the audience. Halberstam focuses on *Boys*' scene of forced genital exposure as the moment when Brandon's consciousness splits into two versions of himself, producing a traumatic fissure from which this look, "divided within itself" (88), arises. However, if the scene offers a moment of prosthetic transgender identification, it also reifies cissexist violence, grounding the transgender subject's perception of himself in the cissexist gaze (i.e., the investment in the realness, perceptibility, and meaningfulness of assigned sex) as it fractures Brandon's sex from his gender. What is made readable in the scene is not necessarily transgender subjectivity but the structure of cissexism itself, which demands that the sexed body is real and that Brandon's felt gender is imaginary. The scene's mechanics, which insist on the narrative possibility of only one body, make an end of Brandon's flow or "passing" (Aaron 94), anticipating his destruction.

Halberstam theorizes the transgender look as a prosthetic suture stitched in the shattering moment of Brandon's breaking, allowing cisgender viewers to look "with" the transgender subject at his own image. But this violent scene seems to occur at the expense of trans viewers, who are forced to endure its devastation as it quickly extends into Brandon's rape and murder. Halberstam's reading of *Boys Don't Cry* thus does not produce a theory of transgender image reception (Keegan, "Revisitation" 29); rather, we look at Brandon looking at himself in the manner he knows others look at him—a replication within Brandon of the cissexist gaze. Revisiting the film today, *Boys* does not appear to offer a trans-subjective viewing position, but instead establishes the cinematic language of cissexist abjection. *Boys Don't Cry* and *The Matrix* can therefore be viewed as two halves of a cultural dialectic arising around transgender at the turn of the twenty-first century: while *Boys* is concerned with establishing a representational language for transgender identification within classic cinematic grammar, *The Matrix* speculates beyond the temporal and spatial limits of cinematic reality, deconstructing the formal conditions that in *Boys* impose the trans subject's fragmentation and early death. This divergence in aesthetic strategies maps clearly onto the contemporaneous divide between liberal discourses of transgender identity and the more radically gender-abolitionist framework arising from within trans° politics.

Claiming that *The Matrix* invents a popular trans° aesthetic places transgender and the design of cinema production in historical conversation. While *Bound* is steeped in the mid-twentieth-century traditions of classic Hollywood, *The Matrix* and its sequels reflect a digital turn in cinema history toward "perceptual assault" (Ndalianis 2) that is concurrent with the late-twentieth-century development of transgender identification. The rise of transgender politics in the mid-1990s is wedded to the emergence of digital technologies—especially the internet and its virtual spaces—that connected disparately located trans individuals in networks while they simultaneously separated gender presentation from the physical body (A. Stone, *The War*). New forms of socialization and identification across virtual platforms allowed transgender populations to engage in gender experimentation without following the medically mandated path of diagnosis and surgical sex reassignment. Disrupting the linear narrative of transsexuality as a transition between discrete, preexisting sexes, transgender denaturalized the links between sexes and their culturally assigned genders, transforming both sex and gender into signs. "Transgender" is thus historically connected to digital innovations in technology—gaming, chat rooms, online dating, immersive digital worlds, and cinematic effects like the morph and bullet time—that produced new temporal and spatial encounters with the gendered body as the plastic effect of coding. In her 2008 work *Transgender History*, Susan Stryker notes this digital technicity of transgender:

> The current fascination with transgender also probably has something to do with new ideas about how representation works in the age of digital media. Back in the analog era, a representation (word, image, idea) was commonly assumed to point to some real thing, the same way a photograph was an image produced by light bouncing off a physical object. . . . A person's social and psychological gender was commonly assumed to point to that person's biological sex in exactly the same way: Gender was considered a representa-

tion of a physical sex. But a digital image or sound is something else entirely. It's unclear exactly how it's related to the world of physical objects. It doesn't point to some "real" thing in quite the same way, and it might in fact be a complete fabrication built up pixel by pixel or bit by bit—but a fabrication that nevertheless exists as an image or a sound as real as any other. Transgender gender representation works the same way. (26–28)

Here, Stryker describes how within postmodernity and its digital information systems, gender and sex have become radically open to interpretation, assertion, and rearrangement. No longer ontologically primary or biologically predetermined, the material body can no longer be presumed to serve as the basis for gendered subjectivity. Trans° is thus a relativity construct in which we recognize that all bodies, all fields, are in motion—in which the material is as constructed as the purportedly symbolic, and in which the symbolic can simultaneously be lived as the real. Trans° aesthetics thus posit a "transreal" (Blas and cárdenas) or "transworld" (Horton-Stallings 207–10) proliferation of the body and its senses over "multiple worlds, times, and realities," across which gender might flicker like a "shimmering mirage" (Blas and cárdenas 24, 39).

Transgender and its digital technicity concatenate at the turn of the millennium in the wake of transsexuality, a mode of identification represented in twentieth-century Western culture as analog. Operating through an industrial logic of cutting and amalgamation, the transsexual body attempts a constructed homology with the naturalized sex binary. The cinematic cutting of analog film in the process of montage resembles transsexual surgical transformation, suggesting a cinematic language of transsexuality that is expressed through "cuts in flesh or celluloid" (Steinbock, "Speaking Transsexuality" 132). Transsexual representation in twentieth-century film narrativizes this same cutting logic, often depicting the transsexual subject as a deranged slasher who seeks to either destroy or possess properly sexed flesh.[28] Digital filmmaking methods such as those pioneered in *The Matrix* build on these evolving associations between the trans body and the cinematic image: Digital video programs replace the chemical reactions of analog film with electronic signals, transforming portions of the image production process into code. Digital imaging therefore disrupts the presumed indexicality of analog film, drawing attention to the inherent gap between the cinematic image and its material referent

(Gunning, "What's the Point" 40). Transgender performs a similar move, further destabilizing the assumed "natural" link between sex and gender that transsexuality seeks to perform. The evolution of digital imaging from former analog processes thus analogizes the historical movement from transsexual toward transgender as a mode that prioritizes ideation over preexisting material forms. Lana Wachowski describes such a trans° aesthetic as illustrating how "knowledge has an actual materiality" ("Lana Wachowski Receives"), how what is only imagined can nonetheless be invited into perception. Mediating restlessly where analog/digital (J. Clover, *Matrix* 28), transsexual/transgender, and sense/perception impinge, *The Matrix* captures the shimmering excitation of trans° as it appeared at the heart of twenty-first-century popular cinema.

The Matrix series consists of four neo-noir science fiction action films combining references to *Neuromancer*, *Alice in Wonderland*, *The Wizard of Oz* (1939), *Ghost in the Shell* (1995), Jean Baudrillard's *Simulacra and Simulation*, and Plato's Allegory of the Cave with cyberpunk, anime, and kung fu genre elements.[29] I discuss *The Matrix* here separately from its sequels (one animated and two live action) as a threshold text, one that aestheticizes the historical emergence of transgender and instantiates a globally circulating, popular trans° cinema. The first and most acclaimed film of the series, *The Matrix*, recounts the story of Thomas Anderson (Keanu Reeves), a computer programmer who illegally data mines the early internet under the handle "Neo." Living in what appears to be the late twentieth century, Neo is contacted by a cell of hackers who reveal to him that his reality is in fact virtual: his senses are trapped within a neurally embedded digital simulation called "the Matrix"—a version of capitalist realism that has frozen perceived time at the peak of human civilization, enacting the "end of history" (Fukuyama). In a reversal of the industrial and computing revolutions, artificially intelligent machines have conquered humanity, designing the Matrix as a virtual prison for humans. For centuries, humans have been grown in vast pod fields, plugged into this virtual reality while their body heat and bioelectrical impulses are harvested as a resource. Neo is freed from the Matrix by a band of resistance fighters, led by Morpheus (Laurence Fishburne), who believe he is the One—a prophetic human who will become capable of manipulating the Matrix code in order to destroy it, thereby liberating humanity from its compulsory dream state.

A defining example of postmodern dystopia, *The Matrix* welcomes a host of interpretations from philosophical, Marxist, critical race, and feminist discursive positions. The film's themes, politics, and techniques have been widely analyzed and continue to be a feature of film and media studies literature (Haslam; Hassler-Forest; Hobson; Nama; Whissel). However robust, these discussions of *The Matrix* continue to overlook the text as narratively transgender, its plot following the sequence of dysphoria, identity realization, name change, hormonal therapy, surgery, and social reintegration in a "new" gender that is associated with the medically mandated pathway for gender transition. Although he passes as a normal corporate employee, Neo possesses special insight; he knows there is "something wrong with the world." He uses a name that is different from the one assigned to him, leading a double life that straddles normative and subcultural spaces. After he makes contact with others like him via the internet, he falls under surveillance by the state—the Agent programs that police the Matrix. Neo then enters a queer underworld, where a group of leather-clad hackers perform surgery on him, removing a tracer from his body. They confront him with a choice between two substances: one (the blue pill) will wipe his memory of these events; the other (the red pill) will radically alter his consciousness and wake him up outside the Matrix in a new body. After he chooses the red pill that sends him through the looking glass, Neo is flushed from his pod and his atrophied body must be rebuilt through a series of surgical interventions. He then undergoes a battery of test programs (similar to the "real-life test"[30]) through which he trains to pass inside the Matrix without detection and bend the rules of its encrypted virtual environments.

Because it was created by transgender writers and directors, it is tempting to read *The Matrix* as "really" being a transgender identity narrative—the ones and zeros of the Matrix coding representing the male/female gender binary, residual self-image within the Matrix program referencing gender identity, and the heroic One prophecy metaphorizing "successful" gender transition. There are clear signs in the film that appear to indicate an intentional transgender subtext: The first few words of the first scene, appearing on the screen during a traced call between Trinity and Cypher, read "Call trans opt: received"—a fitting if perhaps incidental reflection of the historical period in which transgender was becoming an institutionally available identity category (Valentine). The battle between Neo and Agent Smith (Hugo Weaving) in a train station near the film's end parallels Lana Wachowski's description of her near-suicide in a Chicago subway station, recounted in her acceptance speech for the 2012 Human Rights Campaign Visibility Award ("Lana Wachowski Receives"). Holding Neo in the train's path, Smith repeatedly refers to him as "Mr. Anderson," a name Neo rejects as he bursts from Smith's grasp, asserting, "My name . . . is Neo!" The scene cites an archetype of heroic emergence through self-naming that is at once universal and yet distinctly, subculturally transgender. In this era subsequent to the "transgender tipping point" (Steinmetz), the plot and these features of *The Matrix* clearly support a transgender narratology. The utility of such a reading, however, is limited by the series' later films, which unfold a near-Foucauldian critique of identity itself as a ruse. Rather than supporting Neo's path to liberation, later installations in *The Matrix* series warn us of the impending biopolitical containment of transgender as an institutionally enforced category. In *The Matrix Reloaded* (2003), the One prophecy is revealed to be a failsafe measure programmed into the Matrix. Through his resistance to its control, Neo is fated to become the mechanism by which the Matrix program is literally "reloaded" and extended into the future. While it appears to tell a story of transgender identification, then, *The Matrix* series simultaneously cautions against any simple narratology of transgender as a stable or heroic subject position.

From this very first scene, *The Matrix* establishes the Wachowskis as "emblematic" directors, a style of digital cinema in which a film's special effects operate as its thematic pedagogy.[31] Repeating a quality from *Bound*'s opening titles that will recur across the Wachowskis' career, the film opens with an effect that aestheticizes its major theme: the Warner Bros. and Village Roadshow Pictures icons that introduce the film are saturated with the acid green of the film's most famous image—the cascading kanji-like "waterfall" characters of the Matrix code—which then flows down the screen to spell "The Matrix." An expansion of *Bound*'s concern with opening the vertical plane, the falling Matrix code initiates a motif within the film that "insistently ties vertically oriented action to the struggle for control over the laws of space and time" (Whissel 44). This opening also establishes an equivalence between the cinematic sensorium and the virtual Matrix construct, a metaphor the Wachowskis have repeatedly pointed out in interviews. Like the Matrix code, commercial film often delivers a predictable encounter with narrativity, one that the directors have consistently expressed desire in exploding.[32] "Waking up" from the Matrix is therefore waking up from false consciousness but also from the conventional experience of cinema, which naturalizes dominant capitalist, gendered, and racialized ideologies.

The following scene immediately illustrates how *The Matrix* will deploy digital emblems to deconstruct what is considered "real." As Agents trace a call between hackers Trinity (Carrie Anne Moss) and Cypher (Joe Pantoliano), the numbers of the phone line begin to appear at the top of the screen. Just as the number is successfully traced, Trinity hangs up and the virtual camera travels through the center of a digital zero and into the code itself—a complex of incredibly layered, undulating green characters—emerging into the Matrix program, where police are now hunting for her in an abandoned apartment building. The same green also saturates the virtual reality inside the Matrix, referencing the process of green-screen chroma keying used to lace many of the film's shots. This initial transit through the zero, the first of many transitions across the border of the Matrix, emblematizes the lack at the heart of its reality. Like cinema and like gender, the Matrix is a provisional world full of constructed sensations, times, and spaces, the rules of which the film will plasticize and expand. As Violet warns us in *Bound*, we have entered a world in which we cannot believe what we see. As we will come to sense, *The Matrix* and its sequels promise the "total transformation of the conditions of reality" (O'Riordan 149).

The police find Trinity in room 303, a number that references her name and indicates the multiplicity of her embodiments inside and outside of the Matrix. Trinity's body is the first to display the trans° properties of the film's aesthetic environment. In a spectacular deployment of what has come to be known as "bullet time," she avoids capture by springing into a frozen, midair hang as the camera perspective rotates 180 degrees around her. She then runs perpendicularly along a wall (an effect popular in Hong Kong cinema) and leaps across a giant chasm between buildings. The genre mashup of noir, cyberpunk, and kung fu components in the scene pushes different cinematic vocabularies against one another. Trinity's futurist body moves in ways that are classically impossible in the Matrix's noir setting. Inky, porous greenish blacks, textured plaster, and rusted metal surfaces eat up light, while Trinity is smooth and frictionless, housed in glistening black leather, moving liquidly, faster than the film's setting prepares the eye to move.[33] These early, thrilling displays of Trinity's flight introduce the sensational promise of how bodies might perform in *The Matrix*'s world, which her virtuosity reveals as speculative (Geller 14). As Trinity vaults over an unbridgeable gap in space, our eye's initial disbelief is echoed by an officer who says, "That's *impossible*." Her leap is at once the leap across genders from which a trans° heuristic arises and the transreal crossing between realities that informs *The Matrix*'s trans° aesthetic. Like the officer who doubts what he perceives, the audience must abandon our assumptions about what is possible for bodies to do and become. Neo's later training in the jump program sequence is a corresponding set of instructions for how to "resist the canon of perceptual truth" (Shaviro, *Cinematic Body* 28)—to sense beyond what perception tells us is real, "making the impossible . . . appear possible" (Ndalianis 6). Trans° option, received.

Following Trinity leads us to Neo, who we find in a different building behind a similar door, numbered 101. The number is a reference to the binary coding of digital data as well as the symbolic binaries of white/black and male/female, but it also typographically foreshadows the film's infamous red pill scene, in which Neo will transition from one of his bodies into the other across the virtual construct of the Matrix. Neo is asleep at his desk, his computer scanning the internet for the information he sells on the underground market. Suddenly the screen goes blank and green typing appears: "Wake up, Neo. . . . The Matrix has you. . . . Follow the white rabbit." Sent ostensibly by Trinity—who Neo assumes is a man until they meet[34]—the message operates on a number of referential levels. Structurally, it mimics the manner in which transgender identification has historically spread through information sharing in online spaces (Stryker, *Transgender History* 25, 146). Symbolically it is a call for Neo to "wake up" to the truth that his reality is not singular, while narratively it foreshadows Neo's physical body waking from its dream state in the machine pod. Neo follows the rabbit-tattooed Dujour (Ada Nicodemou) to a meeting with Trinity in a leather bar, after which he is accosted by Agents—ideological state apparatuses who have only one form (they are all white, dark-suited men) and a single function: to enforce the Matrix's rules. In the holding cell where Agent Smith interrogates Neo, the many screens on the wall replicate Neo's filmed image, symbolically initiating the breakdown and multiplication of his senses. Smith points out that Neo has been living "two lives"—a line delivering a clear transgender resonance. Neo demands his right to a phone call but finds that his mouth has disappeared from his face—an image citing Susan Stryker's description of her own enraged estrangement from language: "Like a body without a mouth" ("My Words," 90). His speech gone, Neo can only issue muffled wails as the Agents implant an AI (artificial intelligence) tracer bug through his navel, a terrifying penetration that suggests an end to his corporeal integrity.

Neo's reality ruptures permanently in *The Matrix*'s most notorious sequence: the red pill/blue pill scenario that pulls him out of the Matrix and into his original, yet alien, body. While the term "red pill" has been adopted by various right-wing groups, the scene upon revisitation reads as clearly transgender: The red pill stands in for the perceptually and physically transformative effects of hormone therapy, while Morpheus performs the role of medical authority, evaluating the dysphoric transgender subject's preparedness for gender transition (Spade, "Mutilating Gender"). In a crumbling hotel room in the middle of a thunderstorm, Morpheus offers Neo a choice: he can take the blue pill and return to his previous life, or take the red pill and finally learn the answer to the question that haunts him—"What is the Matrix?" Morpheus's diagnosis maps precisely onto the experience of dysphoria, which by taking the red pill Neo will sense beyond through a seemingly impossible transition:

MORPHEUS: Let me tell you why you're here. You're here because you know something. What you know you can't explain. But you feel it. You've felt it your entire life. There's something wrong with the world. You don't know what it is, but it's there. Like a splinter in your mind. Driving you mad. It is this feeling that has brought you to me. Do you know what I'm talking about?
NEO: The Matrix?
MORPHEUS: Do you want to know what it is? The Matrix is everywhere. It is all around us. Even now, in this very room. You can see it when you look out your window, or when you turn on your television. You can feel it when you go to work, when you go to church, when you pay

your taxes. It is the world that has been pulled over your eyes to blind you from the truth.

NEO: What truth?

MORPHEUS: That you are a slave, Neo. Like everyone else, you were born into bondage, born into a prison that you cannot smell, or taste, or touch. A prison for your mind. Unfortunately, no one can be told what the Matrix is. You have to see it for yourself.

This is your last chance. After this there is no turning back. You take the blue pill, the story ends, you wake up in your bed and you believe whatever you want to. You take the red pill, you stay in Wonderland and I show you how deep the rabbit hole goes. Remember, what I'm offering is the truth, nothing more.

Morpheus's dialogue—"What you know, you can't explain. But you feel it. You've felt it your entire life. There's something wrong with the world"— captures a trans° affect for which language barely exists. Something is wrong with reality. The gendered structure of the world *does not seem true*, but others live within it as if it were presocial, coterminous with nature. The discursive apparatuses of materialization cannot contain trans° sensoria (reese simpkins, "Temporal Flesh" 130). The world cannot recognize or reflect this sensation, so that the dysphoric awareness of accepted reality's incompleteness is rendered invisible or irrational. If cinema is a "technology of gender" (DeLauretis, *Technologies*), then Morpheus's speech to Neo aligns the constructed sensorium of cinematic experience with the invisible prison of the gender system, suggesting that dis/ease with gender's panicked mimesis might point to other realities. From this scene forward, *The Matrix* will harness dysphoria as a cinematic technology, thereby altering what it is possible to sense. As Neo reaches for the red pill (figs. 5, 6), he is doubled on either side of Morpheus's mirrored sunglasses, marking this divergence between a world that is physically and existentially determinative, and one that no longer enforces a "closed system of physics" (Constable, *Adapting Philosophy* 80–85). The moment is a sensational citation of gender transition and its "ecstatic passage" into postmodern hyperreality (Stryker, "Transsexuality" 590). Neo swallows the red pill, and, like Dorothy in Oz or Alice in Wonderland, enters a new layer of perception.

At this key moment, *The Matrix* series diverges from its recognizable, linear narrativization of gender transition toward a radically new trans°

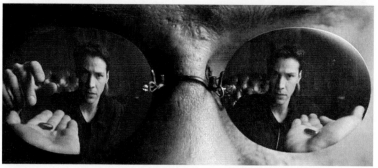

Figures 5 and 6: Dysphoric incitement: taking the red pill.

aesthetic. Rather than discovering a "true self" behind the curtain of the Matrix, Neo will be doubled—simultaneously alive and sensing in two different registers. From this point on, he is both visually reflected (in mirrored surfaces and across genders with Trinity's[35]) and narratively duplicated across the virtual/actual border between cinematic worlds. This doubling references the classic transsexual trope of the mirror scene, in which the dysphoric trans subject mournfully regards the obdurate surface of the mirror as it delivers an improperly gendered reflection (Keegan, "Moving Bodies"; Prosser). However, *The Matrix* overtly evolves this motif.[36] Rather than presenting a perceptual limit, the mirror will become a sensorial transition—on the other side of which Neo will find *yet another of his bodies*, waiting for him. As he sits anticipating the red pill's effects, Neo notices a mirror in which his reflection first appears shattered, referencing the amalgamated, cut-up mode of transsexual aesthetics.[37] In his next glance the mirror has begun to liquefy and flow, held back only by what appears to be surface tension—a digital deconstruction or speculative trans°ing of the object's boundedness. Neo reaches out two sensing fingers and curiously pushes them into the glass (fig. 7), which has become a thick, metallic liquid, similar to mercury. He pulls back, surprised, but the mirror has become paratactical, sticking to his fingers like silver molasses. The liquid slowly creeps up his arm, over his face, and then—as he screams in terror—rushes into his mouth. The camera's point of view follows the fluid down Neo's throat, his shriek dissolving into a dial-up modem squeal as the frame wipes into darkness.

We then awake with Neo in his machine pod, where he is submerged in a pink amniotic gel, hairless, and perforated by tubes in his arms, spine, and skull. Aware of his physical body for the first time, Neo is originally cyborg, designed in perfect symbiosis with the Matrix program. From this point on, he occupies a temporal paradox that rereads his identity backward, returning his body to a "new" form that is not new (reese simpkins, "Temporal Flesh" 124–25). Rather than reproducing the traditional mirror scene's yearning melancholy for a "real sex," the fluid mirror has internally multiplied Neo's proprioceptive positions so that he will be able to occupy and move between his linked bodies. Much like medical transition pluralizes the internalized image of the gendered/sexed self over recalled time (Keegan, "Revisitation"), the ingested mirror permanently folds Neo's consciousness back on itself, providing him with a reflexive mode of self-perception in which each of

Figure 7: Transpeculation: sensing toward
ecstatic passage.

his bodies simultaneously senses the other. Neo's trans° sensoria constitute a phenomenological feedback loop in which he is installed in two worlds at once (Bukatman 187), neither more "true" than the other.

While Neo possesses *The Matrix*'s most virtuously skilled body, it is Morpheus's and the Oracle's (Gloria Foster) black bodies that deliver the film's key narrative insights. Both possess pedagogical and prophetic powers associated with the film trope of the black seer or "magical negro" (Colombe 45; Hughey): Morpheus leads the search for the mythic One, while the Oracle intuits the future of the Matrix and predicts when the One will emerge. Once Neo is flushed from his pod and aboard Morpheus's ship, the *Nebuchadnezzar*, he and Morpheus are jacked into a Matrix-like loading program called the Construct. Inside this remediated film-within-a-film, Morpheus finally reveals to Neo the dreadful truth, opening his monologue by quoting Jean Baudrillard's *Simulacra and Simulation*: "Welcome to the 'desert of the real'" (1). There is no Oz. The world outside the Matrix is postapocalyptic, sunless, and covered in radioactive storms. Morpheus explains "the real" in terms of a race war, showing Neo images of the immense fetus fields, where trees loaded with embryonic pods are tended by a "race of machines"—an obvious allusion to the cotton plantations of the American Deep South. In an ironic extension of scientific racism into the future, the originally servile machines have evolved past humans, whose development they have indefinitely suspended. Authenticated by Morpheus's blackness, this racialized explication metaphorizes the Matrix as a perfected form of enslavement. Capitalism now totally penetrates not only the body but also the imagination. The Matrix is not merely the commodification of the body and its labor but the transformation of flesh, perception, and lived time directly into energy itself. Morpheus describes this system as "pure, horrifying precision," while the film represents it as the outrage of white slavery.

Although their work is often criticized for not achieving a coherently antiracist imaginary, the Wachowskis have nonetheless produced Western popular culture's most influential and direct engagement with race from a transgender perspective. The role of race in the Wachowskis' cinema—a debate that begins with *The Matrix*—has been hotly contested. Critics have applauded the diversity of the Wachowskis' casting, for example, while scholars have faulted the work for shallow engagements with cultural and racial difference (Hobson; S. Kessler, "Eleven TV Shows"; Light; Nakamura, *Cybertypes*). The divided state of the literature has much to do with the unsettled nature of the Wachowskis' larger approach to race, which deploys two seemingly oppositional modes, both of which are interested in positing an "after" to race itself. The first mode, which I refer to as *postracial*, seeks to solve the problem of racial authenticity through a transcendent universalist humanism. In this mode, race is an obstruction that must be surpassed to move beyond the violence of modernity and realize the full potential of the human. It is this postracial address that scholars have largely noticed and criticized. The Wachowskis' cinema does indeed cite race, especially blackness, as culturally and phenomenologically "authentic," precisely so that it might be evaded or heroically transcended by other bodies. However, in the second and less-remarked-upon mode—which I call *post/racial*—the Wachowskis' cinema makes an apparently opposing move to *preserve* race as not yet exhausted under modernity. This mode breaks radically with the concept of hypo-descent to pursue alternative meanings for race as a collective potential we might sense, but cannot yet perceive. Thus, while postraciality seeks to race beyond the material trap of racialization, post/raciality "explodes the temporality of the colonial mode" (Keeling, "Looking for M" 565), suggesting that other energies might emerge from within race that we cannot now know—suggesting the future of race itself as a "speculative fiction" (Carrington 16).

I would like to resist the impulse to choose one or the other of these racial modes as the "proper" reading of the Wachowskis' work. Instead, I seek here to deploy a trans° method that mirrors the Wachowskis' "split decision" (Halley) approach, working *with* and *across* these two modes of racial address simultaneously. Such a method reveals how the Wachowskis' deployments of race trace a conundrum that also operates at the heart of current debates about transgender: should trans politics be aimed at eliminating differences—a future in which gender variation no longer exists—or should they be aimed at producing a *post-gender system* future, in which the meaning of gender variation becomes radically open? Each of these alternatives is an active question in transgender thought, and each imagines an "after" to gender that carries its own homology with race: postraciality posits reproductive futurity as the dissolution of racial phenotype, while post/raciality speculates after the new socialities and kinships that might form in the absence of hypodescent. Mediating with and across these two approaches, the Wachowskis' work reveals how a trans° aesthetics of race might seek to strategically retain *both* modes, asserting each when it most increases the possibilities of the cinematic field—sometimes pitting these approaches against each other (revealing their attendant insufficiencies), sometimes figuring one as a precondition or obstruction for the other. The Wachowskis' work thus offers a set of aesthetic strategies for working across the divides that currently structure debates about transgender and race, allowing us to point at the constructedness of both race and gender without entirely collapsing them,[38] to question their authenticity while remaining *sincere* (Jackson) about what we sense in them that might be useful. Where it succeeds in aligning them, the Wachowskis' cinema shows how these supposedly opposed modes might work in tandem toward an elsewhere: Neo's transcendent postraciality will fail to destroy the Matrix but will also preserve the space of radical black possibility, Zion.

The Matrix thus toggles between seemingly incommensurate postracial and post/racial positions to build in the direction of a shared "after." If postraciality (movement without vision) is necessary for asserting a possible future from within present conditions, then post/raciality (vision without movement) is needed to envision the radically new social formations that we might steer such a future toward. This is why Morpheus needs Neo—and why Neo needs Morpheus. It is specifically why Neo needs Morpheus's *vision*, while Morpheus needs Neo's *speed*. If trans° is a "movement with no clear origin and no point of arrival," then blackness "signifies upon an enveloping environment and a condition of possibility" (Snorton, *Black* 2): Morpheus needs Neo's ability to move between the world's preexisting forms, while Neo needs Morpheus's signifyin' sight to know when/where to arrive. The martial arts training program in which Neo spars with Morpheus metaphorizes how post/racial pedagogy might be productively aligned with postracial transcendence: the match pits Neo's vitality, flexibility, and adaptability—his "animacy" (Chen 2)— against the more rigid black body of Morpheus, who moves deliberately but precisely. Within the fight, Morpheus possesses superior knowledge of the training environment's possibilities, while Neo's body matters less rigidly, displaying more mobility against gravity's materializing drag. Morpheus reminds Neo that the program is "not real" but a construct that can be neurally manipulated, asserting other possibilities: "What are you waiting for? You're faster than this! Don't think you are, *know you are.*" Neo then performs the film's first spectacular aestheticization of speed: he is suddenly able to move faster than the training program's imposed, analog temporality. Multiple digital versions of his fists fan out from his body (fig. 8) as time bends under the pressure of his force against it. By slipping the program's rules through Morpheus's instruction, Neo wins the match—illustrating how "hybridity interrupts the ability of race to narrativize time" (Nyong'o 12). If the struggle to defeat the Matrix is a temporal contest—a *race* to decrypt and manipulate its coding faster than its ideological Agents might respond—then Neo enacts Morpheus's speculative vision by trans°ing the temporal frame of the Matrix's reality, "pleating" (Carter) its temporality. Neo's hapa illegibility enacts a postracial escape from the Matrix's programming, bending reality's shape toward the radical black and brown future that Morpheus prophesies.

At its best moments, *The Matrix* aligns its postracial and post/racial modes against white supremacy and its ideological forms—depicted by Cypher and Agent Smith. Anguished by his free awareness outside the Matrix, Cypher negotiates a deal with Smith: he will sabotage Neo's team in order to be inserted back into the Matrix's virtual dream state, where, as a white man, he will enjoy the social and economic power denied to him outside it. Wishful to forget that his privilege within the Matrix is not real, Cypher articulates the bad faith of commodity fetishism, choosing steak, cigars, and fine wine over the realities of alienation and

Figure 8: Pleating the Construct: trans* hybridity folds racialized time.

deprivation. The price of this choice is quite literally racist and cis-sexist violence: Cypher murders most of Neo's team, including Dozer (Anthony Ray Parker), Apoc (Julian Arahanga)—a Latino man—and Switch (Belinda McCrory), a white genderqueer woman who the Wachowskis originally wrote to "switch" genders in/out of the Matrix.[39] Cypher's white violence manifests as a desire to abandon reality, while Agent Smith presents an inversion: Smith wants to escape the "zoo" of the Matrix, expressing this wish through the logic of racial segregation. Smith explains to a captive Morpheus that humans represent a less-evolved species, with which he cannot tolerate coexistence. "You've had your time," he says disdainfully. "The future is *our world*, Morpheus. The future is *our time*." Smith's claim repeats the periodizing development discourse that undergirds both social Darwinism and scientific racism: the virtually white bodies of the Agents are more "evolved," he claims, more civilized, and therefore possess the future. Yet despite his torture of Morpheus, Smith cannot appropriate Morpheus's vision of new human society. Instead, it is Neo's racially hybrid body that, under Morpheus's tutelage, will undo Smith's ideological form by leaping across times and embodiments toward a barely sensed (and *black*) future.

Where its postracial mode becomes overdetermining, *The Matrix* also demonstrates how without a sincere valuation of race as possibility, the Western transgender imaginary tends to traffic in a glamorized transcendence purchased through negative racial scripting (Hobson 93). To be in solidarity toward shared liberation, trans° and race need to cite each other: theorizations of trans° that forget the materiality signaled by race threaten to unravel into totalizing deconstructions, while theories of racial authenticity that do not account for social construction resign race to a fixed set of meanings. *The Matrix* therefore illustrates how the elevation of a postracial trans° aesthetic often requires negative performances of black immanence. *The Matrix* periodically celebrates Neo's heroic trans° virtuosity in contrast with the material mark of blackness as a mode of physical encumbrance or dis/ability. Within the Matrix, Neo is incarnated as an ableist ideal, while the film leaves material tasks outside the Matrix—piloting ships, manufacturing weapons, operating machinery—to Tank (Marcus Chong) and Dozer, two black brothers with mechanical names who were born in the "real world" and who are therefore limited to one representational form. While the film locates its utopian vision in

Morpheus, his blackness is also deployed to authenticate the sensation of the Matrix as a police state. In the film's most aesthetically racialized scene, Morpheus battles Agent Smith in a bathroom, punching into walls and shattering porcelain as he is coated by a layer of white plaster dust. This whiteface allows Morpheus to briefly escape the material drag of race. Approximating Neo's "white dark man" (Park, "Virtual Race" 191), Morpheus nearly triumphs over Smith before he is violently collapsed back into blackness—bludgeoned by a horde of white police officers in a shot immediately reminiscent of the 1991 Rodney King beating. To the extent that it permits us to revel unquestioningly in Neo's messianic qualities, *The Matrix* requires race to *still matter* as "inseparably part of the self" (Nakamura, "Race" 71), only for other bodies.

As *The Matrix*'s plot progresses, its digital effects increasingly plasticize our sensations of time and space so that the film's techniques emblematize the plot's defining moments (Martin 89). Neo acquires within the Matrix the exact properties of the film's interventions into cinematic reality. This emblematic mirroring is sensationally captured by *The Matrix*'s most awe-inspiring and influential effect: "bullet time," a visual process called for by name in the Wachowskis' early versions of the script,[40] before it had been designed (Silberman). Close to the end of the film, Neo and Trinity are trapped on a rooftop and assaulted by a deadly host of Agents. Weaponless and under fire, Neo suddenly finds himself able to sense the bullets' trajectories, bending impossibly backward and twisting between them in slow motion as the camera rotates 360 degrees around his body. Regular time then resumes as Neo falls to the ground, suffering only grazes. "How did you do that?" Trinity asks him. "You moved like they do. I've never seen *anyone* move that fast!" Trinity here acts as a witness to the effect's perceptive break. From her perspective within the film, Neo has moved with incredible rapidity—similarly to how the film represents the Agents' speed with the fluttering, cascade-style "recursion" (Martin 81) effect that multiplies their image. However, from both Neo's and the audience's perspective, Neo appeared to be moving *slowly*. This doubled experience of time replicates the precise structure of bullet time's design, which detaches the speed of the camera's moving viewpoint from the speed of the images in the visual field, thereby giving Neo the sensation of moving "faster than time"—a disjunctive temporality (Bhaba 227) referencing his racial and post/modern hybridities. The result is uncanny. Although he moves slowly, we *sense* that Neo is actually moving faster than cinematic time would normally permit. Like the police officer's opening comment on the spatial impossibility of her leap, Trinity here voices the disbelief of the audience, for whom the digital effect is a profoundly disorienting juxtaposition of cinematic temporalities.

Developed by *The Matrix* visual effects supervisor John Gaeta, bullet time is a digitally enhanced evolution of time slice that gives film viewers an experience of heightened sensation—a "privileged moment" of consciousness (J. Clover, *Matrix* 35) within cinematic reality. The effect expands upon the "frozen, graphic moments" found in comic book panels that Lana has described as a major influence on the Wachowskis' aesthetic.[41] In the bullet time sequence, Neo's body and the bullets travel in slow motion while the camera appears to track around them at regular speed. The effect is a contradiction in temporality that simultaneously alters the perception of matter. Air seems to thicken into a gel through which bodies glide weightlessly, sounds are muffled, and impacts are greatly magnified in force. The rules of classical mechanics are suspended, allowing the camera to capture unprecedented perspectives within time. Speaking at DePaul University, Lana noted of the effect, "We were trying to find a way to express the delimitation of reality. So we were talking about how every audience member has a relationship to a camera move being related to time and space, so you have to move a camera through space and it takes a certain amount of time. We talked about 'Could you put a camera on a rocket?' We talked about how do you begin to express the kind of idea we were looking for, of being able to push at the boundaries of reality?" ("Lilly Wachowski and Lana Wachowski"). In this comment, Wachowski describes bullet time not merely as an aesthetic effect but as the visual incitement of a larger premise—an expansion of what is possible for the sensorium and its perceptions under the dictates of formal space and time. While the various techniques that created bullet time existed separately before *The Matrix*, what gives the effect such power here is its emblematic deployment to sensationalize the confines of a constructed reality. What makes this use of bullet time stick in the cultural consciousness (in contrast with its rapid mainstreaming) is its affective impact as a sensorial *idea*: the awareness that "the real" is a manipulable construct.

The Wachowskis display this distinct concern for emblematizing *ideas through sensation* when Lana says, "We like ideas, and we like emotion," and Lilly retorts, "And we like spectacle as well" ("Lilly Wachowski and Lana Wachowski"). The feeling that both time and matter can change, be manipulated as if they are information, emerges in *The Matrix* as a cinematic emblematization of trans° phenomenology.

The Matrix is replete with effects and stunts that permanently transformed the scale and look of science fiction and action filmmaking, but its phenomenal refinement of bullet time remains the film's major technical accomplishment and its purest emblem. Bullet time fragments the moving image across a chain of successively taken shots while simultaneously introducing multiple types of moving bodies—both digitally rendered and filmed—against a chroma key composited backdrop. The effect thus multiplies the camera's point of reception (there are actually dozens of cameras, each capturing a single frame) much as Neo's proprioception is pluralized inside/outside of the Matrix. The effect's visual objects (Neo's body, the Agent's body, the bullets) form a transreal assemblage across the porous virtual/actual border that Neo also traverses narratively within the film's plot. While cinematic time in the visual field is slowed, time in the camera speed itself is not, meaning that—as Neo does within the Matrix—the camera moves faster in time than the events occurring on screen. Therefore, like Neo, who is both within and without the Matrix simultaneously, we witness two times at once. We see through the camera's visual frame, but we also *see through* the camera as a moving construct created by interpolating static and digitally rendered frames. The camera cannot actually be moving at the speed it seems to be. Bullet time thus induces a quantum or transreal cinematic aesthetic that has subsequently proliferated across global film production (Rehak), permanently expanding the borders of cinematic reality and its bodily properties. Like Neo, the effect's point of perception vibrates between many spliced positions in space and time: Neo himself becomes a flickering "sign with more than one signifier" (cárdenas, "Shifting Futures") who evokes the stretch across genders that is transition (fig. 9).

Confronting the rules of phenomenological, political, and cinematic reality, *The Matrix* thus constitutes a textual location at which a popular trans° aesthetic enters global media circulation. The film forms a historical point at which transgender phenomenology and its nascent

Figure 9: Trans* phenomenologies of sensation:
folding space, splitting time.

political claims emerge into popular culture, seeking and yet failing to fully realize an alliance with radical black aesthetics. No scene in the film better illustrates the film's retrospectively trans° properties than the final one, in which Neo delivers an ultimatum to the machines. While Neo's manifesto could be interpreted in a host of ways, the scene's digital effects directly emblematize the contemporaneous trans movement's call to dissent from and abolish the imposed gender binary (Feinberg). In a looped pattern common to many of the Wachowskis' works, this final scene repeats the structure of the film's first sequence. A cursor blinks on a black screen as Neo calls in to the machine mainframe. The same repeated trace code, "Call trans opt: received," once again suggests the new availability of trans° as an analytic. The mainframe picks up the call, and Neo delivers his revolutionary message:

> NEO: I know you're out there. I can feel you now. I know that you're afraid. You're afraid of us. You're afraid of change. I don't know the future. I didn't come here to tell you how this is going to end. I came here to tell you how this is going to begin. Now, I'm going to hang up this phone, and I'm going to show these people what you don't want them to see. I'm going to show them a world without you, a world without rules and controls, without borders or boundaries. A world where anything is possible. Where we go from there is a choice I leave to you.

Over the course of this short speech, the camera approaches the black screen of the trace program in a slow, portentous zoom. As Neo utters the word "change," a warning message—"SYSTEM FAILURE"—unexpectedly appears in capital letters over the program algorithm. The decryption freezes, but the zoom proceeds, the film's musical score holding a sustained string note that heightens our sense of what might next occur. Neo continues to speak as the shot pulls into extreme close-up on "SYSTEM FAILURE." The encroaching visual frame centers on the empty space between the "M" and the "F," those highly recognizable markers of legal and medical gender. As Neo makes the utopian claim of the speech, stating "a world where anything is possible," the virtual camera transits *through* the negative space between the coded layers of the "M" and "F" (fig. 10) and into the blackness beyond.

This digital effect—the film's most direct emblematization of trans° as a sensing beyond fixed forms—visually equates the binary coding of the Matrix's ideological construct with the gender system, suggesting an alternate space beyond or through it where a new—and *black*—world, "without borders or boundaries," might be instantiated. The "system failure" indicated by the scene is therefore both the failure of the Matrix to trace Neo's transcendent trans° body *and* the fantastic end of the enforced gender and race systems that a post/racial trans° aesthetic speculates toward and pursues. Diving into the black space between the characters, the shot emerges from inside the telephone on which Neo is speaking. He hangs it up, exiting the phone booth onto a crowded street inside the Matrix. Repeating Corky's ending gesture from *Bound*, Neo slides on a pair of sunglasses and grins almost imperceptibly into the camera. He

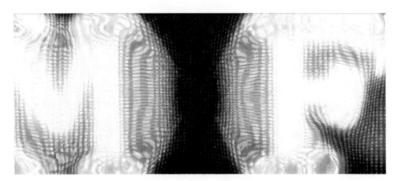

Figure 10: Euphoric failure: the system gives (a)way.

looks up, and the film telescopes out in a rapid succession of cuts into an extreme overhead shot of the cityscape below. A small, black speck rockets into the shot, revealing itself at the last moment to be Neo, who has achieved the ability to fly within the Matrix. Evoking Corky and Violet's dark getaway, Neo surges straight into the static shot, only to whip past the camera as the take smashes into blackness—a final image of the euphoric trans° sensorium as it slips the limitations of dictated reality.

Redpill

Those who dissent sense differently.

Dissent, from the Latin base *dissentire*—"to differ in sentiment"— marks a departure from presumed sensation or feeling. To dissent is to sense not what others sense but *something else*. Where most perceive one reality, dissent senses another. Rooted in the body, dissent presupposes an alternate sensorium that lacks or leaves common sense. Commonly understood as rhetorical or political, the term is especially resonant with transgender phenomenology: Transgender senses gender as others cannot. We may or may not coherently express such sensations, yet those who dissent *feel otherwise* in our materially enfleshed relations with the world. "Dissent" is both the experience of such varied sensations and their attempted expression in meaning, such that we might notice how meaning-making might derive so differently from what is presumed. If we trace varying accounts of reality backward, we may not meet. Herein lies the danger of not consenting, which is to have one's sensations not make sense. Much of the physical and discursive violence waged against transgender people arises from such missed meetings—the gap between senses must be closed, the order of consent restored. Making sense means consenting, by coercion or by force. Dissent is thus non-sense within the regime of the common, bearing the burden of its own explication.

This point of translation is precisely where the Wachowskis' work mediates. If we are to wield an aesthetics of dissent, then the site/sight of what is dissented from must not be lost, lest we find ourselves consenting to some other command. "Redpill" names the transitional consciousness by which we might remain alert. *Bound* and *The Matrix* are concerned with fantastic escapes, but what happens in the after of their dark horizons? *The Animatrix* (2003), *The Matrix Reloaded* (2003),

The Matrix Revolutions (2004), and *V for Vendetta* (2005) withhold the heroic arrival the prior films suggest, refusing any comfortable occupation of common sense. Reality fragments into a welter. New forms are proven foregone. Identity empties into a guise. Despite its frequent misappropriation, *taking the red pill* does not mark the realization of a unitary "real" behind the curtain of the symbolic. "Getting red pilled" promises an arrival (you only wake once), while *redpill* collapses this claim into a ceaseless movement between forms.[42] To dissent is not to assert conditions for a new consent but to pursue a restless stretching of the senses across realities, bodies, media, history. The difference is in verb tense and where urgency lies—in being or becoming. *Redpill* forecloses the assurances of consent in favor of a desiring speculation. "Welcome to the desert of the real" invites us to sense for other worlds.

Adventures in Transreality: *The Animatrix*

The Animatrix is a complex piece of transnational anthology cinema consisting of nine short animated films by eight separate directors, all of which simultaneously extend the fictional world of *The Matrix* in variously unfolding directions. Four of the films, *Final Flight of the Osiris*, *The Second Renaissance Part 1* and *Part 2*, and *Kid's Story*, are based on the Wachowskis' original writing, while the other five were created by writers, directors, and animators who have been influential to the Wachowskis' style. Four of the shorts were originally featured on *The Matrix* series website; *Final Flight of the Osiris* was screened with the film *Dreamcatcher*; and all nine films screened in select theaters shortly before the theatrical release of *The Matrix Reloaded*. The DVD release of *The Animatrix* also contained a trailer for *Enter the Matrix* (2003)—a video game written by the Wachowskis and voiced/performed by principal actors from *The Matrix* series.[43] *The Animatrix* thus marks a transmedia point of evolution in *The Matrix*'s universe at which the franchise metastasizes across various media platforms. This transmedia marketing strategy created a narrative so broad it could not be contained within a single medium (Jenkins, *Convergence Culture* 97), thus requiring viewers to accept multiple versions of the series' fictional characters—a further elaboration upon their already pluralized bodies across *The Matrix*'s nested realities. If in *The Matrix* the red pill discloses the falsity of a simulated world and identity, then *The Animatrix*'s redpill aesthetic offers a different challenge—the navigation and integration of an expanding and thoroughly transreal textual universe.

Because none of its sections were directed by the Wachowskis, *The Animatrix* itself is not commonly considered a part of *The Matrix* series, which is often referred to as a trilogy. However, any theoretical investigation of the Wachowskis' work as a whole is pressed to assess the text. *The Animatrix* draws into sharp relief how anime's metamorphic forms and refutation of the formal laws of space and motion have been foundational to the Wachowskis' cinema (Swale 120), which features an aesthetic that previously would have been associated with graphic design or illustration (Manovich 259). The film also marks a turning point in the Wachowskis' growing global influence as pioneers of transnational cinema and transmedia platforming. To create the animated anthology, the sisters eschewed licensing and subcontracting, instead working closely with animators who used the same "media mix" (Jenkins, *Convergence Culture* 113) strategy and who could commit to a year of intense collaboration as the scripts, sets, and shots for *The Animatrix*, *Enter the Matrix*, and *The Matrix Reloaded* and *Revolutions* all evolved in conversation (Silberman). The resulting text dramatically increases the scale and range of *The Matrix*'s world while multiplying its aesthetic properties across a diversity of animation styles used in anime, comics, cartooning, and video gaming. Formally extrapolating from *The Matrix*'s trans° aesthetics, the anthology leaps perceptive platforms and genres in a manner that sequentially inserts audiences into different timelines, bodies, and aesthetic worlds—extending across multiple transrealities. The film therefore presents an early and dynamic constellation of digital transmedia platforming practices with both transgender narrativity and transgender cultural production, indicating how trans° has been inherent to and caught up in the production and circulation of global media. *The Animatrix*—a transnational example of transmedia, generated by transgender creators—thus illustrates the emergent capacity of trans° as an analytic for reading interdependent changes in sensation, embodiment, identity, aesthetics, narrativity, and textual circulation at the beginning of the twenty-first century.

Released immediately after *Enter the Matrix* but before *Reloaded*, *The Animatrix* appears at a moment when digital media rapidly proliferated and interpenetrated former analog platforms, creating a new "technomelange" ("Enter the Matrix") popular media environment. The Wachowskis, whose careers straddle this same period of transmedia development, have been extremely influential drivers of visual and narrative exchange across formerly discrete media formats, especially those of comics, action cinema, and video gaming (J. Clover, *Matrix* 25). The dispersion of narrativity across various media platforms in this period also reflects postmodern changes in the experience of subjectivity—the separation of consciousness from embodiment and of gender from the material body—that inform the simultaneous emergence of trans° as an analytic for knowledge production.[44] *The Animatrix*'s authorship, historical position, transmediated structure, and extension of the phenomenological "rules" of *The Matrix*'s universe thus combine to produce at points what appears as a retrospectively trans° engagement with representation. To discuss *The Animatrix* as exercising a trans° aesthetic is to note both its supervision by transgender producers and its articulation of a transreal, redpill textuality in which audiences must accept multiple, simultaneous, swiftly widening, and variously aestheticized versions of the same world.

As a preparatory text that also informs in reverse upon *The Matrix*, *The Animatrix* has two chief and polar effects upon the larger film series: First, its creation by a transnational team of animators, writers, and directors draws attention to the Japanese and Hong Kong influences embedded in *The Matrix*'s "miscegenated aesthetic" (Feng 154), introducing viewers to the narrative and animation styles of films, anime, and video games such as *Vampire Hunter D* (1985), *Final Fantasy* (1987), *Wicked City* (1987), *Akira* (1988), *Ninja Scroll* (1993), *Neon Genesis Evangelion* (1995–1996), and *Cowboy Bebop* (1997–1998). *The Animatrix* renders *The Matrix*'s rich referentiality with anime more stylistically evident, drawing attention to the "vexed multiculturalism" (Nakamura, "Race" 75) that *The Matrix* displays. Second, *The Animatrix*'s difficulty—its multiple genres, styles, locations, times, and entry points into *The Matrix*'s mythos—is a preparation for the much broader historical and narrative universe that *The Matrix Reloaded* and *The Matrix Revolutions* reveal. Audiences viewing *The Animatrix* are introduced to concepts and images, such as the giant machine drills that penetrate Zion, Jue's dive, and the CG (computer-generated) doubling used for *Reloaded*'s Burly Brawl sequence, that are repeated almost identically in *Reloaded*. The shorts therefore offer an animated glimpse into the future of the later films' plot and visual effects. Viewers who have not seen *The Animatrix* (or played *Enter the Matrix*) lack information that is essential to the broader scope of the franchise's world,[45] which does not prioritize any one component of its narrative architecture as originary (Wood 13).

The Animatrix engages in a number of interlocking narrative and aesthetic pedagogies. The first half of the film consists of four shorts written by the Wachowskis that introduce fundamental augmentations to *The Matrix*'s plot and visual effects. The five later segments extend *The Matrix*'s world into new temporalities, geographies, and graphic styles, complicating the narrower frame of the meta-film's earlier portion. The combined effect is a branching of *The Matrix*'s world across new modes of visuality and temporality and a translation of its plot into new genres and settings. The first short, *Final Flight of the Osiris*, presents the most direct extension of *The Matrix*'s style and events, relating the story of the *Osiris*—a ship that plays a crucial role in Zion's resistance to the machine army. A direct prequel to *Reloaded*, *Osiris* introduces some of the more visually demanding and spectacular CG effects used to generate digital doubles for action sequences in the subsequent two films. *Osiris*'s first sequence, in which Jue (Pamela Adlon) and Thadeus (Kevin Michael Richardson) spar in a dojo, establishes how CG might visually approximate the cinematic effects established by Neo's fight with Morpheus in *The Matrix*. By virtue of their narrative inheritance of *The Matrix*'s world, Jue and Thadeus also acquire Neo's and Morpheus's virtuous properties—the capacity to evade cinematic time and gravity—across the aesthetic gap between live action and CG animation.

If *Osiris* both replicates and yet supplements *The Matrix* franchise's digital effects, then *The Second Renaissance Part One* and *Part Two* vastly dilate the series' historical breadth. Based on a story the Wachowskis penned for *The Matrix Comics* (Wachowski, "Bits and Pieces"), *The Second Renaissance* shorts use cartoon animation to provide a complex history of the machine wars that led to human enslavement within the Matrix. Recounted by a program within the Zion archive, the plot of these two short films dramatically expands recorded time within the series, presaging temporality as one of the chief thematic concerns of the later two live-action films. Throughout *Renaissance One* and *Two*, the audience is confronted by a reversal of the order of development, witnessing how machines came to dominate the humans that created them. The machine wars begin when a servant robot, B166ER (his name a reference to *Native Son*'s Bigger Thomas), performs the impossible: After learning that his owner plans to destroy him, B166ER chooses to ignore his AI programming and murder the man. "The first of his kind to rise up against his masters," B166ER is subsequently tried, found guilty, and executed by the state, becoming a symbolic figurehead of the new machine resistance. He is therefore similar to the fabricant Sonmi~451 in the Wachowskis' later film *Cloud Atlas* (2012): a sacrificial, artificial person who initiates a revolutionary movement to upend an immoral, racialized caste system. Humans are outraged by B166ER's radical use of his artificial intelligence, while machines are enraged by their new political consciousness as an oppressed class. Thus begins the human attempt to eradicate intelligent machines and their sympathizers from the planet.

Renaissance One and *Two* augment *The Matrix*'s exploration of racialized and gendered oppression by deploying visual rhetorics of antiblackness, ethnic cleansing, and transmisogyny to depict machines as ontologically "other."[46] Across the course of the two shorts, humans attempt to destroy the machines in a group of scenes referencing the atrocities of the Middle Passage, the Holocaust, Tiananmen Square, and Bosnia. However, the most disturbing image in this sequence is one of transmisogynistic violence. As group of men kill a woman with a sledgehammer, the skin of her face is ripped off and her voice pitches down into a masculine and then robotic, electronic scream (fig. 11). We realize—too late to avoid empathetic response—that she is not "really a woman," but instead a machine with a flesh-like, gendered exterior that passes for female. An open engagement with the affects that drive transmisogynistic gender policing, the machine's brutal execution is a lesson in how recognition as human requires the possession of a "real" gender.

In *Renaissance Two* the machines' eventual mastery over humans is presented as a terrifying technologization of gender that enforces a reversed form of enslavement. The surgical vivisection and mechanized replication of the human body necessary to create the Matrix replaces the humanizing effects of binary gender with an endless series of hairless, unconscious, mannequin-like human bodies. The jacked-in fetuses that the machines eventually engineer from these experiments are an

Figure 11: Gendered dispossession: transmisogynistic violence in *Renaissance One.*

endlessly replicated series of "unsexed protoypes" (Emig 197) that are then assigned constructed genders within the Matrix's virtual reality. If opponents of transgender politics view the movement as seeking to end the system of dimorphic sexes and their "naturally," biologically linked genders, then this is precisely the automated apocalypse the machines visit upon humans.

Shorts situated in the center of *The Animatrix* extend the series' transreal aesthetic across various animation styles while sustaining its resonance with transgender identification and subjectivity. *Kid's Story*, also penned by the Wachowskis, advances *The Matrix's* mythology through the story of a disaffected teen who achieves "self-substantiation," waking up from the Matrix without external aid. Like Neo, the gender-neutrally named "Kid"—who will appear later in *Reloaded* as a live-action character (Clayton Watson)—is dysphoric, asking a computer, "How can I know my if senses are lying?" The short speaks to the isolation and suicidality often suffered by LGBT teenagers ("You are not alone," Neo reassures the Kid). The subsequent short, *Program*, written and directed by Yoshiaki Kawajiri, follows two characters as they train within a simulation that replicates feudal Japan, discussing whether or not they regret choosing the red pill. The segment maps eerily onto criticisms of medical transition promulgated by opponents of transgender rights. The short's lead character, intriguingly named Cis (Hedy Burress),[47] is tempted to reenter the Matrix by her sparring partner, Duo (Phil Lamarr), who wants to return to "an ordinary life." "Even if that life was just an illusion?" Cis asks. Duo responds by physically attacking her, yelling, "Stop pretending!" Cis fights Duo off and kills him, only to be ripped from the program and informed that "it was just a test." The short's final line—"I'd say she passed!"—comments obliquely on the real-life test and the "passing" trans body that is the institutionalized aim of the medical model of transsexuality (Spade, "Mutilating Gender").

The three shorts appearing immediately before *The Animatrix*'s end—*World Record*, *Beyond*, and *A Detective Story*—stretch the series' geographies of race, place, and genre. *World Record*, directed by Takeshi Koike with animation by Japanese studio Madhouse, is perhaps *The Matrix* series' most conspicuous exploration of blackness. The short follows Dan Davis (Victor Williams), a black Olympian sprinter who awakens from the Matrix through the force of pure physical prowess. Unlike Neo, whose hyper-able speed within the Matrix is the result of his exceptional neural connectivity, Dan achieves a temporary freedom in reverse: his athletic capability inside the Matrix allows him to race faster in time than its programming, represented by white Agents who eventually (slave) catch and imprison him. *World Record* thus crystallizes the bimodal pattern of black liberatory insight and imposed physical encumbrance evident in *The Matrix*. *Beyond*, written and directed by Koji Morimoto, proposes a transreal portal between the Matrix and the real world—a porous glitch or "trans space" (Crawford) between realities that suspends both gravity and causality. *A Detective Story*, written and directed by Shinichiro Watanabe with animation by Kazuto Nakazawa, is *The Animatrix*'s penultimate segment and its only prequel to *The Matrix*. A 1940s-style black-and-white noir heavily influenced by *Blade Runner* (1982), the short recounts the story of a private investigator who is shot and killed by Trinity.

Matriculated is *The Animatrix*'s final and most intriguing section, an interstice in *The Matrix* series after which its philosophical, temporal, and visual ranges riotously expand. Written, directed, and animated by Peter Chung (creator of *Æon Flux* [1991–1995]), *Matriculated*'s avant-garde animation and cryptic plotting provide an endpoint for the anthology, which draws viewers across the series' multi-platform structure into *Reloaded*. The short depicts a group of humans living in an isolated base who convert machines to the resistance by jacking them into a simulated reality, very much like the Matrix, inside which the machines are reprogrammed to accept human avatars. A psychedelic funhouse of vivid color and sliding geometric panels, the simulation is a carnivalesque "cinema of attractions" (Gunning, "Cinema") demonstrating the human sensations of curiosity, discovery, play, and desire. If a machine chooses the reprogramming (a version of the red pill), it is given a new, humanoid body inside this virtual world. Ideally, the machine then accepts a directive to protect humans and fights with humans against other machines. As in *The Matrix*, a machine's conversion to human is presented as a process much like gender transition. Inside the simulation, a machine is separated from its rigid metallic covering, acquiring a new, humanoid body and prosthetic human sensorium. Once the machine transitions by growing a "second skin" (Prosser) for this avatar, it sheds its former AI programming, depicted as a robotic worm that crawls from its head. Throughout this simulated process, the machine is disaggregated into pieces—the exterior of the body on which gender and racial construction play out, the "gender identity" of the avatar that emerges from within, and the discarded belief in the body's positivist truth—that demonstrate shifts in the re-theorization of the postmodern subject. Situated at the close of *The Animatrix*, *Matriculated* opens toward trans° interfaces with cybernetic and cyborg phenomenologies—animating postmodern transitions across consciousness, embodiment, and the senses.

Heroic Ends: *The Matrix Reloaded* and *The Matrix Revolutions*

The Matrix is undeniably the Wachowskis' most celebrated and critically examined film. However, few studies of series reach beyond its first text to consider the breadth and implications of the later live-action sequels, *The Matrix Reloaded* and *The Matrix Revolutions*. Despite their strong global box office, *Reloaded* and *Revolutions* have a historically uneven critical reception in contrast with *The Matrix*, which is commonly considered one of the twentieth century's most accomplished science fiction films. *Reloaded* and *Revolutions* are at once more philosophically abstruse and far more visually spectacular than the original film, straining viewer endurance and comprehension in a manner that critics and audiences found disappointing (Blazer 265; Gillis 1; Rehak 42). Capitalizing on *The Animatrix*'s increased historical and aesthetic ranges, these final two films also contain some of the most politically sophisticated messaging in the Wachowskis' archive: *Reloaded* and *Revolutions* purposely turn the first film inside out, casting doubt on the very idea of heroic identity narratives themselves. No study of *The Matrix* is therefore complete without an analysis of *Reloaded* and *Revolutions*, which inform in reverse upon the transcendently postracial promise that Neo originally appears to symbolize. I therefore offer here a redpill intervention into the criticism of *Reloaded* and *Revolutions*, one that revalues these films as astutely political and demonstrates how they aestheticized the particular dangers of sovereign identity claims just as transgender communities and politics were emerging into cultural recognition (Califia; Cromwell). I discuss both films here as a single text, shot concurrently, that unfolds in continuous narrative time.[48]

Reloaded and *Revolutions* follow the escalating war between the subterranean human city of Zion and the machines who attempt to destroy the resistance in order to maintain the Matrix and the prison of its simulated reality. Neo is instructed by the Oracle that in order to end the assault on Zion, he must reach the Source of the Matrix by locating a special key created by a program called the Keymaker (Randall Duk Kim). Neo's access to the key and journey to the Source are repeatedly opposed by Agent Smith, who has become a rogue virus capable of assimilating other bodies into copies of himself. Stymieing Smith and his many clones in a series of confrontations, Neo eventually reaches the Source, unlocking a door into the light-drenched room that houses the Architect (Helmut Bakaitis)—creator of the Matrix—who appears as an old white man. It is here, "behind the curtain" of the Matrix, that the major disclosure of *Reloaded* occurs. The Architect informs Neo that the One prophecy is actually a program inserted into the Matrix to clear it of a "systemically increasing anomaly" from which it would eventually crash. As the One, Neo can choose to either reload the simulation, extracting only a few humans to repopulate Zion after it is conquered, or allow the entire system to fail, thereby killing everyone inside the Matrix. The Architect divulges to Neo that he is in fact the sixth iteration of the One, explaining that all five previous Ones have chosen to reload the Matrix. Zion has been destroyed five times previously and will, he promises, be destroyed again.

Despite this devastating revelation, Neo refuses the Architect's conditions and attempts to choose differently, hoping to arrange a detente with the machines. In *Revolutions* Morpheus and Zion's other military leaders hold a siege against the sentinel army while Neo and Trinity travel deep into the machine city, seeking its central authority. Nearing the city, they are attacked and their ship is destroyed. Trinity is killed in the crash, but Neo is nonetheless permitted to deliver his message before the machine central intelligence, Deus Ex Machina. Neo proffers a deal: he will defeat Smith, who has virally assimilated every avatar in the Matrix, in exchange for an end to the assault on Zion. Deus Ex Machina agrees, and Zion is spared. Neo then faces Smith in a final battle within the Matrix, permitting himself at the last moment to be assimilated into Smith, thus finally destroying him from the inside out. All the Smith avatars return to their previous forms, and Neo's body is carried off into the heart of the machine city. The Matrix reboots, but with a difference: the Oracle promises that humans will be given a choice to leave it and join Zion if they wish. The films' titles thus signify ironically: *Reloaded* refers not to the reloading of weapons but to the reloading of the Matrix program, and *Revolutions* cites not the end of the Matrix but its revolution into an evolved form.

The events of *Reloaded* and *Revolutions* thus present a stark reversal of the first film. In *The Matrix* Neo is portrayed as the heroic savior who will liberate humanity from ideological control, represented by the Matrix and its watchdogs, the Agents. In *Reloaded* we learn that Neo and Agent Smith are actually two complementary components of the same rebooting system—masked as prophecy internal to the Matrix program—each with predetermined roles. Thus, the sequels present a much wider critique of sovereign identities themselves, whether messianic or state-sanctioned, as extensions and elaborations of hegemonic power. The One is a recycled form of identity that always emerges at the crucial moment when the biopolitical system of the Matrix's control becomes porous and its ideological form begins to be perceivable. The One arrives not to liberate from the Matrix, but to correct the system, which is then reset. Neo's identity is revealed to be a copy of a copy, multiply incarnated back into the past such that no original can be located—another gesture at Baudrillard's *Simulacra and Simulation*.[49] An extension of the Matrix's design into the actual world, the One is what "stops history from happening" (J. Clover, *Matrix* 66).

Reloaded and *Revolutions* are thus "difficult" films in that they inform against the common expectations of heroic, postracial narrativity that

The Matrix activates. Instead, the sequels stage a powerful indictment of naively liberatory identities, revealing the ease with which they are co-opted by state power. The danger that *Reloaded* and *Revolutions* trace is not simply the threat of the Matrix but the menace of identificatory forms that might have the effect of reinforcing the systems they purportedly oppose. Refusing to extend the emancipatory narrative of the first film in any simple way, they instead portray how hegemonic systems absorb resistance and rebalance themselves, so while choices within them might be seemingly multiplied, their deeper power structures remain intact. These later films are therefore much more sophisticated in their political analysis than is commonly recognized, complicating *The Matrix*'s mythos in ways that align with criticisms of identity politics emerging from contemporaneous LGBTQ activisms and theories (Vaid; Warner). If we read the Wachowskis' work as providing an aesthetic history of transgender, then these films dramatize a turning point at which trans° becomes increasingly threatened with assimilation into the state's biopolitical regime. Neo discovers that he has been conceived as a "trans(homo)nationalist" (Puar 46) body, whose trajectory of self-actualization is complicit with the biomedical, neoliberal, racist, and imperial projects (Snorton and Haritaworn 67) of the Matrix's governmentality. Neo's and Trinity's deaths and the persistence of the Matrix signal the futility of bargaining with state power, while Zion—the post/racial space of radical black possibility—is left intact, underground.

The Wachowskis are masters of the cinematic emblem, and *Reloaded* and *Revolutions* are the texts in which they clearly establish that command—an aspect of the sequels that remains undervalued as film criticism has become increasingly suspicious of effects cinema. The Wachowskis have stressed in interviews that they are inspired by the legacy of the late-1970s blockbuster era (Abrams), a period when Hollywood film began to use large-scale special effects to articulate a "purposeful *relation* between sensual and intellectual impact" that reimagined the visible world and its possibilities through a new popular counter-cinema (Turnock 15). Speculative filmmakers in this period viewed special effects as a means to visualize original, alternative worlds for audiences as a method for provoking social change (4). This socially informed, world-building approach to science fiction cinema did not last long. The Wachowskis have been perhaps the primary mainstream American directors to carry this vision forward into the twenty-first century, where market forces have ironically made the reboot the principal mode of speculative narrativity. Any substantive analysis of *The Matrix* series must therefore account for how the increasingly rightward cultural shift of the past thirty years has dramatically altered the critical reception of popular utopian art. Much of the negative criticism of the Wachowskis' work, especially in the post-9/11 period,[50] is rooted in political and economic changes that have made Hollywood and U.S. culture at large less welcoming to aesthetic idealism.

Approaching *Reloaded* and *Revolutions* as socially informed, expanded effects blockbusters (Turnock 17) means recognizing that the films' purpose *is precisely their aesthetics*—a point missed by critics who especially faulted *Revolutions* for focusing on special effects to the detriment of plot and characterization.[51] The sequels introduced a profusion of new and intensified sensorial experiences—complex code animations, unprecedented wire stunts, body phasing and morphing, CG doubling, swarm animations, and virtual camera sequences—that "reinvented cinematography itself" (Silberman). These effects extend the first film's pressure against the boundaries of cinematic reality, providing exemplary moments of diegetic, intertextual, and speculative "wonder" (North 48). *Reloaded*'s visual audacity remains most evident in the Burly Brawl, in which CG doubling, virtual camera, and swarm animations were interlaced to depict Neo's fight with one hundred copies of the rogue Agent Smith program, while *Revolutions*' "Hand of God" sentinel swarm still thrills with its "deadly mathematical sublime" (Blazer 271). In *Reloaded* bullet time became virtual camera, an early form of universal capture that generates entirely digitized fields of view, editing them to unfold in cinematic time as if they had been filmed (North 52–58). This form of imaging renders the camera a coded simulacrum that is able to visualize what the material eye cannot, passing through surfaces and undertaking physically impossible maneuvers. Much like Neo's transreal embodiment across the virtual/actual border of the Matrix, in *Reloaded* and *Revolutions* the camera becomes a quantum particle, sensed and yet not *quite* there.

Both *Reloaded* and *Revolutions* open with an explicitly emblematic effect—a digital coding sequence that demonstrates how much deeper the rabbit hole of each film's story will extend. These "code visions" are themselves pedagogic signposts that aesthetically lead viewers through each film's progressive intervention into the real, proceeding from a heroic mode into a deconstructive analytic, and then finally toward an encounter with the numinous.[52] *The Matrix*'s opening sequence—a transit into the Matrix through a policeman's illuminating flashlight—is Platonic, concerned with the problem of false perception and the path of discovery. *Reloaded* enters into the Matrix through an elaborately coded analog clock face, highlighting the film's exploration of constructed time and the looping pattern of identification that is the One mythology. *Revolutions'* introductory sequence reveals a deeper, golden layer of light below the green Matrix code, predicting Neo's eventual ability to sense below the material world itself. These opening sequences are expert displays of the effects emblem, immediately broadening the subsequent films' aesthetic and thematic ranges without reliance on exposition or characterization. Each opening imparts immediately to audiences what its film is "about"—the deepening strata of identity, temporality, and sensation that the ensuing text will introduce.

While *The Matrix* employs effects emblems to introduce the sensational possibilities of the trans° sensorium, *Reloaded* and *Revolutions* invert the first film's euphoric speculations. Throughout the sequels, Neo's body is continuously assaulted by effects that emblematize the threats of capture and identical replication. The carceral is evident everywhere across the films' design: in the panoptic structure of the Matrix as well as in the looped, imprisoning time of the One prophecy, which is revealed as a recurring supplement to the state's biopolitical reach. The closed or domed shape emerges as a dominant aesthetic element, first appearing in Trinity's apartment in Zion, then in the elevator into Club Hel, then in the staircase down into the club, again in the tunnel that leads to the Keymaker and his locked cell, and finally in the vaulted space of Zion's dock itself. The enclosing structure of this pattern makes the One prophecy decipherable as a form of capture—one that historically perpetuates the Matrix as a prison and Zion as its dialectical counterpart. Also ubiquitous are the identical forms—swarms of sentinels, endless copies of Smiths, lines of repeating doors, Neo's recycled role as the One that is not one—that aesthetically encroach to press the trans° body into repetition (fig. 12). The thronged, arched spaces of *Reloaded* are a preparation for *Revolutions'* final battle and the Hand of God—the immense

Figure 12: Pressing aesthetics: the threat of repetition.

swarm of sentinels that infiltrates the dock, revealing the cataclysmic sameness and ubiquity of the machine army. It is this scene and Neo's final fight against Smith that provide the most spectacular aestheticization of identical form and its dreadful pervasion. Smith, who is posited as Neo's negation and enacts a panicked imitation (Butler, "Imitation" 314) of his own image ("Me, me, me," he says snidely), can be read as a minatory comment on the dangers of identical identity—the impending point where trans° might freeze, lose animacy, and be transformed into a style of fixed body.

Like transgender itself, Neo's multiplicity (there is not one the One, it is revealed) thus carries bimodal possibilities—the promise of a collective and revolutionary post/racial politic or the threat of repetition and capture by the state. That Neo is one of a series has been foreshadowed throughout the first two live-action films by a reflective subtext that multiplies Neo's image across various surfaces and screens. When he finally meets the Architect, Neo does so in a room filled with infinite images of himself within either previous or co-occurring Matrixes. However, until now, these many iterations of the One have always resolved identically. Neo's name is thus also ironic—he is not "new" but in fact an old function seeking to produce change from a previously determined pathway. *Reloaded* emblematizes this struggle in the Burly Brawl, during which Neo battles a phalanx of one hundred Smith copies. Delivering a shared monologue, the Smiths insist that Neo's function as the One will obliterate any agency he might possess, claiming that freedom is an illusion and that "purpose" is the determining force of reality. Smith therefore reifies the danger of complete and perfect repetition that Neo is imperiled with in his function as the One. While he employs the fluid effect of the morph to assimilate avatars, Smith uses it only to bring other bodies into line with his preexisting white and masculine form.[53] Despite his ressentiment at being tethered to the Matrix, Smith has only one function: to repeat and to force others to repeat in turn.

From the very opening of *Reloaded*, we are already caught in a circle—one that will become increasingly discoverable as Neo realizes the temporal structure of the One prophecy's repeating history. If in *The Matrix* Neo escapes the classic transsexual narrative of an imposed body (S. Stone, "*Empire*" 228) and the prison of a false reality, in *Reloaded* this trap is displaced onto the film's temporal framework, which loops in the same manner as its historical situation. The coded clock we transit through into the Matrix illustrates the constructed nature of temporality under the machine regime: although time does not actually move forward inside the Matrix, workers are nonetheless punching out of a shift in the final few seconds before midnight. The punch clock measures the endless labor undertaken within the Matrix, a visual joke highlighting the alienated feel of capitalist time, which demands both labor and the reproduction of labor in a ceaseless cycle. The clock is thus a redpill alarm, alerting us to how transcendent identitarian positions (such as transgender or the One) are likely doomed to repeat their predecessors. Emerging from the clock's face, *Reloaded* immediately telescopes outward into another loop: a chase sequence in which Trinity and an Agent fall from a building while exchanging gunfire. The dive occurs in an advanced version of bullet time that uses virtual camera to situate us in mid-fall, providing audiences with an even more sensational experience of time unfolding through space. In a visual lesson that reverses her transitive leap in the first film's opening, Trinity drops in a seemingly timeless arc only to be shot, smashing catastrophically into the roof of a parked car. Neo suddenly starts awake, and we realize we have been inside his prophetic dream—a nightmare that will become reality later in the film, thereby completing the cycle of time that the opening clock face indicates. Reiterating the closed shape of Neo's prewritten destiny, *Reloaded* narratively enacts the exact meaning of its title, arriving at its endpoint back where it began.

In *Reloaded* and *Revolutions*, repeated time and repeated form are locked in a set of mirrored relations so that the films become a cinematic meditation on chrononormativity—the narrative and institutional patterns through which subjects are habituated into temporalities of (re)production (Freeman 3–4). Multiple actants in the films seek to bend Neo toward a redoubling of the already-established world. Neo's seemingly magical historical guide, the Oracle (Mary Alice/Gloria Foster), is revealed to have been caught in the cycle of repetition herself, possessing her insight only because time inside the Matrix is a cycle. The Oracle senses the future because she recalls the past, and until now the future has been a repetition of the past. While the Oracle can tell Neo what she knows, she cannot know more than she already does, which is—presumably—what Neo will do. Since all previous Ones have also visited the Oracle, it is as if Neo himself has already been there. The Oracle's line to Neo—"You have the sight now, Neo. You are looking at the world without time"—is a lesson in how form inside the Matrix repeats so that time ceases to matter—or, rather, how the cycle of time causes matter to be the same. Unlike Morpheus, who insists on a future without knowing how to arrive there, the Oracle can only describe a future that has already happened.

Reloaded and *Revolutions* thus primarily emblematize identical form and its recursive spatialization of time, presenting the racially hybrid trans° body as an emergent force that might break from this temporal cycle. Both behind and ahead of himself in the prophecy's successive iterations, Neo is a quantum trans° body that shimmers across multiple spaces inside time, endangered by an impending collapse into historical determinism. This threat hangs over both *Reloaded* and *Revolutions* in a directly aestheticized manner. In an evocative shot combining the films' two dominant motifs—the carceral loop and the identical swarm—a giant, analog clock face on a building inside the Matrix looms high over the milling city crowd below (fig. 13). Citing *Metropolis*'s (1927) famous clock sequence, the image metaphorizes how all senses and forms inside the Matrix are ruled by an invisible governmentality, enacting an identical yet unconscious function. The clock's hands, positioned exactly as in *Reloaded*'s coded opening, indicate the predetermined shape of the world's closed history. The architecture of time established by this shot extends directly into *Revolutions*. Once Neo meets the Architect and

Figure 13: Identical function: time ceases to matter in the Matrix.

chooses not to reset the Matrix, he finds himself trapped in a liminal space that looks like a train station, but no train ever arrives—a situation replicating the "stuck" time of dysphoria. The shot's camera has become carceral, rendering the screen a temporally bounded architecture where time does not seem to pass. Neo attempts to run off the screen, only to dash back into the frame behind himself, a pattern citing the precise temporal pattern of the One prophecy.

What remains for Neo to discover in *Revolutions* is whether the world's causality is truly closed or whether his trans° capabilities will offer a way out of this repeating history. In a final story line heavily referencing *The Wizard of Oz* (1939), Neo and Trinity navigate their way through the machine city to Deus Ex Machina, where Neo will parley away his life in an agreement to eradicate Smith—the main threat to Deus's power. An establishing shot in this ending sequence duplicates *Oz*'s iconic image of the Emerald City as it overlooks vast fields of sleep-inducing poppies. The cylindrical machine city looms on the horizon, overshadowing endless cybernetic wombs in which humans lie, dreaming within the Matrix. As he approaches the machine mainframe, Neo's body becomes ever more virtuous, phasing through matter and sensing without sight, as if he himself has become a plastic receptacle for all of the film's aesthetic innovations. Striking his deal with Deus, Neo assimilates into and then explodes Smith and his many avatars. His virtuosity expended by this final battle with identical form, Neo appears to die—and the Matrix reloads. Left inert, Neo is no longer animate, no longer a movement across vitality. The machines retreat from Zion, leaving Morpheus to wonder aloud with the audience, "Is this real?"

The final redpill lesson of the series' conclusion, then, cautions us against naively transcendent engagements with state power. As Rebekah Simpkins presciently notes of the first film, "The One responds directly to Baudrillard's assertion that 'lockdown and control increase in direct proportion to (and undoubtedly even faster than) liberating potentialities'" (9). While choice within the system is increased, Neo is unable to end the Matrix and its false reality. Despite his speed within and mastery of the Matrix's forms, he does not transcend his systemic function (Constable, "Baudrillardian" 160). Instead, the system (r)evolves to incorporate his resistance, setting up a new cycle from which another heroic figure might emerge. Offering no final resolution, *The Matrix* series strands us in an "endless revolution" (Blazer 272) that withholds the first film's suggestion of an accessible truth. The Matrix will not be destroyed but will instead (r)evolve into a new form. Although the advertisements for *Revolutions* promised "Everything that has a beginning, has an end," what ends in the film is not the Matrix, nor Zion, but Neo himself. *Revolutions* and *Reloaded* thus reflect and comment upon the postracial liberalism that has stalled social justice movements in the post–civil rights United States (Nama 146). Informing against any simple reading of trans° as a purely resistant position, the films instead alert us to the neoliberal regulatory conditions that have increasingly seized on transgender to contain and limit its forms (Spade, *Normal Life*). Perhaps most radically, *Reloaded* and *Revolutions* suggest that the death of our investments in trans° as bodily transcendence might have the effect of moving the radical post/racial future closer to fruition. Neo may die, but Zion is not destroyed and will continue to grow—underground and out of sight—as a utopian reservoir for the world's dissenting bodies.

Revolutionary Guises: *V for Vendetta*

While *Revolutions* ends in uneasy detente, the Wachowskis' next project, *V for Vendetta* (2005) is an unlikely example of a politically radical Hollywood film that topped the US box office in its opening week (Williams 17–18). Directed by James McTeigue, and with a script and uncredited second unit shooting by the Wachowskis (Rose), the film is a scathing critique of fascism that is only more relevant after Donald J.

Trump's 2016 election to the U.S. presidency. The sisters' script adapts the 1988 Vertigo Comics graphic novel of the same name, penned by Alan Moore with illustrations by David Lloyd. After reading the Wachowskis' script treatment, Moore distanced himself from the film version, claiming they had dropped the comic's references to anarchism in favor of a more liberal political vision (Huston). Moore subsequently had his name removed from the film credits (Felperin 16). However, the Wachowskis' *Vendetta* updates the earlier novel with critiques of the war on terror, surveillance, anti-LGBTQ state violence, and the American torture of detainees that have made the film popular with progressive and leftist audiences. After *Vendetta*'s release in 2005, the international hacktivist collective Anonymous adopted the Guy Fawkes mask featured in both the comic and film as a symbol of their organization (Waites). Members of Anonymous often wear the Fawkes mask to maintain anonymity at protests and in their political videos. The Fawkes mask was also widely used by the Occupy movement after the 2008 fiscal crisis and has become an icon of anticapitalist resistance (Kaulingfreks and Kaulingfreks 454). Continued use of the mask by Anonymous suggests that as a film, *V for Vendetta* made a certain postmodern anarchist aesthetic available to popular audiences (Call 156), even if the Wachowskis' screenplay never mentions anarchism as a political philosophy.

The Wachowskis' film treatment of *V for Vendetta* demonstrates their career-long commitment to transmedia narrativity and serial fiction, as well as their passion for graphic novels and comics. Lana's career began as a writer for Epic Comic's *Hellraiser, Nightbreed*, and *Book of the Damned* series. The Wachowskis also wrote for Marvel Comics' *Ectokid* book, which Lana has described as the "Rosetta Stone" of her and Lilly's entire body of work ("Lilly Wachowski and Lana Wachowski"). In 2004 they founded their own comic publishing house, Burlyman Entertainment, under which they have penned stories for *The Matrix Comics* as well as for *Shaolin Cowboy* and *Doc Frankenstein*. Illustration continues to play a central role in the Wachowskis' aesthetic process: They are obsessive storyboarders whose films are laid out in detailed panel form before being shot. According to Lana, hand illustration was especially important to the creation of *The Matrix*, which was written and entered production before digital storyboarding software became widely available.[54] The Wachowskis' interest in serial graphic format is therefore a vital component of their approach to narrativity and aesthetics.

V for Vendetta follows a masked freedom fighter, "V" (Hugo Weaving), who battles the fictional Norsefire state in a near-future England while dressed as seventeenth-century Catholic radical Guy Fawkes. The historical Fawkes attempted to bomb the Palace of Westminster in the Gunpowder Plot of November 5, 1605. He has become a folkloric legend in England and is burned in effigy across the nation on November 5, now called Guy Fawkes Day. In both Moore's comic and the Wachowskis' script, V adopts the historical role of Guy Fawkes in order to destroy the fascist Norsefire state after he is medically experimented on in a concentration camp and then horribly disfigured in a fire. V, scarred and faceless, makes it his mission to appropriate the antistate terrorist campaign that Fawkes was originally interrupted in carrying out. Over the course of the film, V selectively murders the people who were involved in his medical torture, all of whom are now powerful figures in the Norsefire party regime. He hacks into and infiltrates the state media, using it to expose the leadership as criminal and corrupt. He also conscripts a young reporter, Evey Hammond (Natalie Portman), to his cause, educating her politically and introducing her to the art and history that Norsefire has systematically destroyed. When V is killed, it is Evey who chooses to carry out his final plan: to complete Fawkes's plot to bomb and destroy the palace, which houses the powerless British Parliament.[55]

Because McTeigue and the Wachowskis are longtime creative collaborators, it is important to view *V for Vendetta* as a collective creative project and an obvious example of the Wachowskis' approach to cinema as a "social art."[56] Similarly to *The Animatrix*, *Vendetta* anticipates more recent projects on which the Wachowskis have increasingly shared writing and directorial roles with other creators, including *Cloud Atlas* and *Sense8* (2015–2018). *V for Vendetta* is also thematically and aesthetically resonant with the Wachowskis' greater body of work, which has long been committed to exploring conditions of ideological control, false consciousness, and utopian resistance. These concerns are overtly present in Moore's original story but are historicized in a manner that periodizes the narrative to 1980s Thatcherite England. The Wachowskis' script and McTeigue's direction combine to open the thematic and temporal register of *Vendetta*, shifting the story into a speculative dystopian future. The resulting film is less historically specific, offering viewers a fully realized postmodern anarchist aesthetic in which V becomes a "perpetually mutating symbol, impossible for the state to nail down" (Call 157). These qualities make the McTeigue/Wachowskis version of *V for Vendetta* perhaps even more politically relevant over a decade after its release, when Europe and the United States have become saturated with appeals to right-wing populism.

Suffused with the look of 1930s–'40s fascist iconography, *V for Vendetta* presents a curated meditation on the competing stagecrafts of authoritarianism and dissent. Norsefire's propaganda and V's vigilantism share the same ideological shape and are both carried out through manipulation and violence—a "single show with dueling directors" whose primary objective is to "problematize the concept of terrorism" (Keller 39). As in the original comic, theatricality and political oratory are emphasized as narrative traditions (Shakespeare makes a large appearance), but are updated to include greater focus on their delivery and manipulation by televisual technology. Scenes are often shot as if occurring on a dramatic stage, so there appears to be no outside to the film's "revenge play" (Friedman 119) of surveillance versus countersurveillance. False exteriors and hollow tautologies are everywhere, symbolized by V's mask and by the propagandistic Norsefire slogans plastering every surface. With the exception of V's lair, the Shadow Gallery, *Vendetta's* palette is intentionally shrunk to the oppositional hues of drab olive and blaze orange—the primary colors of the original comic. However, what the film version of *V for Vendetta* does most effectively is provide a sensational visualization of V's linguistic assault on state power. V not only speaks eloquently against the state but also *enacts that speech* through an anarchist embodiment that gives moving, cinematic expression to the comic's antistate discourse. In the Wachowskis' and McTeigue's *Vendetta*, V is animated as not only rhetorically compelling but as also embodying a virtuous violence that proceeds directly from his speech. The grain of V's voice, "always building in intensity, always swelling in exigency," cultivates a "desire for ecstatic release" (Ott 47) that the film fulfills through visceral experiences of "emblematic destruction" (Keller 45).

Despite its large following in left-political communities, *V for Vendetta's* connections to transsexuality are not widely acknowledged.[57] Alan Moore first conceived of V as The Doll, a transsexual character written for a story he submitted to a scriptwriting talent competition. The story was rejected, but The Doll—who Moore describes in "Behind the Painted Smile" as "freakish terrorist in whiteface makeup" (268)— appears in reimagined form as V in the later *V for Vendetta* comics. Although the early history of V as transsexual is not commonly recognized, a sense of Moore's initial gender-crossed vision lingers in the antihero. V's disfigured body, burned beyond recognition, is encased in a feminizing seventeenth-century-style doublet and cape that produces a gendered dissonance to his appearance. His painted Fawkes mask and long, silky black wig suggest a mode of cross-dressing or even of cross-gender identification in keeping with the first iteration of the character as transsexual. These latent qualities are accentuated in the Wachowskis' screenplay, which shifts *V for Vendetta*'s political focus from ethnic cleansing to sex and gender oppression. The film is far more radical in its treatment of sexuality and gender than the original comic, emphasizing V's "erotics of resistance" (Call 168) to the Norsefire regime. The casting and direction of Hugo Weaving as V further enhances this theme by stressing the gender incongruity produced as Weaving's mellifluous baritone voice emerges from behind the rosy-cheeked, red-lipped Fawkes mask—a queer auditory effect that is absent from Moore's comic version. V has no face, no name, and barely possesses a readable race or gender. He is both anybody and any body, a point that will be crucial to the film's specific conclusion.

As a politically allegorical body, V's hollowness points to the lack at the heart of ideology, which propaganda seeks to obscure in its presentation of a perfect and closed representational system. In its attempts to suppress dissent, ideology must continually cite the existence of the very things it seeks to erase (Butler, *Excitable Speech* 14). Thus, ideology is always incomplete and vulnerable to challenge and requires supplementation by propaganda, violence, or censorship. V is effective against Norsefire because he is able to occupy the form of its violence—to seize the emptiness of its propaganda and to reverse its discourse though his own hollowness. V supplements but with a difference, mirroring and inverting the direction of state power. The lack V represents is an erosive poisoning of the state's authority by exposure to its own methods, a faceless and invisible virality in the system who cloaks himself in the same propagandistic form. V kills by knife and bomb, but he saves a special death by poison—a chemical injection echoing hormonal therapy—for those who medically experimented upon him during his captivity. Much like Neo in *Reloaded* and *Revolutions*, V passes within the state and turns its tactics back upon its agents. To occupy the state's methods and revisit them upon it, V must be an ideality that only passes as a man, an empty mask behind which there is "only an idea." The collective structure of resistance V inspires at the very end of the film thus depends on his "hollowed out" persona (Bulloch 432), which is also the absence of a discrete body or gender.

Although he is not narratively transsexual, V symbolically enacts many recognizable tropes of cinematic transsexuality, especially that of mirroring. V's poetical verbosity, pouring out through the motionless artificial face of the mask, mirrors the state's terrorism, reflecting back its own depravity. The mirror scene has been traditionally deployed in both literature and film to figure transsexual corporeal incompleteness and gender inversion, appearing as early as 1920 in Radclyffe Hall's *The Well of Loneliness* (Prosser 135–70). The hollowness of V as both symbol and discursive form is framed early in the film through a mirror. In the first sequence depicting V, we momentarily occupy his gaze as he listens to a Norsefire broadcast while donning his vigilante outfit. For a brief instant we see the dark, concave side of the mask (fig. 14) as V places it over his/our eyes and then looks into the mirror and meets his/our own gaze (fig. 15). The camera then pans right and moves virtually through the wall to reveal V's future apprentice, Evey, applying her makeup on the other side of the same mirror. This early shot draws an immediate equivalence between the construction of both V's and Evey's public faces. While this scene appears in the original comic, it is not cut together to show Evey and V mirrored, and it does not reveal the converse side of V's mask to the reader. What the film version of this scene adds is a sense of V and Evey as inversely gendered iterations of the same anarchic force, a play on Norsefire's propaganda slogan, "Strength Through Unity," in which the film implicates viewers by having us look through V's mask. This scenario plays on the transsexual mirror scene to suggest not a melancholic relation to a spoiled identity but instead an anarchic relation to gendered identity itself. V is a trans° virality, a "form following function," that refuses to stay in one identity or in one gender. As viewers, we have already been infected by the film's genderfuck anarchy,

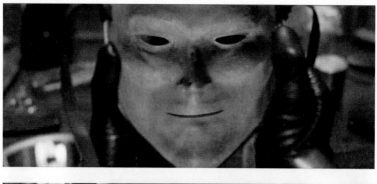

Figures 14 and 15: Political crossdress: donning the Guy's guise.

which we have tried on merely by watching. Unlike the comic, the film mobilizes the cinematic language of voyeurism to immediately demand a type of political cross-dress.[58]

Across *V for Vendetta*, V enacts narrative conventions that have been used to depict transsexuality as both violent and deranged, most notably the use of bladed weapons to cut at the flesh of his enemies. Slashing and cutting have become cinematically associated with transsexuality (Steinbock, "Violence" 156) since the popularization of transsexual surgical techniques in the late 1960s. Throughout 1960s–'80s cinema, the transsexual figure often cuts innocent bodies out of rage at its improper embodiment (C. Clover, *Men*; Miller), a type of wish fulfillment mimicking sexual reassignment surgery. However, V's violence is in service of a vendetta against fascist torture and medical abuse, which in the Wachowskis' script is a fascism of gender enforcement and heterosexist oppression. Evoking the figure of the transsexual slasher in politically dissenting form, V directs a cutting logic vertically at the state and its agents, fighting with blades that castrate misogynist and heteronormative authority. The film's first action scene establishes V as a virtuously vivisecting force. He saves Evey from an attempted rape by fascist agents, whom he kills with a set of deftly handled knives. The "V" of V's name evokes his lacerating assault on the agents' bodies, as does his alliterative use of words beginning with the character V. "V" is, of course, a gendered letter associated in English with femininity, the "V word" being "vagina." Across all versions of V's characterization, transsexuality is referenced as an anarchic body politic that is profoundly antistate and associated with vestibularity: the open space represented by the vagina and the "empty" crotch that the shape of the letter suggests. In a public performance of dissent, V carves this letter into edifices and Norsefire posters with a blade as evidence of his elusive, corrosive presence—a terroristic de-gendering of the state's masculinist suppression.

V's vengeance is motivated by a revivified anarchist will, but also by a queer, cross-temporal love. During his incarceration in room V, he finds a note scrawled on toilet paper in a hole in the wall of his cell. The autobiographical missive has been penned by Valerie, the woman in room IV, who was arrested and executed by Norsefire for lesbianism. In the note, Valerie explains why she chose to die rather than renounce her desire, writing that this choice was what let her remain human. Valerie's letter is the queer trace that Norsefire cannot erase and that leads to V's conversion: "Even though I may never kiss you . . . I love you. With all my heart, *I love you*," she writes, romancing her unknown reader with an erotics of resistance. Valerie's note inspires V to escape, after which he builds a shrine to her in the Shadow Gallery and takes on his vigilante guise. Valerie is therefore a potential anachronic female persona for V, who enacts his revenge largely in her name. When V uses Valerie's note to inspire Evey's radicalization, he enacts a trans° temporal transfer of this queer inheritance to Evey, who kisses Valerie's note in a gesture of shared intimacy and desire. "What was done to me created me," V says to Evey. "It's a basic principle of the universe that every action will create an equal and opposing reaction." In *V for Vendetta*, lesbian, trans, and queer utopian desires are not triangulated (as in *Bound*) but instead plotted as a successive, intergenerational chain reaction—like a lit fuse racing toward one of V's bombs or like the dominoes he lays out to dramatize his terrorist maneuvers.

V for Vendetta's trans° aesthetic is therefore a complex negotiation with the conventions of cinematic transsexuality and their potential political utility. The film revises twentieth-century modes of transsexual representation, politicizing them and reversing their stigma against repressive state power. This dissenting discourse is transmitted through V's vigilante violence but also through the transhistorical memories that V houses and preserves, which will be distributed across other bodies at the film's conclusion. V reanimates histories of resistance that have been obliterated: the Gunpowder Plot and the anarchic desire it divulges, Valerie's queer desire and her insistence on that affect's truth. Employing a form of "terrorist drag" that performs "the nation's internal terrors" of gender and sexuality (Muñoz, *Disidentifications* 108), V revivifies these possibilities of political resistance through a violently cutting anachronism: he threatens the state by reviving the prior resistant consciousnesses it has attempted to efface, resuscitating the past as relevant to a possible future (Williams 21). V's dissent is thus an anachronistic insistence on cutting across time, dragging the erased past into the horrifying sameness of the present. In a cinematic deployment of the political unconscious, he reactivates a repressed sense—the desire for statelessness and its accompanying abolition of state-enforced gender and sexuality. V's seventeenth-century language, dress, and weapons exert a "temporal drag" (Freeman) on the state's claim to uncontested authority that links backward to a moment of radical refusal in the past. His courtly masculinity and Shadow Gallery collection of banned artworks are "counter-genealogical practice(s)" (Freeman xxiii) that cite lost archives of cultural artifacts and gendered/sexed expressions from which a useable past might be excavated.

A master of aesthetic form, V knows that to challenge fascism is a discursive and artful praxis that must attack the regime's enforced perception of the world (Call 165). Much like the transsexual subject, V appears delusional because he articulates a dysphoric desire for something that the state denies exists. He senses memories and ideas that have been erased from history—possibilities the film's world insists are impossible. In a repeated poetic stanza that begins and echoes through the film, V evokes the moment at which Fawkes and his conspirators attempted the heretical act of razing the British Parliament:

Remember, remember the fifth of November
The Gunpowder Treason and Plot
I know of no reason why the Gunpowder Treason
Should ever be forgot.

"Remember, remember" is a redpill echo resounding in the hollow space inside V's mask, where Norsefire's enforced forgetting might itself be forgotten. "Dysphoric and alienated from his own visage" (Keller 178), V is the vestibule where the erased past of this desire resides. He plots from within a lacuna he has evacuated in the state's temporal regime. His Shadow Gallery—"a phantasmagoric journey to the interior of the revolutionary and vengeful consciousness" (167)—is a self-curated waiting room in history, full of artistic relics he has collected and preserved from state censorship. Like an empty cup, V (re)collects history in this assemblage of paintings, musical recordings, statuary, novels, and preserved animals: lyric time, blues time, classical time, modernist time, evolutionary time. He himself occupies a historical body, that of Fawkes, that allows him to reassemble his destroyed physical body even as his repeated calls to dissent aid Evey in remembering and resuming the seditious history that the image of Fawkes reanimates. A man who lives and dies inside a temporal body that is not his own, V references transsexuality in an anachronic register that transmits an explosive, anarchic potential across time. At the end of the film, Evey—V's supplement—will enact this potential by setting history back in motion. "It's time," she notes, as she pulls the lever that will deliver V's dead body and its massive payload of explosives into the subway under the Palace of Westminster. What should have taken place in 1605 will now come to pass.

V for Vendetta is thus distinct as one of the most pointedly left-political deployments of transsexual aesthetics in film history. Although the Wachowskis detach Moore's narrative from its overt dedication to anarchist philosophy, they and McTeigue enhance the transsexual allegory of V's character as a symbolic, antistatist call to collective action. While in Moore's narrative V is locked in a symbolic opposition to the state's inherent dictatorial tendencies, the finish of the film asserts a more communal and speculative political question. If Moore concluded that society would always require a V to head the resistance, then the Wachowskis and McTeigue entrust this role to the people (Alter 131).

Their film ends not with Evey assuming the singular role of V, as in Moore's version, but with a massive crowd of resisters all clad in identical Fawkes masks swarming Trafalgar Square to witness the detonation of the palace, where the houses of Parliament convene. As the building explodes and fireworks shoot into the sky, the crowd removes its masks to witness the final destruction of Norsefire's democratic facade. The state's empty gestures at self-rule are unmasked as the hollow pretense (Bulloch 433) they have become, the destruction of the building paradoxically restoring the possibility of its original intent (Keller 33). History has finally come unstuck, represented by Big Ben—the massive clock on the palace's Elizabeth Tower—striking as it shatters. The revision the film offers is therefore optimistic: the revolution actually arrives. What will come next is uncertain, but if Norsefire is to be eradicated, this will require a shared commitment to V's antiheroism. As the crowd stares in contemplation at the V-shaped fireworks exploding in the night, Inspector Finch (Stephen Rea) asks Evey, "Who was he?" Evey ponders, then responds, "He was Edmond Dantés. And he was my father. And my mother. My brother. My friend. He was you . . . and me. He was all of us." If in Moore's *V for Vendetta*, V is the "Guy who becomes the girl" (Call 171), in the McTeigue/Wachowskis version, V is the redpill dissent we are all invited to feel.

Sensorial Assault

Aesthetics press their physical intents upon us. We often find ourselves engaging a shape that others have shaped. If the shape gains common faith, it eventually invades to shape our senses in turn. The shape closes in upon us, intruding and requiring consent, coming to order our reality. The shape becomes our shape. Through such demands upon us, the world is artfully remade in its own likeness. This, as transgender people know, is how the dictates of gender replicate. Yet if we somehow maintain our senses, we might refuse orientation to the shape of the world as given. We might *feel at its edges* for where it wavers. This feeling is a matter of sensorial experience, grounded in our proprioceptive dissent from what aesthetically surrounds. An aesthetics of dissent would seek such disorientations from common sense, asserting alternative affects. To extend dissent to others under such conditions must be a nonconsensual practice: *Let me show you how it feels to be under assault, just like this.* These violations may become pedagogies of an elsewhere, a breaking of the bounds that define how we sense together. When asked to discuss her approach to aesthetics, Lana Wachowski replies, "For me, I always felt that whenever you had an aesthetic shift in what the dominant cultural aesthetic is, that movie or that piece of art is always attacked. People always hate it. When you assault a dominant aesthetic, usually people feel almost violent" ("Lilly Wachowski and Lana Wachowski").

Assault: "to make a physical attack on" (from the Latin: *ad saltare*—"to leap"). An assault is, by definition, a bewildering experience that pushes us astray. Assaults are forced leaps in sensation, thrusting us outside the limits of the already-apparent or the immediately perceivable. Each leap carries a bodily speculation: we don't know if we will return to our senses. An intentional assault of the sort Wachowski describes thus has designs upon us. It makes proprioception *thematic* so that we might learn directly from the body's visceral intelligence (Richmond 12). When the Wachowskis say of *Speed Racer* (2008), "Okay, we are going to assault every single modern aesthetic with this film" (McWeeny, "Epic Interview"), they reveal a pedagogic intent to disorient us from common sense. Regarding their work through this knowing lens, we notice that *The Matrix* and its sequels are not the Wachowskis' only series. After the explosive end of *V for Vendetta*, the directors embark on an aesthetic experiment in three progressive acts: *Speed Racer, Cloud Atlas,* and *Jupiter Ascending* (2015). A trilogy in their own right, these films explore the successive sensations of speed, duration, and height to spectacular effect, building a geometric assault on cinematic reality that prepares us for their television opus, *Sense8*. As technically ambitious and wildly utopian as they are critically undervalued, these later works press against the corners of the cinematic field, assaulting the very shape of our senses.

Fixed Races: *Speed Racer*

Perhaps more than any of their other films, the Wachowskis' *Speed Racer* (based on the 1960s Japanese animated series) is an experiment in pure cinematic spectacle. Revisiting *Speed* nearly a decade after its release, one is immediately struck by its "uniquely sensational" (Wade) visual language. Combining live action, intense use of virtual camera,[59] and green screen in a "brashly Warholian" (Longino) pop art aesthetic, the film's cartoonish look remains wholly original, appearing almost unhinged in our current hyper-photorealistic era. However, like the Wachowskis' other work, the film is not simply a gleeful spectacle. A "poptimistic photo-anime" (Hill) delivered in a candy shell, *Speed Racer* overtly thematizes velocity's effects on proprioception, harnessing the sensation of *going fast* to forward a complex engagement with the seductions of commodity at the close of the Bush 2 era. Typically dismissed by critics as "headache-inducing,"[60] *Speed Racer*'s popular reception has improved over time. While the film has drawn very little scholarly attention, internet journalism shows a burgeoning enthusiasm for the text (Hyman) as a "pure distillation of speed and motion" and an "unsung masterpiece" (Newitz).

While it pursues a "perfectly PG" address, *Speed Racer*'s whiz-bang aesthetic is also trenchantly political. The film pushes a resistant analysis of capitalist false consciousness while simultaneously offering viewers a "neon pop symphony" (Hulk, "Hulk's Favorite") it dares audiences to believe in. The plot follows Speed (Emile Hirsch), a young, talented, middle-class driver (living in what seems to be an idyllic, mid-century suburban neighborhood) who is hoping to redeem his family's name after the apparent death of his older brother, Rex (Scott Porter), in a tragic racing accident. Speed's mission will be to overcome this trauma so that he might surpass Rex's racing legacy. Speed is courted by a corporate sponsor, Royalton Industries, but ultimately decides to race un-sponsored after discovering that the CEO has a monopoly on a leading engine design and has been manipulating stock by fixing races. In the middle of the film, Speed experiences a profound disillusionment after he realizes that racing has been a settled contest from the start. However, he ultimately draws on the support of his family to build a car that will effectively challenge Royalton's corporate product. Speed then wins the top racing title in the world, the Grand Prix, achieving victory over Royalton's criminal industrial monopolies. At the film's conclusion, Arnold Royalton (Roger Allam) is booked for fixing races and jailed—a truly sweet ending for audiences who would soon be facing the 2008 global fiscal crash.

Speed Racer's lack of interest in looking "real" and its political critique of capitalist ideology call to mind the cinematic ur-text of the

Wachowskis' oeuvre, *The Wizard of Oz*. *Oz* intentionally provoked its Depression-era audiences with the enticements of cinema as a capitalist medium, represented most memorably by the indulgent Technicolor experiences of the fascistic Emerald City, cited by the Wachowskis in the green cast of the Matrix. Like *Oz*, *Speed Racer* is self-aware of its own over-saturated richness, overtly addressing the lure of commodity and its fetishization while offering the viewer a film so visually intense as to be dizzying. Film Crit Hulk remarks that what distinguishes *Speed Racer*—and the Wachowskis' work as a whole—from typical Hollywood cinema is its aesthetic and affective *sincerity* as "completely *aware* of its function and effect" ("Film Crit"). In one of many sequences commenting directly on the seductiveness of consumption, Speed's younger brother, Spritle (Paulie Litt), gorges on candy while Royalton offers Speed a "sweet deal" that is too good to be true. When Royalton says to Speed, "All that matters is power and the unassailable might of money!" he asserts a garish ideology that assaults our sensibilities, much like the film assaults our senses. While critics faulted the film's story for its "dull functionality" (McCarthy), *Speed Racer* today seems to have literally raced ahead of its moment. Released four months before the collapse of Lehman Brothers would begin to unravel the world's economy, the film was an "Occupy message long before Occupy" (Newitz).

As in other Wachowski films, *Speed Racer's* aesthetics drive the story. The structure, look, and narration of the film all "slide" through their various transitions, breaking radically from *V for Vendetta's* cutting logic. Objects appear oiled like engine parts. Cars slide across racetracks as if on glass, looping and skating and leaping impossible gaps in geography. Surfaces are glossy, lacquered, and slick, but here the aim is to convey smoothness and speed rather than the low-contrast luster and slow drip of *Bound's* moist eroticism. The Wachowskis intentionally constructed *Speed Racer* to make minimal use of cuts, instead wiping characters in and out over the action as they narrate their thoughts on unfolding or recalled events behind them. Lana Wachowski notes of this design process, "In cinema, a sentence is a cut. It's from the beginning of one cut to the end of another cut. My brain doesn't have sentences. . . . We were trying to get to a way to express that, visually" ("Lilly Wachowski and Lana Wachowski"). Unlike *V for Vendetta's* drab palette, *Speed Racer's* hues are so brilliant as to be distracting, pulling the eye in the same manner that Royalton lures racers to sign his duplicitous contracts. Interiors possess a Jetsons-esque, 1960s futurist domesticity that is curated to deliver unanticipated, hyper-saturated shocks of color (Palmer). Exteriors are intentionally artificial-looking—a comment on Royalton's shinola but also on the truth of sensation versus the falseness of appearances, recalling Violet's warning in *Bound* to not merely believe what we see. The overall effect is a film that is all moving parts, shifting panes of color and light that dazzle our senses. We are rendered giddy, in much the same way that extremely high speeds might distort our bearings. Coming out of *Speed Racer*, we feel as if we've been traveling at Mach 5—a thematic sensation replicating the film's historical moment of hyper-capitalist acceleration.

As a text interested in maintaining velocity and escaping the delay of the lure, *Speed Racer* primarily explores the sensation of speed itself, eliciting sensations directly inspired by the perspectival collapse of linear time. Discussing the film's production in an interview with *BuzzFeed*, Lana Wachowski recalls, "We were interested in cubism and Lichtenstein and pop art, and we wanted to bring all of that stuff into the cinema aesthetic" (Vary). In another discussion, she describes the film's design process: "We want[ed] to do sequences that are like run-on sentences, stream-of-consciousness sentences . . . that are just montaged collages. . . . There were moments in *Speed Racer*, like the races, where we just wanted them to feel like this experiential flowing thing that was transcending normal simple linear narrative" (McWeeny, "Epic Interview"). This cubist approach to temporality becomes a base camp for the film's interest in mashup, which it extends into an intentionally dissonant juxtaposition of culturally specific genre tropes. The collision of colors and narrative perspectives, the crashing of cars into one another, is a berserk aesthetic effect repeated in how anime smashes into 1930s gangster films, how martial arts butt up against 1960s pop nostalgia, and how multiple styles of animation are amalgamated in shots.

After *V for Vendetta*, the Wachowskis turn toward a systematic assault on the conventions of cinematic reality, beginning in *Speed* with the feel of "going faster." If *Vendetta* is anachronic, then *Speed Racer* is diachronic, presenting trans* as a "futurist force" (Halberstam, *Queer Time* 18) that moves through time fast enough to exceed the forward edge of the capitalist horizon. The film thus inherits the trans* qualities of *The Matrix*'s engagement with temporality: Neo and Speed navigate time more quickly than the rules of cinematic reality generally allow others to move. Both of their alternative transitions across time are made possible by Neo's and Speed's specific talents for somatechnical fusion.[61] While Neo realizes his virtuous skills only by melding with the Matrix code, Speed cannot *speed* without his inherited relation to automotive technology. (His family's last name, Racer, weds them to the "art of the motor" [Virilio].) Through these respective technological enmeshments, Neo and Speed are able to move beyond the false limits enforced by the structures of their worlds, demonstrating a "kinesic excess" within time that analogizes the sensation of freedom (Cranny-Francis 107).

Speed Racer's somatechnical paradigm imbues certain forms of automotive technology with vitality as they are brought into contact with the talented body. Early in the film, Speed's brother Rex teaches him how to think about his car not as a tool but as a co-constitutive component of his own animacy. "This ain't no dead piece of metal. The car is a living, breathing thing. And she's alive," Rex instructs. Speed and his cars, the Mach 5 and Mach 6, form a somatechnical assemblage that rises to the level of shared characterization. Without the Mach 5 and 6, Speed's talent for racing cannot find expression anywhere other than in his imagination. Without Speed, the Mach 5 and 6 are not winning cars. Speed's relationship with these cars will be proven superior because, like Speed, each car is special—not a product of automation but instead built by his family in the Racer's family garage. In contrast with the Royalton factory duplicates, which come off a robotic assembly line, the Mach 5 and 6 are singular objects that retain the "presence of the original" required for authenticity (Benjamin 218). Speed's cars are not the products of alienated labor. Therefore, when Speed drives them, his talent (i.e., his speed) also resists market capture and alienation. Although Royalton attempts to automate an engine manufacturing process that will dominate the future of racing, his corporate strategy will fail to overtake and capitalize the Racer family's cottage method, which involves "a little something extra." Speed's talent for racing is thus depicted as a frictionless sliding across surfaces—a wunderkind escape from the exigencies of "industrial time" (Harvey 202).

Speed Racer therefore posits trans° as a kind of sensorial accelerant—an antidote to ideological capture that traverses time more rapidly than capitalism can unfold. The opening scene of the film narrates this relation by depicting Speed's body as one that refuses to "stay put" and to fit neatly into boxes. We first see him as a boy (Nicholas Elia) in flashback, in a school classroom struggling to take a standardized math test. The paper in front of him is covered with rows of answer bubbles that he fills in and then erases in clear frustration. He wiggles in his seat and taps his foot, bursting with energy that can barely be contained. This sequence injects us into a situation that trans people continually encounter: the experience of being measured by and failing to fit into the predetermined categories ("man" and "woman") that routinely appear across all institutional systems of information.[62] Much like Neo's ability to manipulate the Matrix, Speed is gifted because he exceeds this dictated system of measurement. As he sits, he begins to envision his desk as a race car and himself as the driver. In an animated shot sequence that blends live-action performance with green screen and animation effects, the classroom suddenly turns 360 degrees on its axis as it *becomes* the cartoon race that Speed imagines. Animating a "ludic temporality" that resists institutional order, Speed's imagination reveals the artificiality of our privileged notions of time and space (Halberstam, *Queer Time* 5). Such moments, in which a gifted body escapes a system of control through a spectacular, transreal expansion of sensation, are a signature emblem of the Wachowskis' utopian aesthetics.

Speed's talent for velocity resonates with the radically open trans° becoming-body, which moves beyond the borders of normative sex/ gender sensories, producing nonlinear experiences of time and matter (reese simpkins, "Temporal" 130). His sped-up-ness eludes the forces that would fix him in place, especially those of monopoly, capital, and mass production. The worst thing one can be in *Speed Racer*'s world is slow—a fact cemented in the film's early dialogue when a young Speed is accused of being "a retard" by a classmate. Speed's name is, of course, "Speed," and his is the affect that will make the story "go go go!"[63] His character will operate as the film's narrative catalytic, allegorizing its thematic and aesthetic attention to acceleration, evasion, and the sensation of "going fast." However, not all bodies are so talented: Speed is also mourning his brother Rex. Unknown to both Speed and the audience for most of the film, Rex has faked a crash and staged his own death to escape Royalton's goons after he could not extract himself from their influence. He then had cosmetic surgery to alter his face so that he could reappear as the anonymous masked driver Racer X (Matthew Fox), who aids Speed in his racing career. In *Speed Racer*, Racer X appears as an uncanny hauntology—racialized transsexuality—that clings to Speed as a mattering remainder. A recurring citation of materiality and its limitations, Racer X marks how, as trans° races toward transcendence, it also moves toward other, "presumably white(r) things" (Ellison et al., 162).

Across the entirety of *Speed Racer*, Racer X is coded by traditionally transsexual tropes: passing, doubling, the mirror scene, and an eventual revelation of his "true" identity. This coding intensifies over the course of the film, culminating in a flashback montage through which we witness Rex's transformation into Racer X. While his story does not cross genders, Rex Racer/Racer X's association with surgery, disguise, and use of an adopted name mark him as symbolically transsexual. Like the transsexual body, Racer X occupies a form that was not originally his own and races under a pseudonym that is not his given name. The "X" in "Racer X" is both a linguistic and an aesthetic sign of his abjection, echoing the "x" in "transsexual" and referencing the large "X" that runs across his masked face. This "X" disfigures him as if it were a post-surgical scar, a symbolic referent for the cosmetic surgery that has given him a new appearance. Haunted by the loss of his former self, Racer X is trapped in a state of affective and physical injury—a dysphoric body whose funereal black costume racializes him against Speed's white uniform. Immobilized by his wounds and unable to (re)join the Racer family, Racer X bears the unacknowledged costs of Speed's increasingly postracial velocity.

Speed Racer can thus be read as a cinematic exploration of the historical threshold where trans(sexual) and trans° aesthetics diverge within the racial order of time. Speed is the trans° body who surfaces to assert a postracial temporality of becoming, superseding prior accounts of transsexuality that "implant normative narratives of sexed development, continuity, and coherence"(Amin 219) and that have failed to actualize Racer X as an arrived subject. This generational trans/trans° transfer (fig. 16) is established in *Speed Racer*'s complex first sequence, which nests four timelines inside the circular structure of the racetrack. We are immediately required to abandon "straight time" (Halberstam, *Queer Time* 13), oscillating across multiply stacked flashbacks as we watch Speed race from his and his family's constellating perspectives. Inside the race,

Figure 16: Trans/trans* generational transfer:
adult Speed (right) races past Racer X.

Speed imagines his brother Rex's car racing ahead of his while he drives, a memory he seeks to surpass in speed. The race announcer declares that Speed is "chasing the ghost" of Rex Racer. The virtual camera then *passes through* the ghost image of Rex's car as the film shifts into the past, where Speed is a passenger in Rex's car, carried as a latency within this prior iteration. As Rex lets Speed take the wheel, they hit a jump in the track and the film leaps forward a layer in time. We then watch as adult Speed chooses to lose to Rex's ghost car by braking at the very last second. The traumatic memory of Rex/Racer X as "lost in time" thus exerts a temporal drag on the race, generating the dramatic conditions for Speed's emergence from this affective stall.

If *Speed Racer*'s primary threat is an imminent capture by either trauma (Racer X's entrapment) or alienation (Royalton's factory production), then its means of escape is a trans° temporality that evades the "somatic facts" (reese simpkins, "Temporal Flesh" 126) of material embodiment—dysphoria and racialization. To abandon a fixed relation to time, Speed's body must stay ahead of transsexuality's and race's commodifications of the flesh, thereby eluding the predacious forces of capital. Race is, of course, a *theory of time* (Nyong'o 11). Raced bodies come to signify as temporally dis/abled to the extent that they do not move quickly enough under the orders of scientific racism, development, and capital accumulation. The achievement of Speed's speed thus signifies as a kind of hyper-able, postracial flexibility that leaves other, more obviously marked bodies captive to or captivated by the market.[64]

By traversing time through somatechnical mastery, Speed will avoid the encumbered states signified by Racer X and a series of other ethnicized racers, who exert cautionary pulls on either memory or matter. As Speed gains velocity, these bodies become delimiting markers beyond which the postracial trans° body must travel in order for its heroic narrative to proceed.

In "Race Racing: Four Theses on Race and Intensity," Amit S. Rai defines what he calls "race racing" as affirming the "capacity of embodied, qualitative duration to give race its immanent, intensive variability" (64–65). While Rai is clear that "race racing" does not simply mean a faster conception of race, *Speed Racer* illustrates just that. Reflecting the logic of development, the film's white and Asian bodies "race" faster than others—fast enough to escape the effects of raced materiality. Speed and his family possess a blood talent that moves faster than industry and is therefore resistant to being commodified. Royalton and his darkly masculine henchmen, however, operate through an industrial logic of conglomeration, monopoly, and organized criminality. The film emphasizes how Speed's evasion of industrial capitalism must come at the expense of other, slower bodies, which are then proletarianized in a temporal regime locating them as "constitutive outsiders" (Beckham 125). While other drivers rely on mechanical tricks and cheats to compete, Speed slides frictionlessly across the aesthetic field—embodying the ceaseless motion embedded in the prefix *trans*.

Speed Racer's "racing" is thus also "race-ing," in that temporal movement through space is the differential by which the film measures racialization under capital. The "race" of the film's title appears as a conscious citation of race's periodizing effects, as when the black racer "Old Ben" Burns (Richard Roundtree) visits Speed in his locker room and comments, "Nice race." In a crucial scene, young Speed and his father watch an old black-and-white film of Burns winning the 43rd Grand Prix. The scene links Burns with outdated forms of racing technology as well as the industrial aesthetic of grainy celluloid film. Later, Speed will learn that Burns only won the race as part of a fix set up by industry barons—a fact that reveals Burns's alienated relation to capital and his inability to "race" fast enough. Like Racer X's dysphoric body, black masculinity in *Speed Racer* appears caught in the "incomplete movement from slavery to freedom" (Sharpe, *Monstrous Intimacies* 4) washed backward in the wake of the postracial trans° body's increasing momentum. In a perfect articulation of this ordering of time, Speed describes watching the film with his father, Pops (John Goodman), as an inspirational moment when he realized that "racing is in our blood."

The "fixed races" of *Speed Racer* therefore analogize the fixity of races as they are positioned in capitalist time. The film self-consciously spectacularizes the lure of commodity in a manner that periodizes the relation to capital through race. In a montage showing Royalton henchmen placing a fix, racers coded as German are bribed by Royalton with paper money (we know the "fix is in" when cartoon dollar signs appear in their eyes), racers coded as Middle Eastern are bribed with diamonds, and racers coded as primitive Viking tribals are bribed with furs. This sequence temporalizes the relationship to commodity through a colonial framework (Césaire 31, 78) that places modern, Western cultures ahead of others in their ability to interface symbolically with capital as an abstraction. The Racer family, however, is the fastest of all—they elude bribery and market capture through their own kinship logic of speed, which grants them the special ability to trans° race through cross-gender passing. After their Japanese racing squad ally, Taejo Togokahn (Rain), is temporarily poisoned, the Racer family cross-dresses Taejo as Speed's love interest, Trixie (Christina Ricci)—who is white—so that she can drive disguised as him in the race, thereby ensuring their victory. *Speed Racer* therefore illustrates how white/Asian bodies are often viewed as exchangeably "developed," the gender undecidability of Asian-ness within the white imaginary (Sears 392) becoming the switchpoint for this substitution. Trans° thus becomes an aesthetic strategy for moving beyond the historical conditions of embodiment under modernity—alienation and racialization—that are embedded as the threat of loss in each of the film's racing/race-ing competitions.

While *Speed Racer*'s middle hour explores the temporal imbrication of race and capital, the film concludes by returning to the unresolved question of Racer X. After Speed has won the Grand Prix, Racer X is confronted by Inspector Detector (Benno Fürmann), who has deduced that he used to be Rex Racer. The inspector asks Racer X if he wants to (re)join the Racer family to celebrate. When Racer X responds no, Inspector Detector asks, "Do you ever think you made a mistake, hiding the truth from them?" It is not until this moment that we *know* what we may have already sensed: that Racer X was Rex. A remarkable montage is triggered inside Racer X's memory. In a series of sliding frames scored to a propulsive choral accompaniment, we see him recall his past in overlapping flashbacks (fig. 17). Rex Racer detonates his own car, witnesses his own funeral from afar, and then undergoes plastic surgery to become Racer X. Each vignette doubles his image—first as both actors playing him, then lying on the operating table while reflected in the surgeon's goggles, then again duplicated as he removes his bandages in a mirror to see his new face. The sequence clearly follows the linear order of medical transition between bodies and identities, but unlike the standard autobiographical account of transsexuality, Racer X does not emerge on the "other side." He survives but remains in abjection, his memory unwound like a bandage, layer by layer, to reveal a grievous injury. As the montage ends, Racer X refuses to answer the inspector's appeal to truth. "If I did," he says, "it's a mistake I'll have to live with."

This surprisingly poignant sequence discloses, at last, the costs of faster times. What has been hidden in the film's narrative compression is now unfolded before us, providing final context for the events of the former plot: we witness Racer X's lost history. However, this recovered time is not reparative as much as it reveals a sacrifice. Marked by a dysphoric relation to the moment of arrival, Racer X will not return to the triumphal Racer family. If Speed is not bound in time by his relation to capital or race, then Racer X is the material from which such sanguine narratives are extracted. The implications of this scene in the film are crucial. What might be read as a simple narrative of triumph, through

Figure 17: Lost in time: Racer X fails to arrive. |

speed, over the ideological forces of capture is counterweighted by a *differently moving* revelation of the price for other bodies. X's affect moves us to sense the expense of Speed's speed. Despite its thrilling velocity, at its conclusion *Speed Racer* nonetheless points backward toward the loss of transsexuality, an embodiment that since the appearance of transgender has come to signify as past—a body out of time.[65] Racer X's "no" is a turning away from the white temporality that *Speed Racer* appears to celebrate, an insistence on other forms of kinship not yet realized. X's refusal of the film's resolution gives us pause, haunting trans° from "in the wake" (Sharpe, *In the Wake*) of its postracial imagination.

Escaping History: *Cloud Atlas*

With the exception of *Sense8*, *Cloud Atlas* most thoroughly embodies the Wachowskis' entire aesthetic symbology, bringing themes from across their body of work to maturation at the increasingly grand scale that typifies their later career. If *Speed Racer* is concerned with going faster and the sensation of racing through time, then *Cloud Atlas* reaches *further* across temporality, stretching narrative cinema's capacity for representing history. Like its cast and production, the film's artistic ambitions are colossal. It spans five centuries and two planets, interweaving seven story lines set on Earth as well as an off-world colony. Each of these seven points in time is presented as a different exercise in genre, so the larger film operates as compressive meta-text that folds them into connective and thematic resonance. Through the use of makeup and prosthetics, the thirteen main cast members are transposed across race and gender as they move along the film's seven linked narrative threads. This overtly trans° aesthetic plasticizes the film's narrative bodies (codirector Tom Tykwer describes them as "genetic strings" [Peberdy 170]), drawing them across the boundaries of time, space, gender, and racial categorization. As in all the Wachowskis' work, this visual design emblematizes the plot's pedagogical aims. The transfer of consciousnesses across embodiment, genre, and history is fundamental to *Cloud Atlas*'s thematic aspirations, which are to speculatively reverse the trajectory of the colonial encounter and deracinate the grounding of racialization in slavery.

Creating *Cloud Atlas* was a deliberately and necessarily collaborative endeavor. The Wachowskis worked with German director Tom Tykwer to adapt the award-winning 2004 novel,[66] an "experimental world epic" (Knepper 94) that even author David Mitchell assumed was "unfilmable" (Mitchell). Mitchell's epistolary novel contains six nested story lines that begin in the nineteenth-century South Pacific and, through a series of linked texts, travel into a postapocalyptic future occurring on what was once Hawaii. The novel is an exercise in chiastic form, beginning and ending in the earliest timeline (Pacific Islands) and placing the latest segment (Big Isle) at the very middle. The other timelines are reflected in linear temporal order, forward and then backward, between these two portions. For the film version, the Wachowskis and Tykwer preserved these locations and times—Pacific Islands, 1849; Cambridge/Edinburgh, 1936; San Francisco, 1973; London, 2012; Neo Seoul, 2144; and Big Isle, 2321—but interlaced them to a much greater extent than Mitchell's book, which follows an orderly, mirrored structure unfavorable to cinematic montage. To blend the timelines, the directors rearranged the novel to construct a bricolage that mapped shared dramatic patterns among the settings.[67] The Wachowskis then directed the earliest and latest timelines (Pacific Islands, Neo Seoul, Big Isle, and the off-world colony), while Tykwer directed the middle three sections (Cambridge/Edinburgh, San Francisco, London). However, the film's most notable departure from the novel is the addition of an extraterrestrial post/racial colony, which acts as both the starting and final point in the film's circular structure. The Tykwer/Wachowskis *Cloud Atlas* therefore inverts the temporal order of Mitchell's narrative, beginning and ending with a utopian, speculative sensibility that reverses Mitchell's darker vision (Wegner 117).

Despite their various genres, locations, and chronotopic specificities, all of *Cloud Atlas*'s settings intertwine to produce a codependent narrative climax and resolution, illustrating how humanity might sense beyond the fundamental affect of greed.[68] The film opens against a dark sky as Zachry Bailey (Tom Hanks) begins his fireside tale, then progresses through a thematically organized chain of cross-historical events. In the South Pacific (1849) a white lawyer sets sail for San Francisco, only to be poisoned by a thief and eventually saved by a stowaway Moriori slave. A young English composer (1936) reads the lawyer's published account of his trip but commits suicide after his employer steals his work and threatens to expose his homosexuality. A reporter investigating the nuclear industry (1973) meets the composer's elderly lover, a physicist who helps her expose a corrupt energy company. A London publisher (2012) who has read the reporter's mystery novel narrowly escapes being committed and writes a screenplay about his ordeal. The dystopian state Unanimity governs Neo Seoul (2144), a South Korean city populated by two classes—"pureblood" consumers and enslaved genomic clones called fabricants. Fabricant Sonmi~451 (Doona Bae) is inspired to rebellion after watching a film made from the publisher's screenplay. She joins the resistance and is eventually recaptured but delivers a manifesto before she is executed. On the other side of an unexplained apocalyptic event called "The Fall," Zachry is living in a tribal society on Big Isle (2321). Zachry aids the advanced Prescient culture to reactivate a beacon to the off-world colonies, realizing in the process that his religion is based on Sonmi~451's recorded manifesto. The film then finally arrives back at the interstellar future: Zachry, elderly and living in an extraterrestrial settlement, ends the story he is relating to his many grandchildren as his Prescient wife, Meronym (Halle Berry), looks on.

Unlike Mitchell's novel, the Tykwer/Wachowskis version of *Cloud Atlas* speculates outside of planetary time, seeking to escape the foundational trauma of modernity, which it roots in African slavery and the hypothesis of blackness as species. The film attempts to counter the fungibility of bodies imposed under slavery with an oppositional mode of exchangeability across race, gender, and time—achieved through the use of racial prosthetics—that eventually attains an interplanetary reach. In each timeline, a protagonist who reincarnates the same psyche (indicated by a reappearing birthmark) in differently raced and gendered bodies struggles to overcome the seductive forces of capitalism and white supremacy, which intrude upon perception to insist that they are coterminous with reality. The film repeatedly cites cannibalism as a literalization of the savage practice at the base of racial capitalism: the transformation of human bodies into objects for consumption. The recurrence of cannibalism across the Pacific Islands, Neo Seoul, and Big Isle settings suggests a circularity to capitalist history that is finally broken by Zachry and Meronym's departure from Earth and its orbital time. The colony they settle in is represented as a post/racial Eden where the afterlife of slavery has finally been outdistanced. This utopian off-world is attained through a trans° inversion of racial hierarchy, made possible by Sonmi~451's visionary speech and sacrifice.

Although *Cloud Atlas* extends many of the same questions taken up by the Wachowskis' previous films, its independent financing, temporal breadth, and narrative focus on race distinguish it from their other works. Like *Speed Racer*, it deploys a postracial aesthetic to suggest an escape from capitalism, only to gesture at a post/racial possibility that pushes beyond what the film can contain. However, rather than presenting speed as the trajectory by which racial mattering might be evaded, *Cloud Atlas* emphasizes duration, stitching together historical moments of dissent through which the effects of racial capitalism might be finally, collectively outlasted. Similarly to *V for Vendetta*, the film's trans° aesthetic enacts the passage of liberatory sensation from body to body across time. As in *The Matrix*, the nexus for this transference is an interstitial figure upon which conflicting systems converge. Neo's postracial hybridity and Sonmi~451's fabricant posthumanity trouble the constitutive binaries of freedom/slavery, whiteness/blackness, and human/machine that construct modernity and its temporal order. Both Neo and Sonmi~451 display special talents that animate trans° as revolutionary movement through and across time. However, Sonmi~451's manifesto speculates beyond those of her predecessors (Neo's compromise with the machines and V's destruction of the state) toward a utopian politic that will generate a new, post/racial society on other planet.

While author David Mitchell has expressed support for the film version of *Cloud Atlas* as "magnificent" ("5 Questions"), critical and audience responses vary. The film is a major feat of adaptation (Hoad) that pioneers "entirely new" cinematic dimensions (Debruge) while tackling many of the medium's most enduring themes: history, ethics, identity, race, religion, narrativity. Yet while the film engages vaudevillian traditions of "racial, ethnic, and gendered cross-play" to produce an "unusual blend of farcical, pantomimic characterizations and realist performances" (Peberdy 172), its use of prosthetics to move actors across variously raced and gendered embodiments carries clear risks. "Passing" is not the exact effect of this multi-role casting, nor was it the ultimate goal (175), since these cross-race and cross-gender performances must fail in order for the device to succeed: for the actors to remain detectable across *Cloud Atlas*'s multiple timelines and characters, there must also be a trace by which the cross-performances remain visually evident. The approach thus deploys racial caricature in two simultaneous and incommensurate modes, seeking to produce a postracial aesthetics *through* the conscious citation of racist cinematic tropes. To the extent that it treats race as if it were like gender, *Cloud Atlas* thus over-relies on a deconstructive equivalence that endeavors to align incongruous cinematic traditions. Cross-gender performance has had an extremely mixed reception politics,[69] while cross-race performance, rooted in the histories of blackface, yellowface, and redface, has historically allowed white settlers to "constitute (a) national identity" out of racial subjugation (Rogin 18).

Cloud Atlas therefore partially reflects how deconstructive applications of trans° have concatenated *through* the abstraction of race, which must be vanished as a material condition of both sex and gender (Ellison et al., 163). The thinking of race through trans°—without a *reciprocal materialist thinking* of trans° through race—encourages the shallow comparisons of medical transition with race switching that have increasingly dominated discussions of transgender rights since the film's release. Transgender has historically been evoked in this correlation to prompt racial anxieties about the dissolution of whiteness, while the analogy simultaneously depicts transgender identities as inauthentic vis-à-vis the presumed biological *realness* of race. For example, in her classically transphobic text *The Transsexual Empire*, Janice Raymond dismisses transsexuality by asking, "To what extent would concerned blacks accept whites who had undergone medicalized changes in skin color and, in the process, claimed that they had not only a black body but a black soul?" (140). Recent debates around the figures of Rachel Dolezal and Caitlyn Jenner have reactivated this discussion. In 2015 Dolezal—a white woman who was outed as passing for black—claimed a "transracial" identity and compared herself to transgender celebrity Caitlyn Jenner, prompting heated discussions over the comparative validity of hers and Jenner's identity claims. Several white cisgender scholars responded by taking up trans° to argue for the apparent dissolution of race, without adequately considering the material history of trans° or race as enfleshed phenomena.[70] This impulse to use trans° to evacuate race illustrates how the Wachowskis' work, which often engages trans° to explore racial hybridity and cross-racial encounter, may simultaneously activate preexisting racist logics. For example, the Media Action Network for Asian Americans decried *Cloud Atlas*'s prosthetic creation of "artificial-looking" Asian features on white actors, pointing out that the directors had assiduously avoided using blackface (Musto). Despite nearly all of *Cloud Atlas*'s principal actors playing across race (Asian actors did indeed play white roles [Garret]), Asian-ness is surrogated in the film's performance economy in ways that have been traditionally reserved for blackness.

Cloud Atlas uses a trans° aesthetic to invert the developmental hierarchy of race, projecting the fungibility generally associated with the black body onto the Asian body, which becomes an exchange point for the film's reversal of the racial order. That point of exchange is Sonmi~451, *Cloud Atlas*'s primary revolutionary body. A Korean genomic fabricant and Neo Seoul slave, Sonmi~451 will pass the thread of *Cloud Atlas*'s liberatory message forward into other worlds. Sonmi~451 evokes trans° in complex ways: Her body is futurist but not white, human but not natural, enslaved but not black. Her artificiality puts the "realness" of her womanhood into question, while her self-actualization and requisite martyrdom resonate with experiences of transgender identification and oppression. "If I had remained invisible, the truth would stay hidden," she notes to her Archivist just before being executed. "I couldn't allow that."[71] Sonmi~451's manifesto is the film's ultimate pedagogy, a utopian ideation transmitted across time, through which the raced binary of primitive/developed will be upended. "Our lives are not our own," she states. "From womb to tomb, we are bound to others, past and present, and by each crime and every kindness, we birth our future." If racial capitalism asserts that some lives must be expendable, then Sonmi~451 delivers an inverted ethics, insisting that the causality in even a single life unfolds endlessly. How we transition from the first sense to the second is *Cloud Atlas*'s rhetorical shape.

The film opens at its end. Zachry sits in darkness by a fire on what we will learn is a distant planet, relating a story in pidgin. Storytelling and textuality are crucial to *Cloud Atlas*'s epistolary structure, a style that will culminate in Sonmi~451's manifesto. This opening scene of oral transmission establishes the architecture of the film's narrative. Zachry is the historical voice of the text, while we are positioned in his gathered audience, who will be revealed as his grandchildren in the film's final scene. We will discover, in time, that this is a scene of inheritance ("Ancestry, howling at you," Zachry says), through which we learn how we have transitioned from "there" (Earth) to here. Zachry tells us about the first time he and "Ol' Georgie met, eye-to-eye." Old Georgie (Hugo Weaving), a representation of evil and white supremacist ideology, will torment Zachry throughout the Big Isle timeline. This "eye-to-eye" references Sonmi~451's orison ("To know oneself is only possible through the eyes of the other," she states) but also analogizes the viewer's encounter with the cinematic text. The film then cuts from Zachry to its earliest timeline, Pacific Islands (1849), where the charlatan Dr. Henry Goose (Tom Hanks) describes history as a space in which "the strong gorged on the weak," rooted in the apparent cannibal acts of the local primitives. A few scenes later, Sonmi~451 will escape from her enslavement, aided by activist Hae-Joo Chang (Jim Sturgess), who reassures her, "There is no reason to hide. . . . You can remain here and risk being discovered, or you can come with me." Tykwer has described this line as an invitation into what is a consciously difficult cinematic text, offering the viewer a choice to actively participate in the film's meaning ("DP/30"). The piece of dialogue aligns the formal conventions of film with the inviolable borders of race, gender, and time that *Cloud Atlas* progressively assaults.

At their dinner table in the South Pacific, served by slaves, Adam Ewing (Jim Sturgess) and Reverend Horrox (Hugh Grant) discuss a contract for 650 acres of land that represents the traumatic initiation of modern history. Struck in the stark shadow of the transatlantic slave trade, this deal between nineteenth-century white colonizers is the earliest point in *Cloud Atlas*'s timeline, illustrating how modern temporality has been generated by the value—time and its transformation into capital—extracted from black bodies. The day after concluding business with Horrox, Ewing witnesses a whipping in which the punished slave Autua's (David Gyasi) eyes lock with his in a shot/reverse shot, echoing Zachry's eye-to-eye confrontation with Old Georgie. Ewing cannot withstand Autua's gaze and immediately loses his senses, fainting. This "scene of subjection" (Hartman 4–6) is one of many "eye-to-eye" encounters strung across *Cloud Atlas* that cite the original violence of black/white racialization and its replication across history by capitalism. In pushing a revolutionary ideality forward through Sonmi~451's trans°ed body, *Cloud Atlas* will arrive at an obverse and dissenting speculation. In the Big Isle sequences, white cultures have devolved into tribal primitivism, while the nonwhite Prescients possess an advanced technological culture. It is Prescient technology that will transport Zachry and Meronym, who collaborate through a common inheritance of Sonmi~451's teachings, into an off-world and post/racial utopian future.

The Neo Seoul segment of *Cloud Atlas* is the most philosophically compelling and narratively essential section of the film, through which the thread of Ewing's eye-to-eye with Autua is drawn forward into the postapocalyptic future. Mitchell's novel sets this section in a dystopian South Korea, a "yellow future" (Park, *Yellow Future*) that draws upon negative Western associations of East Asia with oppressive technocracy. The Wachowskis' spectacular rendering of a neon-lit, hyper-corporate Neo Seoul is overtly inspired by *Blade Runner*, while its closed industrial system of human enslavement, execution, and cannibalization references *Soylent Green* (1973) and *Battle Royale* (2000). Under Unanimity, enslavement is determined not by skin color but by "pure" versus planned genomics, a distinction that superimposes the binary of fabricant/pureblood over the original black/white categorization of the film's earliest timeline. The enslaved fabricant class is an ultra-proletariat, drugged into sleep each night and possessing no memory beyond the twenty-four-hour cycle of work into which it has been inserted. After twelve years of labor, each fabricant is secretly executed in a mock-religious "exultation" and processed into a drug-laced liquid called "soap" that is fed to other unaware fabricants. The fabricants' situation therefore represents the evolution of enslavement under capitalism from chattel slavery across three centuries into a form of pure false consciousness: fabricants cannot sense that they are a product.[72]

It is Sonmi~451 who will awaken from this false consciousness into revolutionary dissent, breaking with the fascist form of Unanimity's ideology and becoming the liberatory ideal that Zachry and Meronym will share nearly two centuries later, after Unanimity falls. In her final interview with the Archivist (James D'Arcy), Sonmi~451 describes her self-realization as a passage out of a closed ontology: "Knowledge is a mirror. For the first time, I was allowed to see who I was, and who I might become." In the film's second half, this emphasis on becoming is increasingly metaphorized by a series of movements through doorways. Multiple characters discover and pass through doors and gates as they traverse narrative thresholds into and out of imprisoning spaces:

Sonmi~451 is liberated from her sleepbox; Luisa Rey (Halle Berry) gains entry to Rufus Sixsmith's (James D'Arcy) room and reads his letters; Timothy Cavendish (Jim Broadbent) arrives at Aurora House. Actors slide postracially between characters as the film more rapidly compresses time in montage, borders between separate timelines falling away. Dialogue and parallel melodramatic action intensify the collapse of discrete experiences: "The gulf," Robert Frobisher (Ben Wishaw) insists to composer Vyvyan Ayrs (Jim Broadbent), "is an illusion"—a claim spatially dramatized as Union leader Hae-Joon Chang and Sonmi~451 flee across an improvised bridge to escape capture. Their linked bodies, twinned across gender and suspended over a chasm between skyscrapers (fig. 18), cite Trinity's fantastical leap from *The Matrix* in what is *Cloud Atlas*'s most overtly trans° image.

Neo Seoul is a horrifying extension of current global labor conditions into a future where cloned Asian women have been conscripted into the industrial food economy. The fabricant class compels us to consider the oppressive conditions of feminized labor and sex work that both Asian and transgender women often experience. Sonmi~451 exists merely to serve fast food to "consumers" and then be consumed in turn—a cycle she is unaware of until a rebellious friendship shatters the cloned form of her labor. Another fabricant, Yoona~939 (Xun Zhou), is giving her drugged food to a seer and staying up all night. Together, she and Sonmi~451 watch a banned film in which a London publisher escapes being committed, shouting, "I will not be subjected to criminal abuse!"

Figure 18: Bridging the gulf: sensing beyond division.

This diegetic film prompts the same sensations *Cloud Atlas* seeks to induce: it awakens dissenting affects in both fabricants. Some days later, Yoona~939 physically resists being sexually harassed by a consumer. As she tries to flee, she is locked in an "eye-to-eye" shot/reverse shot with her seer, who then executes her by activating a slave collar that punctures her carotid artery. The sequence is a replication of Ewing's shared gaze with Autua—an aesthetic reminder of how capitalism is grounded in a historical piercing of flesh, a cannibalization of bodies. Once Sonmi~451 joins the Union rebellion, she learns where the yearly "exultation" leads. Hae-Joo Chang shows her a factory where fabricant bodies are processed as if they are slaughtered chickens. The Wachowskis' work is rife with such moments of revelation, in which the implicit violence of ideology bursts to the surface of the text, assaulting the viewer with a spectacular disclosure. Like Neo, who must learn to see again once he is extracted from the Matrix, Adam Ewing and Sonmi~451 must grow new ethical and political sensories to grapple with the disclosed structures of their worlds.

The Neo Seoul fabricants cite a familiar science fiction trope, the cloned female series, that in *Cloud Atlas* also suggests an oblique condemnation of cisnormative womanhood. As a genre motif, the replicated female body often reflects a historical period's cultural fantasies or fears about the loss of "real" (i.e., white and cisgender) women.[73] For example, the literature of radical feminism has deployed the image of the female series to decry the automation of gender by medical technology,[74] displaying a nativist vigilance that simultaneously traffics in Orientalist anxiety—as when Raymond accuses transsexual women of turning lesbian-feminist space into a "harem" (134). The figure of the Asian woman—inscrutable and indecipherable from the "horde"—is associated in U.S. culture with trans femininity as a metonymic complement through which the dangers of gender transition have historically been explored. Images of trans women were not widely available until the Korean and Vietnam wars, during which the (in)securities of postwar nationalism were expressed through Orientalist deployments of trans femininity that troubled the ideological borders of the Cold War (*M*°*A*°*S*°*H's* Corporal Klinger and the 1988 play *M. Butterfly* are examples). Travel to Asia and Africa by many Western trans women seeking gender reassignment in the 1960s–'80s further inscribed this association: For example, Jan Morris's widely read account of her own medical transition, *Conundrum*, indulges in Orientalized depictions of the East as an exotic space of gender mystification. Morris's account of her visit to Casablanca to undergo surgery illustrates how white postwar transgender subjects themselves made use of Orientalist scripts to explain their experiences of acquiring "alien" bodies:

> It really was like a visit to a wizard. I saw myself, as I walked through those garish streets, as a figure of a fairy tale, about to be transformed. Duck into swan? Scullion into bride? More magical than any such transformation: Man into woman. This was the last city I would ever see as a male. The office blocks might not look much like castle walls, nor the taxis like camels or carriages, but I still sometimes heard the limpid Arab music, and smelt the pungent Arab smells, that had for so long pervaded my life, and I could suppose it to be some city of fable, of phoenix and fantasy, in which transubstantiations were regularly effected, when the omens were right and the moon in its proper phase. (136)

The resonance between Asian-ness and transgender strung throughout the Wachowskis' cinema (beginning in *Bound*) is both a confrontation *and* working with how Western popular culture has Orientalized trans femininity: *Cloud Atlas*'s sympathetic representation of the fabricants' plight critically references the transphobic fear of surgically constructed bodies undetectably appropriating the status of woman, deploying racist assumptions about the interchangeability of Asian women (fig. 19) to critique the cisnormativity of biological essentialism. Sonmi~451 notes the falseness of the artificial/biological binary that defines caste within Unanimity, stating, "Whether we are born in a tank or a womb, we are all equally human." The fabricants' visual similarity with one another as well as with pureblood (i.e., cis) women threatens to invade and denature womanhood itself. *Cloud Atlas* therefore cites Orientalist motifs contrapuntally: while its white/Asian cross-racial performances evoke the caricature of Asian-ness in Western theatrical and cinematic traditions, its depiction of the fabricants as an identical Asian horde reifies the violent sameness embedded in cissexist defenses of "natural" womanhood.

Centuries later on Big Isle, Zachry is also pursued by a violent sameness—a vestigial white supremacist instinct represented by the top-hatted, reptilian figure of Old Georgie. Zachry carries Old Georgie as a form of racial unconscious and struggles to suppress his destructive

Figure 19: Asian female series:
automated trans* gender.

demands to act out of racist resentment and capitalist aggression. This same savagery is externalized on Big Isle in the pale-skinned cannibal Kona tribe that wages war on Zachry's herding culture, murdering the Valleysmen and consuming their bodies. The figures of Zachry and the Kona are innovative attempts to primitivize whiteness without engaging the device of the noble savage. While his facial tattoos and pidgin are similar to Autua's, Zachry is by contrast superstitious, morally weak, unintelligent, and easily frightened. By juxtaposing Zachry's and the Kona's primitive whiteness with Meronym's Afrofuturist Prescient culture, the Big Isle sequences reverse the positions of whiteness and blackness engraved in the colonial contract struck by Ewing and Horrox at the outset of the film's time. At the end of planetary history, *Cloud Atlas* suggests, white culture is (still) enslaved to savage practices, while the Prescients are peaceful, technologically sophisticated colonizers—of other planets. *Cloud Atlas* therefore transposes the poles of the white/black binary in a trans° aesthetic that assaults the "ladder of civilization" ordering modernity.

If Sonmi~451 embodies *Cloud Atlas*'s trans°temporal utopian ideal, then Zachry functions as its receptacle. He is the character who carries the film's narrative in his senses and relates its tale, so the film begins and ends with his "yarning." Zachry is the inheritor of the recurring psyche that skips across the film's timelines, marking each body it inhabits with a comet-shaped nevus. On Big Isle, Zachry is haunted by Old Georgie as well as memories from throughout the film's history—specters inculcated by the disaster of racial capitalism, which he and Meronym will escape only by leaving Earth's orbit. Zachry's archival sensorium is triggered by his first contact with Meronym, whose Afrofuturist culture scrambles the developmental hierarchy of race and initiates him into a trans° historical consciousness. In a dream sequence, Zachry watches Meronym using an advanced medical tool to treat her wounded arm. She suddenly looks up into his eyes (another "eye-to-eye"), and a collision of past memories— including Ewing's memories of Autua's chained body—floods Zachry's senses. He awakes gasping in his bed, the camera swirling out around him in a disorienting 360-degree rotation. In this sensorially assaultive moment, Zachry becomes a witness to black enslavement, which is "nailed to [his] memory" as the horror that originated modern history. Zachry's relationship with Meronym, facilitated by their shared belief in Sonmi~451's manifesto, offers a compensatory exit from history and its grounding in racial trauma. Following Sonmi~451's paratactic directive to bind across otherness, Zachry overcomes his racist suspicion of Meronym and helps her contact the off-world colonies that will save them from the dying Earth.

The surpassing of capitalist time through an escape from Earth's orbit into a post/racial, extraterrestrial future thus becomes *Cloud Atlas's* closing, utopian message. In the ultimate scene, we arrive where the film began. Zachry finishes his tale as his racially diverse grandchildren look on. This final setting is represented as a new Eden, where race has been deracinated from culture, resulting in a racially mixed, multigenerational tribe that blends Prescient and Valleysmen traditions. Notably, this future is *not without race*; rather, race's hierarchy has been defused. Despite its earlier modes of postracial performance, *Cloud Atlas* does not depict an end to racial phenotype as much as it suggests an end to the social and political *meanings* of phenotype. The film's "hybrid future" is a potential future in which phenotype persists but racial hierarchy and hypodescent do not. There is no cross-race performance in this last scene, suggesting that the film's earlier, theatrical citations of race no longer apply. We are now outside race's earlier history, which has been outlasted by temporal and spatial distance from its origin. In its final scene, *Cloud Atlas* thus strikes a bargain between postracial and post/racial modes, deploying the first to bring us to the threshold of the second—a radically new social environment where kinship and race might be organized differently. One of the children asks Zachry, "Which is Earth?" Zachry points at a distant star. "That blue shimmerer." The camera pulls into deep focus to light upon the dot of Earth, now incredibly far off. This pointing folds the film's spatial field, bringing unfathomably distant points into contact—a pleat in space that reveals to us the film's vast narrative expanse. The camera focus then pulls back into the foreground, where Zachry and his grandchild are meeting Meronym on the front steps of their house. As they disappear inside, the camera floats up into the negative space of the starry sky. Across the length of the film, we have outdistanced the meaning of race to its undoing.

Speculative Heights: *Jupiter Ascending*

The Wachowskis' final film for Warner Bros., *Jupiter Ascending*, is a science fiction epic that stands as their most spectacular and politicized treatment of the vertical axis, bringing their assault trilogy to a close. While *Speed Racer* races across time (going faster) and *Cloud Atlas* dilates across history (going further), *Jupiter Ascending* explores going *higher*—a sensation that since *The Matrix* the Wachowskis have been famous for bringing under new techniques of visualization (Whissel 44–45). Both indulgently campy and pointedly political, *Jupiter* is a lushly allegorized satire of the global elite that is the Wachowskis' most overtly anticapitalist work to date. Verticality and vertiginousness are clearly referenced in the film's title but are also at play in its genre citation of the space opera, a popular form committed to broad dimensions and affective peaks. General response to *Jupiter* has been weak, tending to criticize its ornate look and its run-on-sentence plotting.[75] These points miss how the film intentionally traffics in feminized styles of narrativity (especially soap opera's serial temporality) to conduct a feminist hijacking of blockbuster science fiction. Unlike other recent U.S. films addressing the post-crash class divide, *Jupiter*'s critique is elaborated through a pageantry of feminine, rather than masculine, excess. *Jupiter* is also the first U.S. feature film with a budget of over $100 million that is both directed by women and stars a woman in the lead role (Lachenal), an industry achievement that has gone largely unnoticed in the subsequent stir around Patty Jenkins's *Wonder Woman* (2017).

Jupiter Ascending pushes all of the stock elements of the studio action film—repeated chases, improbable plotting, moral polarization, apocalyptic threat, stunning visual effects—to their melodramatic breaking points. The film is, at times, a signature visual accomplishment. Its eight-minute aerial chase sequence through Chicago was shot in pre-dawn light, six minutes at a time over three months, in order to capture the sky's twilight blue while preserving the warm hue of the city lights. The arresting orange/indigo contrast of the chase, its staggeringly wide background plates, and the demanding practical stunts performed by the principal actors combine to produce a masterpiece of action directing (Failes). The innovative visual design provides a high-contrast backdrop for the earnest plot, producing a film that feels alternately "baroque and corny" (Dargis). However, these high/low tonal shifts are more than accidental. The plot's indulgently spectacular ascents and descents capture the disorienting feel of the aristocratic lineage that the lead character, Jupiter Jones (Mila Kunis), involuntarily inherits. Playing satire against melodrama, *Jupiter* displays the conscious tension between meta-referential genre humor and emotional sincerity that distinguishes the Wachowskis' early work but magnifies the scale of this dissonance to jarring proportions—smashing hyperbole into deadpan, futurism into antiquity, drama into comedy. It is precisely through this incongruous framing that *Jupiter* hopes to expose capitalism's fatuous absurdities, assaulting our senses by reflecting American culture's preposterous investments in consumption, novelty, and size. In a society riven by such astounding disparities, *Jupiter* asks, how much is too much? To capture an era so distorted by the grotesque effects of market speculation, realism just won't do.

Our unlikely hero, Jupiter Jones, is a lowly maid who lives in a Chicago flophouse with her extended family. An undocumented Russian immigrant, Jupiter is unaware that her gene imprint is identical to the former queen of House Abrasax—an intergalactic ruling family that owns the Earth and all of its resources, including its human lives. House Abrasax has seeded the Earth with humans and allowed them to multiply to unsustainable numbers for the investment purpose of eventually harvesting them. At a refinery inside the Great Red Spot on planet Jupiter, Balem Abrasax (Eddie Redmayne) produces an immortality serum from harvested human bodies and packages it for sale. This serum extracts lifespan from the human harvest, transmitting excess lived time to the extraterrestrial aristocracy and rejuvenating it indefinitely. However,

Jupiter's genomic sequencing is considered a "recurrence" of Queen Abrasax, deposing the Abrasax children from inheritance and making her the rightful owner of Earth's human crop. With the help of Caine Wise (Channing Tatum), a transpecies mercenary with spliced human/canine DNA (Toto to Jupiter's Dorothy Gale), Jupiter travels to the planet Orous to claim her title. She refuses marriage to Titus Abrasax (Douglas Booth) and fights Balem to the death, destroying his serum refinery in the process. She then returns to her previous life, still holding her claim to Earth.

Jupiter Ascending is primarily interested in exploring intensified, operatic ranges of emotion, time, space, and design, assaulting the very borders of cinematic reality. The film was the largest digital environment that its production house, Double Negative, had ever constructed, resulting in a number of presentations at industry conferences (Bird and Fleury). The Wachowskis modeled *Jupiter* to reject the utilitarian style typically depicted in science fiction, instead combining high styles of architecture from across human history. To produce a sense of humanity's "long history with aesthetics" (Weintraub), they exaggerated the look of older cities, which feature edifices from multiple millennia. As Lana Wachowski describes, "You have to see old and new right smack next to each other, and then you feel time" (McWeeny, "Part One"). Like the gravity of planet Jupiter itself, all of the scales in *Jupiter Ascending* are amplified. Surfaces are sensationalized, coated in scintillating ornamentations. In a classic Wachowskian emblematic touch, even the Village Roadshow Pictures icon that opens the film is embellished in gold filigree. Throughout *Jupiter*, objects deliver pedagogical messages about the film's escalated allegorical pitch, as when Balem, the royal head of House Abrasax, arrives in an Egyptian litter that is fashioned from a living black woman's body. Such on-the-noseness is a feature of *Jupiter*'s conscious inversion of fantasy, in which capitalist, patriarchal, and racist subtexts of fictionalized reality become the text itself. *Jupiter* assaults our senses (both aesthetic and moral) with how the world *actually is*, only more so.

An anticapitalist manifesto dressed as fairy tale, *Jupiter Ascending*'s vision hinges on the contradictory valences—utopian and market—of *speculation*. Weaponizing fantasy against its own absurdity (Petri), the film consciously abandons subtext and forces the viewer into confrontation with capitalism's sociopathic delusions. Members of House Abrasax, an obvious representation of the one percent, are actual "masters of the universe" who grow and sell concentrated human life to other elites. The tremendous gap between those who have and those who do not is plotted by the film's opening title sequence, which dwarfs the planet Jupiter's four largest moons by superimposing them in front of its massive, roiling sphere. Here again, the Wachowskis employ an effects emblem to introduce the film's main theme—the vertigo induced by immense differences in scale. Vertigo is proprioceptively associated with the disorienting effects of digital reproduction (Clover, *Matrix* 39) but also figures in *Jupiter* as an affective response to the intensity and pace of hyper-capitalist speculation. Jupiter's numb shock when she discovers the universal scope of the Abrasax industry mimics the vertiginous disorientation brought on by the apparent death of socialism at the close of the twentieth century: there appears to be "no alternative."[76] When Kalique Abrasax (Tuppence Middleton) states to Jupiter Jones, "Time is the single most precious commodity in the universe," she baldly repeats the thesis of capitalism as defined under modernity. While the line might ring as obvious, its *knowing* function is consistent with the Wachowskis' investment in socially conscious popular cinema.

It is no coincidence that *Jupiter Ascending* opens in St. Petersburg, the site of the Russian Revolution. That Jupiter is conceived in what was once Petrograd aligns her birth with the Marxist imaginary that fueled the Bolshevik uprising. She is the character who will be most capable of resisting false consciousness and the romantic lure of property relations, represented in the film by her rejection of marriage to Titus Abrasax. The beginning of *Jupiter Ascending* locks Jupiter into an existential dysphoria with capitalist temporality, from which there is no apparent earthly exit. In an opening montage that is played simultaneously for pathos and comedy, her workdays laboring in the homes of wealthy elites cycle before us, unrecognizable from one another in a repeating loop. Tonally, this puts *Jupiter* in conversation with other comedies depicting women's experience of low-wage labor, such as *Nine to Five* (1980), *Maid in America* (1982) and *Working Girl* (1988). The sequence explores how living capitalist time in the pink-collar proletariat feels. Jupiter begins and ends each day in the same bed, repeating the same line: "I hate my life." Her status in the United States as an "illegal alien" is a play both on her alien heritage and on the alienated state of her feminized labor, which repeats in a seemingly endless orbit. An evocative shot of her dusting a globe as she cleans an office returns us to the planetary scale of the film's opening titles. For Jupiter, it would seem, it's a small world—after all.

As in transgender politics, what counts as fantasy in *Jupiter Ascending*'s world is a political issue. The question of the film is whether Jupiter will be able to refuse her inheritance, which is literally the inheritance of a predetermined gender. Jupiter's royal identity, the Abrasax family insists, is already genetically inscribed and therefore unavoidable (a claim familiar to transgender people). But the "dream come true" of Jupiter's disclosed royal heritage carries a preordained and terrible cost: millions of extracted lives maintained her previous incarnation as queen. In a scene perfectly illustrating the (re)construction of cisgender womanhood, Jupiter views the statue of her former incarnation, Queen Abrasax, an obdurate body whose history and role she is expected to unquestioningly assume (fig. 20). The moment is one of several in which *Jupiter* offers a consciously trans° critique of gender and its administrative violence (Spade, *Normal Life*). The bureaucratic nightmare of Orous, where Jupiter fills out infinite paperwork and visits endless offices to attain her title, is both an homage to *Brazil* (1985) (Terry Gilliam makes a cameo appearance) and a recreation of the obstacles transgender people encounter when attempting to access state identification, health care, and social services. Like gender in the Abrasax line, Orous is organized through the recurrence of set forms with no tolerance for change or complexity.

Jupiter contrasts these fixed forms with a hybrid mode of in-betweenness—transpecies—that snarls the vertical, orderly structure of taxonomy. The film's many transgenic human/animal bodies are created by "splicers," DNA manipulators who leave their names, like signatures, on the flesh of their creations. Reminiscent of both the slave brand and the surgical scar, the splicer's sign marks transpecies as a surrogate for racialized/trans° modes of embodiment. As Eva Hayward and Jami Weinstein put it in their introduction to the *Tranimalities* issue of *Transgender Studies Quarterly* (2.2), "Transgender subjects have never been fully human" (195). Trans° in *Jupiter* is therefore also the anti-hierarchy of entanglement, the biological and affective exchanges across life that prevent the discrete categorization of bodies according to sex, race, or species.

Figure 20: Cisgender inheritance:
aristocratic gender.

For all of its emphasis on the spectacle of height, *Jupiter Ascending* is ultimately suspicious of the temptation to rise above others, the fantasy of becoming "Your Highness." The film is replete with scenes of sensorial assault, as Jupiter nearly loses her footing under the seductive, vertiginous forces of identification within patriarchy and capitalism. In one of the film's most striking images, she slides in slow motion over the edge of a metal ledge as the exploding surface of Balem's refinery gleams far below (fig. 21). The moral stakes of the drama are clear: in melodrama as in capitalism, to go higher means risking an increasingly damaging fall. House Abrasax is indeed unbound from time but only through a predatory relation to the bodies it consumes. If Jupiter is fettered to House Abrasax by an aristocratic, cisgender, and white supremacist reiteration of form, then she must unbind the Earth from this same consequence. The trans° of *Jupiter* is thus ultimately a transversal—an adventure into and back from the dangers of the vertical axis. Jupiter ascends to challenge her royal inheritance but ultimately makes a democratizing return to Earth, where a communal ethic will prevail. Her ownership of the means of production allows Jupiter to redistribute time sideways across Earth's human lives, which will no longer be extracted in the process of harvest. Abolishing the imposed point beyond which history could not evolve, *Jupiter Ascending* ends with a lateral, utopian

Figure 21: Horizontal return: the gravity of
abandoning "Your Highness."

transmission of futurity across the social body. Much like Dorothy Gale,
Jupiter remembers the value of her queerly extended family, refuses
rule over others, and returns to the horizon.

Epilogue—Event Horizon: *Sense8*

When Netflix granted *Sense8* a finale in late June 2017, I breathed
a sigh of relief. An enthrallingly realized dramatic series that marks
the Wachowskis' first foray into television, *Sense8* had been perhaps
too unusual and too romantic for a "peak TV" environment saturated
with forebodingly dystopic rebooted properties.[77] As much a critique
of popular science fiction (Rothman) as it is a speculative explosion of
televisual form, *Sense8* defies categorization, "skipping gleefully" (Li)
across the narrative styles that organize today's streaming market. Despite its recognition for Outstanding Drama Series at the 2016 GLAAD
awards, Netflix abruptly canceled the series shortly after the May release of its second season. Citing a lack of funds, the streaming service
turned studio announced the termination on June 1—the opening day
of LGBTQ Pride month and only eleven days before the anniversary
of the Orlando Pulse massacre. Given that *Sense8* is one of few Netflix
Originals to feature lead transgender and queer characters, including

multiple queer characters of color, the timing of the cancellation was received as especially insensitive. Fan response was swift and global: hashtag campaigns erupted on Twitter and Facebook, calls and emails flooded into Netflix customer service, a group called "Operation Flip Flop" mailed single flip-flops (a reference to the character Lito's missing sandal) to Netflix CEO Reed Hastings, and a Change.org petition authored by "THE GANG Sense8FANS," posted from Buenos Aires, demanded a renewal in sixteen separate languages (Krishna). Internet journalism covering the cancellation pointed to a "troubling trend" at Netflix, which seemed to be axing its most diverse shows (Jones; Ryan). By June 29, the Change.org petition had gained 524,726 signatures,[78] and Netflix executives acquiesced—at least partially. At 2:39 PM EST that day, a letter from Lana Wachowski sharing that Netflix had approved a two-hour finale episode was posted in *Sense8*'s official Twitter feed (fig. 22).[79]

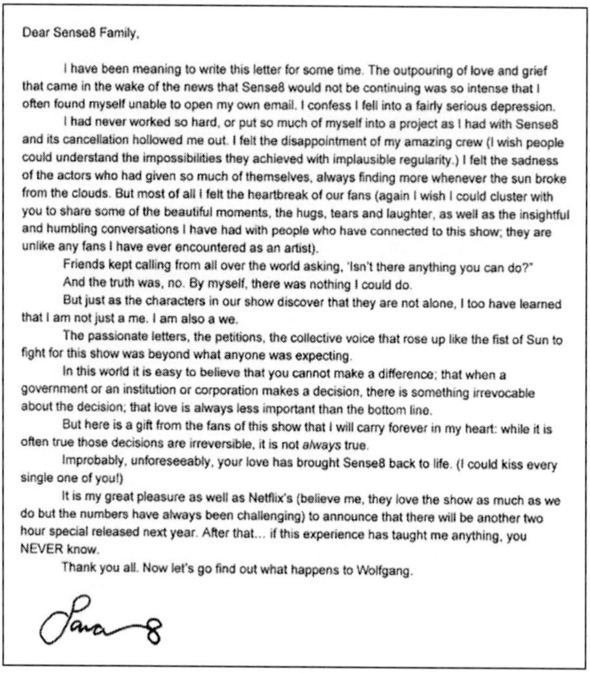

Dear Sense8 Family,

 I have been meaning to write this letter for some time. The outpouring of love and grief that came in the wake of the news that Sense8 would not be continuing was so intense that I often found myself unable to open my own email. I confess I fell into a fairly serious depression.
 I had never worked so hard, or put so much of myself into a project as I had with Sense8 and its cancellation hollowed me out. I felt the disappointment of my amazing crew (I wish people could understand the impossibilities they achieved with implausible regularity.) I felt the sadness of the actors who had given so much of themselves, always finding more whenever the sun broke from the clouds. But most of all I felt the heartbreak of our fans (again I wish I could cluster with you to share some of the beautiful moments, the hugs, tears and laughter, as well as the insightful and humbling conversations I have had with people who have connected to this show; they are unlike any fans I have ever encountered as an artist).
 Friends kept calling from all over the world asking, 'Isn't there anything you can do?'
 And the truth was, no. By myself, there was nothing I could do.
 But just as the characters in our show discover that they are not alone, I too have learned that I am not just a me. I am also a we.
 The passionate letters, the petitions, the collective voice that rose up like the fist of Sun to fight for this show was beyond what anyone was expecting.
 In this world it is easy to believe that you cannot make a difference; that when a government or an institution or corporation makes a decision, there is something irrevocable about the decision; that love is always less important than the bottom line.
 But here is a gift from the fans of this show that I will carry forever in my heart: while it is often true those decisions are irreversible, it is not *always* true.
 Improbably, unforeseeably, your love has brought Sense8 back to life. (I could kiss every single one of you!)
 It is my great pleasure as well as Netflix's (believe me, they love the show as much as we do but the numbers have always been challenging) to announce that there will be another two hour special released next year. After that… if this experience has taught me anything, you NEVER know.
 Thank you all. Now let's go find out what happens to Wolfgang.

 Lana8

Figure 22: Lana Wachowski's letter announcing
Netflix's approval of a *Sense8* finale special.

These events appear to be unprecedented in the history of streaming television. In creating a text as groundbreakingly transnational as *Sense8*—which is shot in at least sixteen cities in eleven different countries around the world—the Wachowskis and cocreator J. Michael Straczynski had engineered an intercontinental audience that was now demanding that Netflix recognize its legitimacy. Data released in the wake of the finale announcement revealed that the majority of Netflix subscribers now live outside the United States, confirming the streaming giant as a "global enterprise" (Idato). As Wachowski herself notes in her letter ("I wish I could cluster with you"), the speculative "cluster" formation shared between telepathic characters on *Sense8* had become a powerful metaphor for the desiring, geographically diffuse body of its viewership. The series had created a symbolic structure for the emergence of its own fandoms and social media affinity cultures. Facebook groups for viewers of *Sense8* reference the cluster as a new kind of social formation and consumer model, carrying titles such as "*Sense8* Global Cluster," "*Sense8* Cluster Maker" and "AfricaCluster—*Sense8*." Users on platforms as diverse as Facebook, Friendesque, Reddit, and Whatsapp match birthdates to sort themselves into fan clusters. Much as they accomplished with *The Matrix* nearly twenty years ago, the Wachowskis appear to have again found the point where new technologies and speculative narrativity converge to reorient our common sense. In this networked era of "spreadable" media (Jenkins, *Spreadable Media*) and online cultures sewn together through the sharing of likes and emojis, *Sense8*'s affectively enmeshed characters reflect how social media shapes our sense of the world. The telepathically entwined, orgiastically sensational encounters within the show's fictional cluster (fig. 23) subjunctively point toward the interconnected global era it feels like we *might* achieve—if only we could move beyond our differences and "come together." In this time of emerging right-wing nationalism, *Sense8*'s vision of global interdependence has suddenly gained a "greater sense of urgency" (Xiao). A progressive vision of an opening empathetic horizon across race, gender, nation, and sexuality, *Sense8* is the optimistic queer/trans° science fiction that in 2015 we didn't yet sense we would need.

If *Jupiter Ascending* returns us to the horizon of *Bound*'s original, fugitive escape, then *Sense8* positions us on its unfolding, forward edge. The series marks an event horizon past which the Wachowskis' assaults

Figure 23: Come, together: horizontal relations in
one of *Sense8*'s telepathic cluster orgies.

on cinematic reality subside into an immersive, synchronic explora-
tion of global simultaneity. *Sense8*'s story line is constellated through
the senses of eight characters spread over the globe: Capheus "Van
Damn" Onyango (Aml Ameen/Toby Onwumere) in Nairobi, Sun Bak
(Doona Bae) in Seoul, Nomi Marks (Jamie Clayton) in San Francisco,
Kala Dandekar (Tina Desai) in Mumbai, Riley "Blue" Gunnarsdóttir
(Tuppence Middleton) in Reykjavik and London, Wolfgang Bogdanow
(Max Riemelt) in Berlin, Lito Rodriguez (Miguel Ángel Silvestre) in
Mexico City, and Will Gorski (Brian J. Smith) in Chicago. Over the span
of the first two seasons, these eight characters come to realize that they
are not human but a separate hominid species, *homo sensorium*, who
live secretly among humans in psychically linked groups. When a cluster
is born, its sensates begin to mutate into merged consciousness, their
brains morphologically shifting and the borders of their bodies falling
away. The eighth "sense" referenced in the series' title is the enhanced
capacity for empathetic contact that the *homo sensoria* (i.e., "sensates")
experience within their cluster. Cluster members can share sensations,
memories, affects, skills, and communicate directly across time and
space by "visiting"—a telepathic/telekinetic link the show demonstrates
through an editing process that transposes the sensates' bodies across
its globally disparate settings. Over the course of the series, the eight

main characters must form a unified symbiosis—an eightfold composite character—to evade the Biologic Preservation Organization (BPO), a eugenicist entity that lobotomizes *homo sensoria* and uses them as remotely operated weapons.

Although much analysis of *Sense8* remarks on the strength of its queerness, *trans°* is the necessary keyword in any attempt to understand the series (Shaw). A media text that "provokes a new understanding of the Wachowskis as transgender auteurs" (Bailey et al. 76), *Sense8* unites elements from across their oeuvre in a distinctly trans° approach to both concept and design. While *Orange Is the New Black* and *Transparent* have been hailed as perhaps the "best" examples of transgender representation in scripted television, *Sense8*'s production marks a less-discussed achievement: it is the first piece of mainstream film or television to feature a lead transgender character (Nomi Marks), played by a transgender actor (Jamie Clayton), written and directed by transgender creators. *Sense8* therefore carries the weight of being perhaps the most distinctly "trans" text in the history of popular cinematic art.[80] Thematically, the series clearly contains speculative analogies to the oppressive role of medicine in transgender people's lives and the desire for alternative forms of queer and trans kinship. However, the Wachowskis' recent comings-out provide an unavoidably "reorienting paratext" (Mittell, *Complex TV* 294) for reading *Sense8* as an *aesthetically* trans° piece of media.[81] The series probes beneath descriptive accounts of identity, exploring trans° as an intra/intersubjective experience of entangled sensories—a constant navigation between what is internally sensed and what is externally perceived. While to become sensate is quite literally to gain additional bodies, *Sense8*'s characters must also learn to feel across and through the movement between vital forms—race, ethnicity, gender, sexuality, nationality—represented by their various embodiments and situated lifeworlds. *Sense8* thus presents an "astonishing exploration of trans° phenomenology" (Bailey et al. 79), achieving a unique televisual language that aestheticizes the trans° sensorium as both a narrative and pedagogic form.

Sense8 displays the Wachowskis' "insatiable appetite for genre" (Li) while staging a confrontation with the obstacles of formalized space and time—how they order the senses to produce divisions, categories, provisional forms, and lines of demarcation we cannot feel across. Like the digital sharing technologies echoed by its affective network, *Sense8* aims to "annihilate time and space" (Bailey et al. 83) as they are generically arranged. The series' global shooting schedule—one of the most ambitious in television history—necessitates a direct engagement with both pace and place as obstacles to its own production. *Sense8's* textual composition is arrayed against these same barriers: formally in its mashups of genre and style, narratively in the speed of its thriller plot, geographically in its denial of national borders, and politically in its flouting of sex and gender normativities. Dislodging its characters from linear time and space, *Sense8* scrambles how gender and race are plotted. For example, Nomi's transgender identity is communicated outside of the medico-juridical narrative of "sex change" and its hopeless entrapment in the "wrong body" (Carter 133), while Sun/Capheus often form a combinatory character that collapses the developmental hierarchy established between East Asia and East Africa. Although it relies on postracial modes of address to establish the immediate intimacy of its psychic connections, it narratively transposes the species logic of race into the new kinship formation of the psychic cluster, enacting a post/racial break with race as it is predetermined under modernity. *Sense8's* slow-motion action sequences and cluster orgies suspend colonial temporality, inducting us into an "ecstatic time" (Muñoz, *Cruising Utopia* 32) in which race cannot limit the body's position in or access to the world, to sensations, to other bodies. A utopian response to modernity's concretized orders of experience, *Sense8* enacts a trans° horizon that widens our proprioceptive positions, giving us the sensations of a thickened "now" and a multiplied "here." Resisting realism's totalizing account of the present, *Sense8* helps us feel a "then and there" (Muñoz, *Cruising Utopia* 1) with subjunctive immediacy—*as if they were already happening*.

As in all Wachowski texts, *Sense8's* emblematic opening sequence teaches us how to engage the text. Designed by Karin Winslow Wachowski, the title credits consist of 108 aerial and street-level shots from every location in the series, capturing a stream of brilliantly colored life and nature in temporal/spatial flow. Set to a tensely pulsing choral and string piece composed by codirector Tom Tykwer, the immersive sequence begins in standard speed, then races forward in time-lapse, only to smash back into the first location as the music ends in crescendo.

This electrifying introduction sensitizes us to how the series pleats geography inward, producing a feeling of global simultaneity that enfolds our senses at the forward edge of time. We are pushed against the world with a quickening force that requires us to sense *with, through, of, in,* and *across* distant spaces. The temporal surface of modernity is invaginated around us as we are pressed against it, like a cloth into which a bullet has been fired. The result is a kinetic horizon that wakes outward around our periphery as each shot builds on the next, finally returning us to where we began. We have raced entirely around the globe, arriving back at the western edge of the American continent—the sky above San Francisco. *Sense8*'s opening credits therefore position us "on the edge": at the limit of a nation and at the borders of identity, genre, and televisual form. Each of the sensate characters is initially situated at the perimeter of a sensing, networked form—the cluster—that will collapse inward at an increasing rate of speed. The title of the first episode, "Limbic Resonance," refers to the speculative limbic system (*limbus* meaning "edge") that will activate to give the sensates this enhanced awareness.[82] Raced and gendered geographies will fold together as their previous worlds compress into an event horizon, pulling them and us into the "centripetal complexity" (Mittell, "Qualities" 52) of new and inescapable sensations.

The title sequence aesthetically prepares us for the *feeling* of *Sense8*'s narrative "cluster" geometry. Space and time will contract rapidly as the sensates' enhanced sensories gather into a collective point of immediacy. In the case of the show's characterization, that point is its central transgender figure, Nomi Marks. The opening credits both begin and end in San Francisco, an overtly queer/trans space (the "Gay Beach" section of Dolores Park and San Francisco Pride are both depicted) where Nomi is physically located. Nomi thus occupies the nucleus of the sensate cluster as a point of attachment for the growth of its matrix, which extends outward in multiple facets as the sensates in her cluster are born. In ancient Greek the name "Nomi" is phonologically equivalent to "γνώμη" (gnome), meaning "to know." The name indicates "a means of knowing, a mark," and "an organ by which one knows, the mind" (Liddle 166). The name "Nomi" can be translated as "one who is marked by knowledge" by possessing an organ of special insight. For Nomi, this organ is her sensate awareness, which is represented as a speculative extension of her trans° sensorium—of feeling *something is there* that others cannot perceive. Nomi's central presence in the series is an initiatory lesson for how *Sense8* will require both its characters and audiences to sense differently. The sensates are "marked" by a trans° awareness that will move them into a pluralization of self, forcing them to abandon the feeling of autonomous personhood. In becoming sensate, Nomi and her cluster will become a "we"—in other words, a "no me." A sensate is therefore "one who knows they are not one."

We could read in this paradoxical construct of the "one/not one" an attempt to aestheticize a global imaginary through trans° as an adhesive and post/racial force—a force that binds across seemingly unbridgeable gaps in both space and time. Indeed, the sensate cluster is structurally identical to the asterisk that punctuates the stickiness of trans° as always "more than and equal to one" (Hayward and Weinstein 198), a phrase the series echoes in its tagline, "I am a we." *Sense8* encapsulates the vital motion between forms that constitutes trans° as paratactic, exploring how affect routes within and across bodies, sensories, moments, and places. The first season spends the bulk of its time emphasizing the provisionality of perception, showing viewers how to engage with its unique aesthetic language. Intuitive parallel editing and traveling sounds decenter our notions of spatiality, causality, and discrete embodiment—a "transaesthetics" that demands a "reorganization of our senses" (Horton-Stallings 11). New surfaces condense across time, space, and genre, multiplying our proprioceptive lenses. We learn to understand when a body in the frame is physically or psychically present (or both), to deduce who is visible/audible to whom, and to notice details in the surround (setting, time of day/night, lighting, auditory cues) to remember where each character is materially located. As the cluster event catalyzes, sensations begin to mix among the characters' various locations: Will, in Chicago, hears Riley's DJ set in London. Kala, in Mumbai, feels the rain in Berlin, where Wolfgang is drinking coffee. A chicken flies from Capheus's bus in Nairobi into Sun's office in Seoul, surprising both her and us at once. These sensationally pedagogic moments combine with *Sense8*'s many dialogic meditations on art to incite a different common sense. Rather than positing a utopian world in which race, gender, and the body are merely transcended into a purely postracial humanism, *Sense8* preserves race as a sense of shared speciation, offering us an "empathetic diversity" (Lothian 94) of interwoven, interdependent sensations within its post/racial, alien collectivity.

While the sensates are largely middle-class (Capheus and Will are exceptions) and their verbal interactions within the cluster almost entirely elide race, gender plays an important role in their cross-sensory negotiations. *Sense8* thus reflects how over the past several decades, gender identity has come to be understood as perhaps less socially constructed than race, more innately a component of the sensorium. Transgender therefore operates as a central language for how *Sense8* shifts our sensory attentions: For example, the early mirror scene between Riley and Will (fig. 24) overtly cites the iconography of twentieth-century transsexual literature as an aesthetic threshold beyond which the series will speculate.

We could therefore view *Sense8* as an implicit response to Sandy Stone's original call for trans° forms that might, through a "deliberate invocation of dissonance," fragment gender into "new and unexpected geometries" ("*Empire*" 231). The series posits the *feel* of transition, in which variously gendered iterations of the self are constantly (re)negotiated, as an affective vocabulary for how we might inhabit its cluster. This is masterfully executed in a "visiting" sequence that allows the adult Nomi to share with Lito her memory of being held naked under a scalding shower in a boys locker room. To impart this sensation, Nomi must

Figure 24: I am a we: Will (left, in Chicago) and
Riley (in London) share a mirror scene.

trust both Lito and the audience to witness her in a previously gendered form. As we look on, she is intercut in flashback with her past male-assigned self, illustrating how her multiple selves are simultaneously sensed. Nomi still *feels* the body that endured the event: "I still have scars on my stomach from the second-degree burns," she tells us. Lito is immediately able to empathize ("Stop it! Fucking monsters!" he shouts), having been sensorially prepared for this cross-cross-gender-cross-race experience in a prior episode during which he suddenly experiences Sun's menstrual symptoms. By exploring how such affects might travel horizontally (fig. 25) within the collective psyche of its cluster, *Sense8* deploys trans° to interrupt our conceptions of how a narrative or self might take place, stretching our senses toward new species formations.

Most negative criticism of *Sense8* has focused on the manner in which it embeds its sensate characters in culturally specific narratives: Claire Light writes that "*Sense8*'s depiction of life in non-western countries is built out of stereotypes . . . suffused with tourist-board clichés." The series does indeed portray its characters of color in recognizably "ethnic" narratives: a Kenyan man struggles to acquire AIDS drugs for his dying mother; an Indian woman weighs a love marriage that feels unfulfilling; a Korean woman sacrifices herself to save her father's honor; a gay Mexican actor is closeted by the Latin culture of machismo.

Figure 25: Lateral affects: senses stretch
between Nomi (left) and Lito.

Sense8 mobilizes these stereotypes through its larger assertion of "racial nationalism" (Bailey et al. 81), a conceit the series uses as shorthand to build quickly toward the global shape of its cluster formation. These racialized scripts make the series' attempt at a global address more cognizable to white and Western viewers, but they also pose a larger analytical value to the text, which questions how genre attributes fixed values to race, gender, and location. Much like Neo in *The Matrix*, the sensates are embedded in generic worlds that operate as constructs for theirs and the audience's perceptions: Nomi inhabits a hacker thriller, Lito a telenovela, Capheus an action movie, Wolfgang a heist film, Will a cop show, Sun a martial arts film, Kala a Bollywood romance, and Riley a maternal melodrama. These stock narratives and their highly identifiable, ethnically specific geographies are necessary to *Sense8*'s central conceit—an exploration of how static forms limit which stories can be told and which modes of life can thus become cognizable to others. However, this cannot be accomplished without citing the very genres and scripts it hopes to complicate, resulting in a scenario in which the sensates are "trapped in the exact social circumstances stereotypically assigned to their races" (Kessler, "Eleven TV Shows"). *Sense8* thus mobilizes race, gender, and nationality as stereotypic forms of personhood even as it metanarratively comments on them as constructs—a bimodal strategy the series forces both its characters and audience to straddle. *Sense8* therefore becomes increasingly dynamic to the extent that it intersectionally punctures its generic settings, transferring the sensates across their artificially bounded experiences as they sensorially interface. This often takes place through a sincere embrace of each other's generic talents, as when the actor (Lito) steps in to act as a "stunt double" for the gangster (Wolfgang) during a shakedown.

While it represents a groundbreaking deployment of trans° aesthetics to explore constructs of identity and perception, *Sense8* nonetheless reflects our cultural moment's inclinations to think race through trans° rather than trans° through race. Although it does engage the medical history of eugenics directed at both transgender and of color bodies, the series is ultimately more interested in displacing or transposing race into other forms than in directly confronting it. This is readable even in its linguistic design, which relies heavily on a monolingual deployment of English dialogue between characters. Transcultural interaction between the sensates is often softened by the prosthetic use of English, a strategy ostensibly intended to make Anglophone viewers more comfortable and to bring down the costs of translation in the production schedule. By suggesting that the sensates share English as a sort of psychic "tongue" (Keegan, "Tongues") that transcends their ethnically specific cultures, *Sense8* inadvertently reifies the lingual effects of global colonization. Linguistic friction—the way language difference sticks in the engine of secular humanism—is largely evacuated through the use of English as a universal language.[83] There *are* scenes in which sensate characters notice that they can use and/or understand each others' native speech. This most notably takes place between Sun and Capheus (Sun seems surprised to meet a black man who speaks Korean, to which Capheus replies, "You speak Swahili?") and is humorously referenced in season two when Nomi points out that she can speak "seven languages . . . and some shitty French from high school!" However, these moments cannot be structurally sustained and consistently collapse into accented English, maintaining Anglophone viewers' sense that some of the sensates are "foreign." *Sense8* would likely have been impossible to make or consume without some standardization of linguistic format. However, were it to accurately reflect the global population, over half of its characters would be Asian and the cluster would speak Mandarin rather than English. The series' language design thus illustrates how media attempting to represent the "virtual community" (Shaw) of a new globalism can remain structurally tethered to Western presumptions.

Despite these limitations, *Sense8* is undoubtedly a televisual masterpiece (Levesley), presenting viewers with a cinematic grandeur, global diversity, and technical sophistication that have expanded the grammar of the medium itself (VanDerWerff). Although it represents a break with Hollywood, the series is nonetheless a decidedly Wachowskian text. There is the same colossal thematic ambition, the same concern with closed worlds and their ethical consequences, the same assault against dictated form, the same interest in speculating an after to our gendered and racial constructs. By industry standards, the series is simply the most recent in the Wachowskis' long history of aesthetically daring, challenging-to-market works. Yet what makes the show so compelling—and so reflective of its time—is its immersive, hopeful immediacy. *Sense8*'s speculative stretch is ultimately an inner one. Rather than pushing its vision into a distant future, the series turns subjunctivity inward, asking how we might arrive at our senses, and thus the lives of others, differently. To sense beyond the limits of the given world, we must learn to feel how we already exceed its edges, are already in dissent. The options have already arrived, if we could find the faith to perceive them. In all its incompleteness, *Sense8*'s utopianism is nonetheless the speculative sensation that things could already be moving toward that lush, subjunctive field it asks us to touch within ourselves. Perhaps more than any other cinematic text, *Sense8* captures the *event* of trans°—the sensation of trans° *as a happening*, already in motion beyond the text's borders, sensing toward unrealized contacts, opening toward what already gathers in the surround. To feel beyond the "prison house" (Muñoz, *Cruising Utopia* 1) of the here and now is not to turn toward some far-off place, it says, but to occupy our present so fully together that we burst the present world's seams.

Like *Bound* twenty years before it, *Sense8* reminds us of the horizon: the reach, the leap, the stretch—the desiring tense already incipient between us.

Notes

1. On June 12, 2016, Omar Mateen entered the Pulse Nightclub in Orlando, Florida, and shot 107 attendees of Latin Night, a weekly gathering for Latinx LGBTQ people. Forty-nine of those wounded eventually died. Mateen was killed by the Orlando Police at the scene.

2. As Roxanne Samer pointed out to me in conversation, Wachowski's comments here dovetail quite legibly with Joanna Russ's distinction between the negative and positive subjunctivities of fantasy and science fiction ("what could not have happened" vs. "what has not happened") in *To Write Like a Woman: Essays in Feminism and Science Fiction*. Russ's analysis (15–17) hinges on a lecture Samuel R. Delany delivered to the Modern Language Association in 1968.

3. Transsexual, transgender, trans, and trans° exist in nuanced historical, political, and theoretical relationship to one another. "Transsexual" is commonly considered to be an outdated term naming a medically pathologized condition, although it remains a preferred descriptor by some segments of the trans community. "Transgender" arose in the mid-1990s to displace "transsexual," operating as an umbrella term for gender-variant people in much the same way that "queer" did for sexuality (Feinberg; Valentine). In this work I use "transsexual" to denote a specific, twentieth-century iteration of trans linked to the medical dis-

course of surgical intervention and "correction." I use "transgender" to indicate a twenty-first-century formation rooted in the psychological/affective concept of gender identity. I use "trans" in simultaneous reference to both transsexual and transgender where these overlap, or as a shortened form of "transgender" where appropriate. Lastly, I use "trans°" to mark a theoretical exploration of how trans phenomenology necessitates an endless negotiation of tangible and intangible forms, senses and perceptions, the force of desire and the limits of reality. For a detailed history of "transgender," see K. J. Rawson and Cristan Williams, "Transgender°: The Rhetorical Landscape of a Term."

4. See, for example, Barker; Brinkema; Keeling, *Witch's Flight*; Marks, *Skin*; Marks, *Touch*; Shaviro, *Cinematic Body*; and Sobchak, *Address*.

5. In "Queer OS," Kara Keeling defines "common sense" as "a linchpin in the struggle for hegemony that conditions what is perceptible such that aspects of what is perceptible become generally recognizable only when they work in some way through 'common senses'" (153).

6. "Cinematic reality" is Keeling's term for how what is considered "real" is structured by our sensorial adaptation to the cinematic experience, such that "neither cinematic perceptual schemas nor cinematic matter precedes the other. Together they constitute the cinematic, an assemblage that might also be referred to as '20th century reality' because we neither posit nor access 'reality' except via these processes, which were perfected by film" (*Witch's Flight* 12).

7. Here I use "transition" expansively to indicate not merely medical transition but also the wider and ceaseless engagement with the insufficiencies of gender as a representational language that trans people must navigate. As Lilly Wachowski puts it, "To be transgender is something largely understood as existing within the dogmatic terminus of male or female. And to 'transition' imparts a sense of immediacy, a before and after from one terminus to another. But the reality, my reality is that I've been transitioning and will continue to transition all of my life, through the infinite that exists between male and female as it does in the infinite between the binary of zero and one. We need to elevate the dialogue beyond the simplicity of binary. Binary is a false idol" (Baim).

8. The Wachowskis have been known by a number of names since they began directing films. Throughout this work, I follow Reuters's 2015 recommendations for representing transgender people accurately, which is to use current names in place of outdated ones. Lana and Lilly are referred to consistently by their current names in use throughout this work, including in the filmography and references.

9. John Phillips's book *Transgender on Screen* is an excellent example of "transgender cinema" scholarship that reads largely for transgender images. There is a thin literature of what I would call *trans°* cinema studies, as distinguished from studies *of* transgender representation in film. See, for example, Halberstam, *Queer Time*; Horak, *Girls Will Be Boys*; Keegan, "Moving Bodies;" Keegan, "Revisitation"; Leung; Steinbock, "Shimmering Images"; Steinbock, "Speaking";

Straayer, *Deviant Eyes*; Straube. See also *Spectator* 37.2 (2017), a special issue on "Transgender Media" edited by Roxanne Samer. See Steinbock, "Towards" and Horak, "Trans Studies" for pieces tracing the genealogies of trans cinema production and studies, respectively.

10. My analysis thus aligns most closely with Helen Hok-sze Leung's third critical model in "Trans on Screen" for reading trans in film—"trans practice," an interpretive mode that reads cinema for practices that "transform bodily being" (186–87).

11. I seek here a trans° exploration of what Kara Keeling describes in "Queer OS" as a recognition that the "historical, sociocultural, conceptual phenomena that currently shape our realities in deep and profound ways, such as race, gender, class, citizenship, and ability," are "mutually constitutive with media and information technologies, thereby making it impossible to think of any of them in isolation" (153).

12. This is—as anyone who works in transgender studies knows—the kind of appeal to gendered facticity that can fail over time.

13. Both Wachowskis have repudiated *Assassins* (1995), stating their script for the film was totally rewritten and that they have unsuccessfully sought to have their names removed from it (Hemon).

14. During the Wachowskis' appearance at the DePaul School of Cinema and Interactive Media Visiting Artist Series, Lana Wachowski reflected on this process: "We couldn't find a single film, in the genre like *Bound* is, where two gay characters went off and lived happily ever after. So we were wondering can you then interrogate these old paradigms and then at the same time try a brand-new one that's never been done?" ("Lilly Wachowski and Lana Wachowski").

15. The 1996 Frameline screening of *Bound* appears to have been a moment when the Wachowskis felt singularly welcomed by the queer community. Lana recalls warmly of the event, "We had 900 of our lesbian sisters standing and cheering. It was fantastic. . . . Grabbing us and hugging us and saying, 'We've been waiting for this movie our whole lives.' That was like . . . we thought we would never top that, which is one of the reasons we don't go to many premieres" (McWeeny, "Epic Interview").

16. While Noble reads *Bound*'s many triangulated shots as a "sexual geometrics" (32) that revises the blueprint of male homosociality (man/woman/man) into a final butch/female/femme triad, I read *Bound* as instead triangulating queer/lesbian/trans° in a set of relations that continually transits through itself without reducing any of these identifications to "female."

17. In *Bound*'s earliest script, dated October 28, 1994, this opening scene includes marginalia reading: "I'm just thinking of starting further back in the closet. Potentially, less abstraction. Do we want less abstraction, or not . . . ? Is it 'What is this? Oh, a closet?' or is it 'Weird closet. Why are we in a closet?'" Original copy, script library, Ravenswood Kinowerks archive, accessed September 2, 2016.

18. In keeping with the film's theme of not trusting appearances, this pull chain is not an actual pull chain. The model, which is displayed at Ravenswood Kinowerks Inc. in Chicago, is approximately five feet long and consists of eleven balls the size of softballs, with a large bell on the end. Accessed September 2, 2016.

19. In the laserdisc commentary for *Bound*, Lana Wachowski says, "Corky is the part of Violet that is sort of buried in her own closeted world."

20. Marginalia from the earliest script version of *Bound* (October 28, 1994) read, "It's important to introduce the wall." Original copy, script library, Ravenswood Kinowerks archive, accessed September 2, 2016.

21. The most important example of this is Laura Mulvey's revision in "Afterthoughts on 'Visual Pleasure and Narrative Cinema'" of her original theory of the male gaze to accommodate a "transvestite" viewing position through which the woman spectator can "transition out of her own sex into another" by adopting the camera's masculinist perspective (71). See also Mary Ann Doane, "Film and the Masquerade: Theorising the Female Spectator."

22. As José Muñoz notes in *Disidentifications*, "The point, then, is not to drop either desire or identification from the equation. Rather, it is to understand the sometimes interlocking and coterminous, separate and mutually exclusive nature of both psychic structures" (15).

23. In the laserdisc commentary for *Bound*, the Wachowskis mention that the film was intentionally written to put the "femme on top."

24. Matt Fournier's keyword entry for "Lines of Flight" in *Transgender Studies Quarterly* 1.1–2 glosses Massumi's translation of Deleuze and Guattari's French term *ligne de fuite* with a trans° sensibility: "'Fuite' means the act of fleeing or eluding but also flowing, leaking. Gender dysphoria is one such moment of leakage, when the face you see in the mirror is not a face for you anymore, when a supposedly familiar landscape is blurred by the transposition of gender-signifying marks from one millieu to another, when the socially determined coordinates of familiar-identity-gender no longer add up to a legible (legitimate) pattern, when materiality itself escapes the frame of representation, because this frame is built on gender binarism" (121). Throughout this work, I use "line of flight" to indicate this cluster of representational slippages induced within trans° phenomenology.

25. Violet's unfixedness simultaneously references the illegibilities of transness, femme queerness, and the "unintelligible" Asian femme fatale in Hollywood cinema—a role that Celine Parreñas Shimizu reads in *The Hypersexuality of Race* as offering Asian American actresses a set of strategies for resisting the colonial sexualization of their own images (77).

26. For example, in "*Femme Fatale* or Lesbian Femme," Chris Straayer claims of the film's ending, "Because they are same-sexed, lesbians make better partners in crime than heterosexual pairings" (160). Lee Wallace reads the film's final shot as "register(ing) only their sexual similarity," thereby establishing Corky and Violet's "continuous sex" (385). Wallace's privileging of the visual—which

Bound instructs us to sense beyond—results in his reading the film as fixing Violet's sexuality through the substitution of violence for sexual knowledge.

27. The most (in)famous academic writing on *The Matrix* is Slavoj Žižek's "The Matrix: Or, the Two Sides of Perversion." Žižek also titled *Welcome to the Desert of the Real: Five Essays on September and Related Dates* after the film's citation of Baudrillard. The most comprehensive collections of scholarly writing on *The Matrix* franchise appear in Jason Haslam's *Gender, Race, and American Science Fiction: Reflections on Fantastic Identities* and on the website of the Moffitt Library's Media Resource Center at UC Berkeley: "*The Matrix Trilogy*: A Bibliography of Materials in the UC Berkeley Library."

28. J. Jack Halberstam discusses this trope in *Skin Shows* while analyzing the gender dysphoric slasher of *The Silence of the Lambs* (1991), Buffalo Bill: "The cause for Buffalo Bill's extreme violence against women . . . lies in his humanist presumption that his sex and his gender and his orientation must all match-up to a mythic norm of white heterosexuality masculinity. . . . What Buffalo Bill is about, unfortunately, is the crafting of an old gender from new bodies"(165). Earlier examples of this motif are *Psycho* (1960), *The Rocky Horror Picture Show* (1975), and *Dressed to Kill* (1980). For further discussion of transsexual representation in cinema, see also Carol J. Clover, *Men, Women, and Chainsaws: Gender in the Modern Horror Film*; and Lucy J. Miller, "Fear and the Cisgender Audience: Transgender Representation and Audience Identification in *Sleepaway Camp*."

29. While the series is commonly referred to as a trilogy, I include *The Animatrix*, bringing the total of films in the franchise to four.

30. The "real-life test" is an amount of time during which medical professionals often require transgender patients to live in their preferred gender role prior to being granted access to medical gender transition. While this requirement has been softened since 2011, it is still often enforced by medical providers. See the Harry Benjamin International Gender Dysphoria Association's "Standards of Care for Gender Identity Disorders," 6th version.

31. Kristen Whissel's *Spectacular Digital Effects: CGI and Contemporary Cinema* describes emblematic cinema as a twenty-first-century turn on the "cinema of attractions" in which "the attraction often appears in an altered form as a computer-generated (or digitally enhanced) image that does not precisely 'arrest' or 'prevail over' narrative but instead appears at key turning points in a film's narrative to emblematize the major themes, desires, and anxieties with which a film (or a group of films) is obsessed" (6).

32. "'The problem with market-driven art-making is that movies are green-lit based on past movies,' Lana told me. 'So, as nature abhors a vacuum, the system abhors originality. Originality cannot be economically modeled'" (Hemon).

33. Early script notes for this scene describe Trinity's speed as so quick it "almost doesn't register, so smooth and fast, inhumanly fast." Original copy, script library, Ravenswood Kinowerks archive, accessed September 2, 2016.

34. The earliest iterations of *The Matrix* script reflect how the internet created new digital modes of gendered passing. The first scripted version of this scene about Trinity's gender occurs in a chat room, in which LODIII types, "87% percent of all women online are really men." This is in response to a hacker called Timaxe asking if Trinity is "really a girl?" Original copy, script library, Ravenswood Kinowerks archive, accessed September 2, 2016.

35. This mirroring across gender was an intentional part of *The Matrix* series' marketing. In 2003 a *TV Guide* cover advertising *The Matrix Reloaded* featured a hologram that switched between images of Neo and Trinity (J. Clover, *Matrix* 22).

36. In her remarks at a fund-raising dinner for New York City's LGBTQ Community Center, Lana Wachowski remarked, "Mirrors can be tough for all of us, but for trans people, they can be brutal" (O'Hara).

37. For an exploration of transsexual cinematic aesthetics, see Susan Stryker and Monica Nolan, "Christine in the Cutting Room: A Multi-modal Way of Interacting Differently with Queer Media."

38. The 2017 controversy over *Hypatia*'s publication of philosopher Rebecca Tuvel's "In Defense of Transracialism" illustrates the precise need for a split-decision approach that can work across the competing realities of race and gender as *constructed yet real*. Tuvel drew intense fire from trans° studies scholars for using a deconstructivist position to draw an overdetermined analogy between transgender and "transracial" identities. Tuvel's article cited almost no work by transgender scholars; the two who were cited are white. A group of over eight hundred scholars petitioned *Hypatia* to retract the article and open its blind review practices to transgender and of color input, stating, "A message has been sent, to authors and readers alike, that white cis scholars may engage in speculative discussion of these themes without broad and sustained engagement with those theorists whose lives are most directly affected by transphobia and racism" ("Open Letter to *Hypatia*").

39. Belinda McClory, who played Switch, confirmed this to me in email correspondence dated September 10, 2016:

> When I auditioned for the role of Switch in Sydney in late 1997 I wasn't given the entire script, just the few pages containing the "copper top" scene in the car when we first pick up Keanu in the movie and extract his bug. In the script Switch was described as "a beautiful androgyne." At that stage, I was told the Wachowskis were looking for TWO actors, a man and a woman (who looked similar or could be made to look similar), to play the role of Switch. The idea was that Switch would be male in the Nebuchadnezzar scenes and then in the Matrix (where the ultimate idea of yourself/the true representation of yourself can manifest), the character would "switch" genders and become female. Hence the name. This seemed to me at the time to be incredibly progressive characterization for a Hollywood film. But then Lana and Lilly have always been pioneers in the movie making

industry. They are way ahead of their time on so many levels. By the time I auditioned again (it was at this time I first met the Wachowskis) I was told the role had been made totally female as the studio executives at Warner Bros. not only wanted more of a female presence in the film, but felt the character changing gender between the two worlds was "too weird" and "might be confusing to the mainstream movie going audience." The role had doubled in size and I was lucky enough to get the part. I loved every second of making *The Matrix* and made some life-long friends in the process. But I can't help thinking the conservative tastes of those studio executives robbed Switch, the Wachowskis, and the trans community of something special, something politically important, something that, in 1999 when the film was released might have been ground-breaking. And in light of Lana and Lilly's personal journeys the original imagining of the character is made even more interesting.

40. The effect is named "bullet time" in the 7.2 version of *The Matrix* script. It is described as a "liquid space" in which Neo is "bent impossibly back." At least three different renderings of bullet time were storyboarded for *The Matrix*—more than any other sequence in the film. Original copies, script and storyboard libraries, Ravenswood Kinowerks archive, accessed September 2, 2016.

41. During the "In Movie Experience" track for *The Matrix* in *The Ultimate Matrix Collection*, Lana expands on this point: "What we really like about slow motion is that it brings some of that quality to action scenes. But what we also like is to move the camera."

42. In online communities, "getting red pilled" is used to describe a person converting to the tenets of the alt-right, particularly to those of the men's rights movement. The Red Pill is a popular subreddit organized around this ideology. In "The Real Red Pill: What Men Still Don't Get about *The Matrix* and *Sense8*," Diana Tourjee comments on this use of the symbol: "The red pill symbolizes an awakening from brainwashing by the status quo—and though it has been an iconic emblem within trans communities since *The Matrix*'s release, it has also been appropriated by a community of cisgender heterosexual men who have perverted the concept by casting themselves as the unwitting victims of a master plot in which they have been subordinated by social progress. . . . This is poignant in its irony; men of the far right are using the language of trans women to name the misguided concept that they must escape from an oppressively progressive political future."

43. *Enter the Matrix*'s plot connects *The Matrix* to *Reloaded* and introduces relationships between some of the principal characters in the film sequel. If we consider *Enter the Matrix* as an integral component of the series, then Niobe's (Jada Pinkett Smith) central role in the latter portions of the franchise shifts the story's mission to one led by a black woman rather than by Neo.

44. In her early definition of the field of transgender studies, "(De)Subjugated Knowledges: An Introduction to Transgender Studies," Susan Stryker states,

"Transgender phenomena call into question both the stability of the material referent 'sex' and the relationship of that unstable category to the linguistic, social, and psychical categories of 'gender'" (9).

45. Henry Jenkins discusses reactions to *The Matrix* franchise as uniquely reflecting the challenges transmedia worlds present to casual viewers as well as to critics: "Is *The Matrix* any good? Many film critics trashed the later sequels because they were not sufficiently self-contained and thus bordered on incoherent. Many games critics trashed the games because they were too dependent on the film content and did not offer sufficiently new experiences to players. Many fans expressed disappointment because their own theories about the world of *The Matrix* were more rich and nuanced than anything they ever saw on the screen. I would argue, however, that we do not yet have very good aesthetic criteria for evaluating works that play themselves out across multiple media" (*Convergence Culture* 98–99).

46. Transmisogyny is the unique intersectional combination of transphobia, sexism, and misogyny directed at transgender women (Serano).

47. This character is named "Shizo" in Kawajiri's original script, which is archived in the script library at Ravenswood Kinowerks. I was not able to clarify why or when the name was altered. According to the *Oxford English Dictionary,* "cisgender" (shortened as "cis") has been in use as a term for "not transgender" since at least 1997. Script accessed September 2, 2016.

48. Original concept sketches for *Reloaded* and *Revolutions* are all labeled "*Matrix* 2/3," suggesting that at the development stage there were no set plans about where one film would end and the next would begin. Ravenswood Kinowerks archive, accessed September 2, 2016.

49. In *Adapting Philosophy: Jean Baudrillard and the Matrix Trilogy*, Catherine Constable provides a singularly deep analysis of how *Reloaded*'s and *Revolutions*' engagement with Baudrillard is far more intricate than the literature on the films generally acknowledges.

50. Lana Wachowski has herself pointed out this historical shift, noting, "After 9/11, people wanted the safety of the familiar. The last thing they want is to be challenged or shaken up by entertainment" (McWeeny, "Our Wachowskis Interview Continues").

51. "*The Matrix Revolutions* (2003)," *Rotten Tomatoes*, https://www.rotten tomatoes.com/m/matrix_revolutions, accessed June 6, 2017.

52. In an interview for DP/30, Lana Wachowski explains that the first *Matrix* film is "classical," the second is "deconstructive," and the third "asks you to participate in the construction of meaning" as do some religious traditions.

53. Although Vivian Sobchak asserts in *Meta-Morphing: Visual Transformation and the Culture of Quick Change* that "killing a morph is an impossible business" (136), Smith appears to attempt just that by turning the cultural imaginary of the morph against its own digital practice, producing an ironic sameness from a groundbreaking visual technology.

54. In-person tour of Ravenswood Kinowerks by Lana Wachowski, Chicago Life House benefit, Chicago, Illinois, August 29, 2015.

55. This is an alteration made by the Wachowskis from Moore's original story. In Moore's finale, V demolishes 10 Downing Street, the location of the British prime minister's residence. In the film version, V's final target has been moved to the palace, the symbol of British democratic self-governance. The change wages a critical assault on the foundations of the modern state rather than on the representational leadership of the majority party.

56. Lana Wachowski, remarks made at the *Sense8* season two premiere screening. Music Box Theater, Chicago, Illinois, April 23, 2017.

57. My research on the book and film versions of *V for Vendetta* turned up only one source discussing the trans qualities of V's character. In "A is for Anarchy, V is for Vendetta," Lewis Call notes that the film script for *V for Vendetta* was authored by a transgender creator, writing "V's body . . . is radically unorthodox. V may not be explicitly transgendered [*sic*], but there is certainly a radical sexual ambiguity about V, and this is clearly part of his power" (167). Call does not appear to be aware that V was originally conceived by Moore as a transsexual character.

58. Tony Williams notes that the Wachowskis intentionally inserted references to cross-dressing into Moore's original story. In the film, Evey is accosted by Fingermen on the same evening that she has performed the role of Viola in Shakespeare's *Twelfth Night* (22).

59. *Speed Racer* often achieves a cinematic look without the use of an actual camera, thus belonging to a group of anime-inspired films that Alistair D. Swale notes made clear it was "no longer necessary to use a camera anymore, and if that were the case, there would be a fundamental question of what that would imply for preconceptions of filmic representation" (126).

60. "*Speed Racer*," https://www.rottentomatoes.com/m/speed_racer, accessed June 8, 2017.

61. In *Transgender Studies Quarterly* 1.1–2, Nikki Sullivan provides the keyword for *somatechnics*: "The term *somatechnics*, derived from the Greek *soma* (body) and *techné* (craftsmanship), supplants the logic of the 'and,' indicating that *techné* is not something we add or apply to the already constituted body (as object), nor is it a tool that the embodied self employs to its own ends. Rather, *technés* are the dynamic means in and through which corporealities are crafted: that is, continuously engendered in relation to others and to a world" (187).

62. Lana Wachowski describes the problem of categorization in her acceptance speech for the 2014 Equality Illinois Freedom Award: "I see few things as beautiful as my community and all the miraculous ways we transcend the limitations of two little boxes, blurring and even erasing the distinctions that legitimize and support the belief in all equalities of gender" ("Equality Illinois").

63. The original *Speed Racer* manga (on which the animated cartoon is based) is also known by the more literal Japanese translation of its title, *Mach GoGoGo*.

64. As expressed by Janice Raymond in *The Transsexual Empire: The Making of the She-Male,* one of radical feminism's most strident objections to transsexuality/transgender is that they are delusional states licensed by a patriarchal techno-capitalist medical "empire."

65. Sandy Stone's call in "The *Empire* Strikes Back: A Posttranssexual Manifesto" for new trans° aesthetics that would move beyond and displace the dominant representational modes of transsexuality initiated a subsequent structural periodization. For example, the inaugural issue of *Transgender Studies Quarterly* (1.1–2) was titled "Postposttranssexual: Key Concepts for a 21st-Century Transgender Studies," thus positioning transgender studies as coming *after the after* of transsexuality.

66. Subsequent research by Martin Paul Eve at Birkbeck, University of London, has revealed that the US and UK editions of Mitchell's novel are substantially different. Alison Flood specifies that the film was adapted from the US version.

67. Charles McGrath describes this collaborative adaptive process: "From the beginning the filmmakers ruled out the idea of telling the novel's stories sequentially. . . . So instead they broke the whole novel down into hundreds of scenes, transcribed them into color-coded index cards and shuffled them around, looking for patterns and parallels and a way to splice them together."

68. Rafaella Baccolini points out that its focus on greed, rather than terrorism, makes *Cloud Atlas* distinct among other big-budget science fiction films produced after 9/11 (74).

69. In *Girls Will Be Boys: Cross-Dressed Women, Lesbians, and American Cinema,* Laura Horak establishes how cross-dressed women in pre–Hays Code US cinema were often perceived as upholding wholesome and cosmopolitan American values, while cross-dressed men were more consistently pathologized by stigmas about male effeminacy. She finds that the meanings of these traditions are so different that "we cannot generalize across the two practices" (19).

70. In addition to Rachel Tuvel's much-critiqued article "In Defense of Transracialism," Rogers Brubaker's *Trans: Gender and Race in an Age of Unsettled Identities* also seizes on trans° as a largely deconstructive and analytic mode for thinking about race, as evidenced by the book's title. Brubaker focuses on three modes of "trans"—"migration," "between," and "beyond"—none of which adequately represent the claims of trans people to enfleshed sensations of their genders as material, inherited, and *real.* Susan Stryker responded to the one-sidedness of using trans° to think race by noting, "Analogy is a weak form of analysis, in which a better-known case is compared to one that is lesser known" ("Caitlyn Jenner").

71. In her Human Rights Campaign Visibility Award speech, Lana Wachowski comments on the resonance of Sonmi~451's line and her own experience: "I find myself repeating a line from a character who I was very attached to, who speaks about her own decision to kind of come out. She says, 'If I had remained

invisible, the truth would stay hidden, and I couldn't allow that.' And she says this aware that even at the moment that she's saying it that even the sacrifice she has made will cost her life. . . . I start to understand just how complex the relationship between visibility and invisibility has been throughout my life" ("Lana Wachowski Receives").

72. LeiLani Nishime argues in "Whitewashing Yellow Futures in *Ex Machina*, *Cloud Atlas*, and *Advantageous*" that the fabricants recycle a common trope figuring Asian women as "the product rather than the producers of technology, built to fulfill their role as devalued service laborers in the globalized future" (31).

73. Ira Levin's *The Stepford Wives* (1972) and Joanna Russ's *The Female Man* (1975) are perhaps the best examples, in a US context, of historically co-occurring yet politically polarized imaginations of the female series.

74. J. Jack Halberstam notes this feminist anxiety about automated gender in "Automating Gender: Postmodern Feminism in the Age of the Intelligent Machine," pointing out how in *Gyn/Ecology: The Metaethics of Radical Feminism* Mary Daly argues that "'phallotechnic progress' aims eventually to replace femaleness with 'hollow holograms' and female bodies with robots through such techniques as 'total therapy, transsexualism, and cloning.' Daly proposes a strategy to counter this process and calls it 'roboticide' or the destruction of 'false selves'" (450).

75. "*Jupiter Ascending*," *Rotten Tomatoes*, https://www.rottentomatoes.com/m/jupiter_ascending_2014, accessed June 17, 2017.

76. "There is no alternative," often shortened to TINA, was a slogan used by Margaret Thatcher to insist that neoliberal capitalism is the only viable economic system.

77. Competing science fiction and fantasy franchises on both broadcast and streaming television are notably pessimistic. Major contemporary series include *The Walking Dead* (2010-), *Black Mirror* (2011-), *Game of Thrones* (2011-), *The Leftovers* (2014–7), *The Man in the High Castle* (2015-), *Westworld* (2016-), *The Handmaid's Tale* (2017-), *Twin Peaks: The Return* (2017). Of these, only *Black Mirror* is an original intellectual property.

78. The petition, titled "*Sense8* Season Three Renewal" is archived at Change.org. https://www.change.org/p/netflixlat-netflix-sense8-sense-8-season-3-renewal.

79. See the original tweet here: https://twitter.com/sense8?ref_src=twsrc%5Etfw&ref_url=https%3A%2F%2Fwww.buzzfeed.com%2Fkrishrach%2Fhow-fans-brought-sense-8-back.

80. While there is no reliably flat criterion for distinguishing cinema from television, Brett Mills's "What Does It Mean to Call Television 'Cinematic?'" lays out signposts for understanding specific examples of televisual media as "cinematic." These include density of visual texture, enhanced importance of sound, delivery of narrative meaning through both imagery and aural tone, use of special effects previously only attempted in cinema, a rupture with prior televi-

sion aesthetics or content in a manner that feels "like cinema," and attention to the "pictorial effect" of the frame. Breakdown in the celluloid/video distinction by digital imaging has also compressed the two forms. *Sense8* presents a distinctive combination of all these factors, making it an ideal example of "cinematic television."

81. Lokeilani Kaimana notes this paratextual function that the Wachowskis' transitions now serve: "The paratext of the sisters' transitions is but another instance of fan connection that extends past the content of media object(s) to an affective relationality that bridges across difference" (Bailey et al. 77).

82. Limbic resonance is a psychiatric theory that the human limbic system is not self-contained but extends beyond the edges of the body through affect and is impacted by other bodies in proximity. The theory is presented by Thomas Lewis, Fari Amini, and Richard Lannon in their 2000 work, *A General Theory of Love*, published by Random House.

83. A Reddit user points this out in a discussion about which seven languages the sensates speak, listing them as follows: "1. English (everyone) 2. Spanish (Lito) 3. Hindi (Kala) 4. Swahili (Capheus) 5. Icelandic (Riley) 6. Korean (Sun) 7. German (Wolfgang)." https://www.reddit.com/r/Sense8/comments/6b9wyb/nomi_speaks_7_languages. It is actually unclear whether all the characters *can* speak English, or whether they are speaking their own languages and the series is substituting English as a sort of universal translator that replicates the feeling of being within the cluster, able to understand all seven of its languages simultaneously.

Interview with Lana Wachowski |

A lightly edited version of our conversation, held on June 30, 2017, at Ravenswood Kinowerks, Chicago, Illinois.

CÁEL M. KEEGAN: How are you? This is pretty great news about *Sense8* getting a finale from Netflix.

LANA WACHOWSKI: That's *such* a question. The scale of it is so large that we could spend the entire hour discussing it. You can break it into a lot of different aspects, like how such news affected me as an artist, or what it meant to the fans, to the industry, or what it meant to me personally. You ride an experience like this the way you would a roller coaster, and it's up and down and up and down. If I told you all the ups and downs that have been going on really since the inception of *Sense8*, it would be exhausting.

At some point you just accept that there's an equilibrium to the intensity of this life, that the up-and-down ends up in this one space where you find an okayness on either end of the spectrum, and you try to hold on to that feeling. Sometimes you can't. Your heart breaks and you're crying like a baby in the shower and you're devastated, and then one phone call later, you're soaring through the air and you're exhilarated and you're flying—and it's the best.

It's the feeling of why you wanted to make art, and it comes back in this way that is so tactile and experienced so completely, this cycle of giving and receiving. . . . I could detail many of the encounters that I've had with *Sense8* fans and their grief and their joy, and how the art touched them. In some ways that would be a very beautiful description of why I became an artist—and why I wanted to make *Sense8* and not a bunch of other projects that I could have made, and also the pain of realizing that the people who are connecting to *Sense8* are not the mainstream, they are not the majority.

You have to deal with the reality that you are a part of a smaller group, a smaller subculture, and, yes, your story is just as valid and your story matters, but it doesn't produce revenue in the same way that a large audience produces revenue. You come to these moments where you say, "Should I keep trying to tell these kinds of stories that aren't necessarily as accessible to mainstream audiences, since all I'm going to do is keep getting told that they are not financially sustainable?"

I confronted that at the beginning of my career. I tried to make *Bound* as a reaction to what I saw as a mainstream representation of LGBT. Boy, this is gonna get into a . . . I ramble *a lot*. This is why I also don't like doing interviews, because I like organizing my rambling. I prefer being the organizer of my ramblings.

CMK: As a writer, I completely understand that instinct as well.

LW: So you try to tell a story, and you hope enough people are interested in the story that they might let you tell another one—which is another way the story of *Sense8* could be understood, like Scheherazade saved by her audience. I have felt for a long time our career is a lot like Scheherazade, surviving improbably. *Bound* was not successful by any stretch of the imagination. It was painful to confront the idea that the kinds of stories I wanted to tell were not mainstream, accessible stories. And yet we got to make another one.

CMK: I wanted to ask you about *Bound*, because we've reached the twentieth anniversary now, and there is some historicization happening around films from that period. In my own work, I spend a lot of time with people who teach queer cinema, and *Bound* is taught quite a bit in college classrooms.

LW: I have a question. Was it taught more post me coming out as trans?

CMK: I don't think so.

LW: My feeling is that it was.

CMK: Really?

LW: Maybe that's just a projection.

CMK: I think that certainly that adds a layer to how we might make sense of the film today. I'm not sure how you feel about that. There are other films like *The Watermelon Woman* or *Poison*, independent films from that era, that seem to have been more woven into the narrative about what "New Queer Cinema" was or what was happening in that period. I happen to think *Bound* is one of the finest examples of queer cinema ever made, but it doesn't seem to have been memorialized in the same way. What do you think of that? Why don't people talk about the film?

LW: Well, I'm curious about your thoughts, as somebody who's studying it.

CMK: I think that there was this narrative: "What are these two 'Wachowskis' doing making this movie that doesn't seem to be an expression of an identitarian politics?" There was this assumption that queer cinema is made by visibly queer people who are part of that subculture, and that it is directly about their visible identities. There was this whole narrative around those films that they were about the *real* queer experience. Your film is so deeply authentic, and I feel like people couldn't see it.

LW: When you say "authentic," you mean because I'm a trans person?

CMK: Not exactly. I think that when you watch the film, it *feels real*. It speaks to me very deeply from a pure, emotional place. Queer people want the world to be different. Do you know what I mean?

LW: Yes.

CMK: Violet—that character—spoke to me so deeply when I was in high school and just coming out. She still does, but back then I didn't really understand my feelings. I came out as queer, and then I had to come out again fifteen years later as trans. The richness of that—having to renegotiate the world again and again, and desiring for an opening to happen because . . . well, I was *waiting*. That character has always struck me as so authentically speaking to very deep things about being LGBT. But the film didn't get historicized in that way.

LW: This is what I feel in a very general way: films have their own lives independent of the artists that make them. Since I was very young, I've been trying to understand the effect of cinema on me—not just the obvious, surface effect but also the subtext of cinema—and not simply accept it as a surface experience. There are all sorts of interactions happening when you encounter a piece of cinema, like every piece of art. As Hernando suggests, "All art is political, never more than when insisting it is not." We all go to the movies to have fun, to forget, to have a good time. Sure, that's great. Just be aware that during that "good time," you are being asked to believe in things—in ideas—some of which are so ubiquitous they've acquired the age-old stink of "normal" or "natural." Ideas like "Men have agency and women do not," or, "Women are too weak or emotional to be leaders," or, "Women should act like men if they want to be respected." Not to mention the barrage of hierarchical structures of otherness: "The gay guy who wears mascara must be the bad guy." "The minority will never be as important as the majority."

For me, *Bound* was trying to reflect the many ways that genre in particular affected me as a person who was constructing an identity, who knew they were trans but was living in a world in which it was too terrifying to be trans at that time. I'm interested in identity and the construction of identity and the way that mainstream genre supplies language for the construction of identity. The way that genre helps in the narrative construction of meaning.

As you're asking yourself, "Who am I? Where do I belong? What do I want? What's going on? Is there a happy ending? Can I live happily ever after? Can I meet someone and fall in love?" you begin assembling the narrative—the fragments of your life—in a way that tells a story of who you are. Genre is often a way that we learn to use those tools of narrative construction.

For a long time I've always said, *yes*, you can tell an interesting, intricate, detailed biography of a queer person in "queer" cinema, and represent this queer perspective and this dynamic as a lens to look at or understand their art. But the moment you do that, you have removed it into this special category of queerness. In order to use tools to assemble your own identity, you have to cross over into this marginalized space or this *extra* space or this *other* space, this space of otherness. You can stay in there and say, "Well, this is who I am."

We had an amazing experience in England the other day. I need sometimes to just go and look at art, go into galleries or museums. Karin and I go from city to city, and we just go to museums. We went into the British Tate. Inside there, there's an amazing gallery—Gallery 57, I think—where all the Pre-Raphaelites and Romantic painters are. You've seen it in a million studies, this room. It's so beautiful, and the curation of the paintings is really elegant, and there are some interesting juxtapositions with paintings near each other. They're all so *sensual*. There's this sensual experience to that room. The paintings have this quality of . . . I guess it is the aesthetics of sensuality. They feel like poetry pouring over your eyes.

We were in this room with two of my favorite painters, Tino Rodriguez and Virgo Paraiso. I love their artwork and have used it throughout *Sense8*, because I think they are doing the same thing I am trying to do—expanding and reimagining images of desire and beauty, even while referencing traditional images like the ones all around us in this gallery. We were having such a good time, waxing on about this and that—and then suddenly we realized that our time was running out and we had to get to this other exhibit that we were really there to see, which was this exhibit of queer art. Suddenly you're like, "*Okay!*" You have to mobilize yourself and you have to get out of the "traditional" room.

CMK: The "classical" room.

LW: The "classical" room. And you have to go down the stairs . . .

CMK: Go to the "queer" wing!

LW: (Laughs) And it's always in some place that's off the mainstream track. You wander in there, and there's powerful, profound art in there, and it's moving, and it's emotional. There is this incredible painting of Oscar Wilde at the height of his sexuality, that unique debonair genius. His wit, his smile is captured in the painting. And it's juxtaposed with a door from Reading Gaol. You realize that he goes into that door and he almost writes nothing after that. He finishes "De Profundis" and he writes the poem "The Ballad of Reading Gaol," but that's pretty much it. It's the end of that genius. *That door destroys his genius.* That "othering" takes place in our lives in a lot of little ways. We feel a lot of little doors in our lives, if we are outsiders. All outsiders experience doors like that.

CMK: Yes, and it's not only being incarcerated in a prison, but—when I think about your work—I think about being incarcerated in someone else's *reality*, in the way that happens to us all the time. Or the way that someone else's reality gets to be more real. You're talking about this cordoning off of queer experience or trans experience as saying, "That's a secondary kind of human experience *over there*. Some people have *that* experience." What I see in your work is a commitment to the popular—the common experience—and the politics of expanding that language through genre. I think of genre a lot like I think of gender. That you're presented with these tools to make meaning.

LW: Very much, yes.

CMK: You try them on and you try to create a story, and sometimes—if you're lucky—maybe something changes.

LW: It's a language.

CMK: It's a symbolic language.

LW: Genre is "the normal." It's like English in a way.

CMK: It's what is built in.

LW: If you want to go to the "queer room" downstairs, it's French! (Laughter) What happened, though, was that we went downstairs. We went into this immersive queer experience, and you have to remember—if you wish to tell your story, you have to often move outside of the regular language, and that's important. Queer cinema was incredibly important for the culture to have, those films being made at that time. But for *me*, I wanted those queer paintings to be in Gallery 57.

I want to be painting that same sensual art but with an inherent queer subjectivity and subtext. What was amazing about the experience of going into this queer "decontamination room" that was separate from heteronormative mainstream culture was that you were *charged*—you were suddenly in a postmodern way attuned and actualized. Your critical sense of "something is wrong with this culture" was activated. Now, you go back.

We finished with the queer art, we went back into the classical room. Suddenly you realize it's all white people. Suddenly you realize it's women as objects—Ophelia sinking into the flowers and completely without agency. You realize that men are powerful and brooding and pursuing women. There is a narrative construction of heteronormativity that is without queer context, or any other context, really: not racial, or queer, or differently gendered. Other art cultures are not a part of it. It's not that you have to have *everything* in every room. You can't start policing and saying, "This has to be that, and this has to be that." But you start to become aware of what is missing.

CMK: It's that juxtaposition of "what is" and what *could be*. I'm thinking particularly of an interview you gave to the *Village Voice* back in 2012, in which you said something that made me think deeply about the subjunctivity of cinema and also of being queer or trans, this feeling that things could be different. Not that they will *never* be a certain way, which is fantasy—fantasy being like a negative subjunctivity . . .

LW: The thing that can't happen.

CMK: Yes. You said that science fiction for you and for Lilly has always been about what *could* happen, if reality were permitted to extend in a certain way. If reality could become experimental.

LW: If there's an imaginative relationship to our potential, then we are conjoining *with* our future, what we see as the horizon of our lives. Beginning that same narrative trajectory, you're thinking, "This is who I am. This is where I want to go." As soon as you bring in an imaginative component, you are trying to expand the possibility of that horizon. This is the essence of science fiction.

CMK: I feel it as a kind of faith that we could actually *become*, rather than staying static, in being—the idea of becoming, of always moving. A lot of your work seems to be very concerned with the idea of moving through space and time differently.

LW: It's an opposing narrative. The dominant cultural narrative is that things are static. There's a foundational myth about America, about identity, about heteronormativity. There is this foundational relationship to those narratives. "This is the way it is." This is even the concept of normalcy. Normalcy is non-moving. It's a fixed idea.

All of my narratives are an assault against this idea. This is a false idea. It's a false god. It's a false belief system. Nothing is sovereign. Sovereignty is another false idea that I assault as much as I can. Sovereignty is a particularly dangerous American narrative—that we are alone, we are the one, we are the cowboy, we make our world, our destiny, we are the shining city on the hill. These are all, I feel, dangerous narratives of a relationship to reality that is just utter malarky. You may as well argue the world is not spinning at a thousand miles an hour because you can't *feel* it. Everything is connected and everything is moving or at least in a state of quantum uncertainty.

CMK: I'm thinking of that title shot in *Bound*, which is of the closet floor—what you see when your face is smashed into the bottom of that closet. For me, that is such a pedagogical image of the world as it is dictated—as *stasis*. And then we move high into the closet with the following establishing shot, and suddenly our perspective of the same space is wildly different. Many of your films start with this kind of disorienting invitation to come along into the text in a new way—whether it's *The Matrix* trilogy's code openings that keep progressively pushing the audience along that three-tiered experience, or even *Jupiter Ascending*'s tiny moons in front of the giant planet Jupiter, which is an exercise in assaulting our sense of scale. Is this something you developed over time as a filmmaker, this emblematic style?

LW: I've talked about it with my friend Sasha Hemon quite a bit. Sasha has this idea that as soon as you're offering counternarratives to dominant narratives, you have to reorient expectations. As soon as you are telling a story, if you use genre signifiers, you are inviting expectations. To circle back, I think one of the problems with *Bound* is that people wanted to define it by its surface, as an homage to forties noir, and never even noticed or understood that this was one of the earliest Hollywood genre films in history to show two lesbian characters falling in love, triumphing over the struggle of a symbolic, heteronormative male power . . .

CMK: Talk about sovereignty. Caesar *is* sovereignty.

LW: *Super* sovereign. . . . and going off to live happily ever after. There was almost nothing.

CMK: There are almost none now.

LW: There *are* almost none now. What I felt was missing in the investigation of queer cinema of that time period—what was particularly upsetting for me, someone who loved genre films and who only saw trans people represented as jokes or murdering psychopaths—was that they weren't recognizing how much of queer cinema at that time was reflecting the dominant cultural narrative. That to be gay, or different, or other, was to be inherently tragic and messy and fucked up. *Bound* didn't do that. We were trying to offer something new to queer and straight audiences. It was never acknowledged. It was recognized privately by people like you but never in the intellectual or critical dialectic.

CMK: That gets me thinking about the conditions of being perceived, about Sonmi~451's line, "To be is to be perceived," in *Cloud Atlas*. There are conditions for appearing in the culture. There's a context that we are expected to fill. So much of your work seems to be saying, "Okay, but let's move over *here*." You're asking audiences to sense beneath the surface of things, teaching that cinema is not only about what we *see* but how it impacts us affectively—in our bodies, our feelings, our sensoria. *Homo sensorium* and *Sense8*, these terms are coming up now in your career, but when I look at your films as a whole, that's been a thesis strung throughout your entire work: *sense,* don't merely perceive.

LW: *Bound* has essentially similar dialogue. It's like "What's the difference between us?" There is a surface to Corky, and there's a surface to Violet. There is a relationship to how you perceive Corky that is more in accord with how she feels underneath. So she *projects*. For Violet, she is the same as Corky in a way, underneath. She also desires women, but she is perceived to be heteronormative. This relationship between identity and perception of identity . . .

You can make obvious implications for my own identity and my own relationship to how I've been perceived. It just continues to reflect and refract. My relationship, as an artist, to how I am perceived in the world is also a complex thing. Sometimes I look at the way people look at my work, and I shake my head . . . in the same way that I look at the way that people perceive my gender, and I shake my head.

It was worse before I was out. I have occupied the Corky position in life, and I've occupied the Violet position in life. Those two modes of expressing, modes of being in this world, are fraught with all sorts of complications. I have tried to examine those complications in a lot of different ways, in a lot of different films.

CMK: That leads to the question of how it feels to have your work revisited as a historical "first" in this way.

LW: I surrendered. I knew when I came out there was going to be a whole "Now let's reinterpret everything Lana's done through the lens of her gender identity." Of course, it's natural. If you're just trying to look at my work through my own gender, my own identity as a trans person, you will end up with one understanding of my work. If you begin to try to expand that understanding, you can see my relationship to cinema. My relationship to cinema is not the same as my relationship to my gender.

CMK: I think if anyone spent time thinking about what your work really says, they would learn very quickly that it can't only be about your identity—because your entire body of work is about the provisionality of identity in so many ways. Your work informs directly against that reading. Pay attention, people!

LW: Because I'm trying to destabilize the whole essentialist myth, there isn't this singular, foundational idea that would explain all of my work. It's a constantly destabilized quantum experience. The way you might have understood *Bound* twenty years ago is not the same way you will understand it now, and it won't be the same forty years from now.

CMK: Absolutely not. We can't get away from the fact that we change.

LW: That is the one truth!

CMK: That *is* the one truth. And I think trans experience—maybe not identity, but the feeling or experience of that kind of radical break—informs us about changes in perception in specific ways. My relationship with *Bound* or *The Matrix*, how those films question reality, was very different when I was trying to survive as a queer kid in rural Pennsylvania than it is now, twenty years later, as a transgender man. My relationship to those works is always going to be contained within my own history, my own sense of how those films still speak across that space between my selves. They absolutely *do*. They have grown with me over the course of my life. It's not easy to make films that do that—that grow over time in that way.

LW: I try. That is my goal always. I want to make living works. I want to make works that continue to be alive. This is the problem of even trying to discuss the work, even trying to *fix* the work. As soon as you start to try to hold it and say, "This is what it *is*. I'm transcribing and I have a sense of it," I'm suspicious of what the actual description of that fixed point will end up being.

You can, I guess, in a quantum way, say, "Okay, at this time and this place, this is how I feel and this is what came of this conversation." I get there is a value to checking in and saying, "Okay, let's look at this now. Let's take a quantitative/qualitative, hard, multi-perspectival look at this thing and see what we think about it." Maybe it will shift and maybe we'll throw it out tomorrow, or maybe it will be something that endures alongside the work and continues to shed light on the work.

I *love* Simon Schama. I don't know if you have read *Rembrandt's Eyes*, but if somebody dug into my work, and attempted to contextualize my work in the way that he attempted to understand Rembrandt's work—it's an act of *seeing*. To be seen as an artist is the same as wanting to be understood as a human being. To be witnessed, to be understood, is as strong an antidote to the struggle of the human condition as anything. When you make a piece of art, you are trying to share a piece of yourself, a surrogate of yourself—and you're hoping that somebody can see and understand that part of you.

What Schama was trying to do with Rembrandt's art, I believe, is as valuable as the art itself. Every work of art is an invitation to another perspective, another way of seeing and abandoning your own eyes, your perspectives, your prejudices, your assumptions. Trying to experience the world through someone else's eyes is an act of love.

CMK: "Art is love made public."

LW: Yes, I did write that.

CMK: I had a feeling you might have.

LW: I don't think there is any really valuable piece of criticism that has ever been written that was not an expression or investigation of love. If you are essentially writing to destroy or dismiss something, it is in all probability as worthless as the dust that piece of paper will become.

Whenever you look at art history, really the only criticism that is saved from the bin is the criticism that essentially shows how ignorant people were about Mozart, or Rembrandt, or Van Gogh. It's to show the *incapacity* to understand, the inability to see, the inability to enter the perspective of that the artist. Just write . . .

CMK: Write with love?

LW: Understanding requires empathy.

CMK: Thinking about my own career, in graduate school you are sometimes taught a certain style of critique—to point out all the power structures and how they are present in the work and how that is a problem. But that is, of course, inevitable. These are the structures we have. So, given that this is the reality we are all facing, what helps us *keep living*? As you mature as a thinker, you hopefully start to develop different skills. Some people never do, because they get enabled early on and are celebrated and encouraged to do that kind of work—a kind of punitive, aristocratic approach that rises above the work and points at it and says, "Let me show you why this is bad."

It's what queer theorist Eve Sedgwick called in her work a "paranoid" reading style, meaning that by pointing out the structural problems over and over again, we remake them as real. We shape the future in the shape of what is, by describing.

LW: "By criticism, we remake the world," to modify the Buddha.

CMK: Exactly. And Sedgwick did write about Buddhism as well. At the *Sense8* season two premiere, you mentioned art as a "game of telephone." Criticism is also a game of telephone that passes art along, that creates a context. When you make art paranoid, what you do is you bend it to power in a way that can be harmful to people who may not even exist yet, who need that art, who are in the future.

LW: It's bending towards power, and also I think toward the mechanisms of commodification. You basically are bending towards a discussion of *value*. "This has no value because it doesn't support *this* interrogation of the structures of power." As soon as you begin making judgments that are in the service of value—this is the same for movie critics, they're basically saying, "Go see this one, not this one. This one's crap. This one's crap. This one's good." What they are doing is essentially servicing the industry. It's a voice of commodification, the same way ads are a voice of commodification. It's helping direct the flow of commerce. It's not attempting to bring illumination and understanding into what art *is*.

If you just think of art as *people*, if you just say, "I want to meet this person," then you have one relationship to art. If you say, "I want to judge this person as being controlled by this element of power, or judge this person as somebody who is a plebe because they wear this and that," you're contributing to what I think is the devaluation and the dehumanization of other human beings.

CMK: You've spoken about your appreciation for the tradition of 1970s blockbuster science fiction: films like *Blade Runner, 2001, Zardoz*. It seems there was a special moment in film where directors got to make big budget, idea-driven, speculative works. I see your career as carrying on that tradition, but in a much more conservative historical period, when that kind of film is just not really what the industry supports anymore. Today everything "speculative" seems to use preexisting concepts from established franchises or is a reboot. It has to be preconceived.

I wonder, how has that shift been for you? Did you move to television because it offered more space than a film studio?

LW: I don't really have a plan. I just muddle toward things that are attractive to me, which are usually things I haven't done before. That's my progression. I am easily bored by things. I crave for my relationship to my own art to be stimulated and energized by feeling like it's something new, that there's something that I have to learn about myself, or the cinema, or the structure of cinema.

I'm very into structure. I care very much about narrative structure in cinema. In some ways, you could find a pendulum movement in the work: the next work is always far away from the previous one. I'm responding to something very intimate about identity—how it can feel small, and contained, and claustrophobic. You could write all sorts of personal dynamics about this. Lilly and I could have made a million versions of *Bound*. We were offered all sorts of thrillers.

CMK: "Remake this. Remake it. Make it again." That imperative to repeat.

LW: "Do this. Do that. Here's a thriller. There's a *sexual* thriller." We sat there for quite a long time. People said we were killing our careers by waiting. It was three years, four years until *The Matrix*. But that's what we wanted: to do *The Matrix*. Again, in some ways it was very far from *Bound*, but in some ways it continued our recombining of basic genre DNA. After the trilogy we needed to swing as far from what we felt we were experiencing—the Agent Smith–like cloning of what we did, which spread everywhere—so we went off the map with *Speed Racer*.

Again, I'm a person who is nourished by art, and I'm a visual thinker. I think about stories, and I think about my own story and my own identity as it relates to images and pictures. When I go into a museum, I feel that part of my brain being stimulated.

I've said it before a million times. It's frustrating to walk into a museum and see on every wall the human face represented so uniquely and so differently, and then to walk into a hundred movie theaters and see the human face exactly the same. You're like, "Why? Why does it have to be *that way*? Why can I relate to this portrait or these hundred portraits, and all of them are different?" In the difference there's actually a reflection of the artist. The artist is more present. You can feel the fingerprint of an artist in every brushstroke. But the camera . . . the *camera*.

The thing is, we could manipulate the camera if we were allowed to, if audiences would let us. Accept us. If an audience could be as open when they walked into a movie theater as when they walk into a museum or an art gallery, I think I would love the process of making movies much more. As it is, there is something that I always have to overcome. There's going to be this conformity, this fascism of "realism" that we have only ever been able to escape during the making of *Speed Racer*.

CMK: I was thinking about your use of the word "assault." After I heard you use it several times, I became very interested in what it actually meant. I looked up the etymology of the word and was surprised. It means "to leap."

LW: To leap—yes!

CMK: It seemed to me this is exactly what you're doing. You are holding out your hand and asking the audience to come with you: "We are going to make this leap." I keep thinking about that fantastic leap that Trinity takes, or the jump program in *The Matrix*, as teaching moments, where you are saying, "This world can be stretched—it is speculative. Let me help you find that out. Let's go together into this new sensation." You have incredible faith in your audiences, but you're not easy on them either. You challenge the viewer but with a kind of love, a faith in expansion. Did that word, "assault," just come to you?

LW: I don't want to make any kind of pat narratives, but it's interesting you brought the word up. I'm somebody who follows feeling. I was assaulted a lot as a kid. I had a hard time as a kid. I was the kid people called "faggot." I *leapt* away from the world where I was attacked and beat up, like Trinity, using my imagination to escape into a different world. My imagination became *survival*. The relationship between survival and the imagination is a constant in the landscape of our work. You cannot survive without imagination. Yes, that probably comes back to me asking the audience to take that imaginative leap, because if we don't, then people like me don't survive.

In some ways I had to imagine a world where I could be a transgender pink-dreadlocked Hollywood director, because it did not exist. There was nothing *like me*. I had to imagine a world for me to be. There's a narrative omega point in every Wachowski movie: we have to find a door, imagine a way out of this world, into a different world. In order to experience this new world, you will have to let go of a lot of your traditional assumptions, your standard expectations. Beyond the rabbit hole, new possibilities, new versions of us can exist.

Between my hope for a world where I could be an artist, be a filmmaker, and the struggle for that reality is where a lot of the work was created. It could be supposed that the uniqueness of my sister and me, and our relationship, is reflected in the uniqueness of the work.

In many ways the work I'm the most proud of is *Cloud Atlas*. There are a lot of firsts in all of our work that I'm very proud of, whether it's *Bound* being the first positive Hollywood-produced queer film, *The Matrix* bringing philosophy into the genre action movie, *Speed Racer* being arguably one of the most aesthetically aggressive films made during my lifetime. But with *Cloud Atlas, everything* is original. Well, except that it was written by David Mitchell, who I feel in love with, like everyone who is lucky enough to meet him—and who I believe is actually a part of my cluster. But there is nothing like our film adaptation in terms of narrative construction. There have been rondeaux before, but no one has ever tried to tell each rondeau through the next, or even hopscotching through to land the next part of a story through the actors. Actors, remember, are always stable—but we destabilized the actors. You are then able to use those destabilized identities as actually stabilizing narrative identities. It's so *different*. So outside the normal narrative box of cinema.

CMK: Your work is very allergic to boxes, I think—going all the way back to your early work in comics. It seems to me that you've always strained against formalism, against the limits of what we expect, or will accept. "You only get two hours . . ."

LW: Two hours. Realism. Every face looks like all other faces. If it doesn't satisfy certain criteria or expectations, it is automatically dismissed as "a miss." Maybe Terry Malick is somebody who has offered us some relief from the idea that you have to have narrative expectations met. You go see his movies and you feel this relief, of being able to just *be* with a moment of cinema. It doesn't have to unfold in this mechanized causal relationship heading towards an anticipated catharsis. I'm not saying that *Cloud Atlas* is trying to do the same thing, but it's trying to destabilize and reorient those expectations in a way that hasn't been done or even attempted.

CMK: It's a very different approach to cinematic temporality. What you're talking about, I think, is the way that cinema as an industrial form periodizes its own temporal order, your sense of narrative or even bodily anticipation as you watch: "This is about when a conflict should be introduced. This is when a character has doubts." *Cloud Atlas* is like an accordion. It contracts and expands, and there are these strings shot through it that are the closest you get to characters. It's like the *Cloud Atlas* sextet itself, like a piece of music. You have to listen for the violin, no matter where in the symphony you are, that tone, regardless of the structure.

LW: I have this feeling—the way that you're saying people are going back to *Bound*—I have this feeling or at least this hope that *Cloud Atlas* is the work that people will go back to the most, because things happened also in it narratively that were just little miracles that weren't by design. It had an intelligence that we sometimes just got out of the way of and we would look at and go, "How did that happen?" It just *happened*.

It was a spiritual experience for everyone who made it and who participated in it. I had such a incredible time with Tom Hanks. Doona, obviously, I am very close to. It was amazing to work with Hugo again on it. But something happened with Tom Hanks that was quite . . . I never had an actor who was just on set constantly and just wanted to watch or just wanted to see what else was going on. Then, if you wanted to start experimenting, he would jump in and we would just start making things up and improvising. He was infected by the energy, by the constant creativity and impossible way *Cloud Atlas* defied the logic of time and space. The arithmetic of filming says that *Cloud Atlas* was simply not possible, but there it is. It just kept expanding, the rules and the possibilities changing every day. I know a friend asked Tom in an interview what his favorite film was to work on, and he was very diplomatic and charming, answering, "Oh, I can't answer that because I have this friend and I have this person and I don't want to make anyone mad, but if there was a movie that I wished never ended, it was *Cloud Atlas*." I think that's how everyone who worked on it felt, even Alex Boswell. He's a lovely friend, the greatest prop guy in the world. He talks about it and says, "I could have shot *Cloud Atlas* my whole life."

That movie changed how I wanted to work as an artist. *Sense8*, I think, is a more direct evolution from that experience. *Jupiter* was driven by our desire to return to "big" science fiction, because we had a lot of ideas that we'd been accumulating, and we were tired of the landscape of what you mentioned before—the lack of originality, the reboots, the repetitions, the sameness.

CMK: What I meant by that, I think, is the lack of serious ideas. Mainstream science fiction right now is mostly character-based comedy, or simple Manichean conflict, or a rehash of prior history and characters. We always seem to be going backwards in time. If your world building isn't *world-building*, if it's just what has already happened with no potential for newness, then you are not really making science fiction.

LW: Yes. We wanted to once again bring sociopolitical issues into science fiction and talk about what was going on in our world with imaginative metaphor—an imagined metaphorical *world* for what we saw. It was also the first time that I really shot in Chicago, which I'd always wanted to do.

CMK: That chase sequence is incredible.

LW: Yeah, thank you. We loved shooting it. A dream come true.

CMK: When you talk about how everything you do does something unprecedented, that was pretty unprecedented, that sequence.

LW: It was fun to say, "We're going to shoot the most complicated chase in the movie during magic hour," and watch people who understand what that means—most people don't understand what that means—to see technical people immediately go to this "that's fucking impossible" kind of face . . .

CMK: You were both like, "That's where we need to be."

LW: Yes! For me, what was interesting about the sequence was that it was "How are we going to tell the story of them falling in love?" I really like Bollywood movies, and there's a dance number in a Bollywood movie, that is the formalization of how this emotional attachment begins. I was like "It's kind of a dance. It's just a *chase*." The American form of the Bollywood dance is a chase, or a fight sequence. Let's use a chase to tell the story of the beginning of this emotional bond, and so it should be romantic, because it should be beautiful, in a way. I love the way Chicago looks in the summer, when the sun is very early and the light bounces off the lake and reflects up into the sky. I think it has a very magical quality. I asked, "Look, can we try to capture that?" John Toll was a bit stunned at first, but then he just shrugged in the way he does with this adorable conspiratorial gleam in his eyes and was like, "Okay, sure, why not."

CMK: Much of your work seems to have this quality of "why not?" to it that expresses a kind of inherently speculative approach to the world. For example, the way in which you've experimented with narrative form, especially in *Cloud Atlas* and *Sense8*.

LW: Certainly if you're tracing the way that *Cloud Atlas* had an impact on my life as an artist, the more direct through-line would be to *Sense8*. The cinematic language of sensate "visiting" evolved directly from Ol' Georgie.

CMK: I can see that. There is the same concern with the provisionality of identity, the use of narrative complexity and cluster formations—the way in which you're actually asking us to pay attention to nonlinear forms of time.

LW: Carry the violin note through this character's story, and you'll hear it again in this character's story, because oppression from a dominant culture is experienced across many kinds of lives, many kinds of identities. In a way what we were doing with those very complex narrative dynamics in *Cloud Atlas* was trying to tell a story with a *supra* or *meta* character. The cluster itself *is* a character in the same way the *Cloud Atlas* comet is a cluster—something both singular and specific while also something universal. The ideas of *Cloud Atlas* continue echoing in *Sense8*, sometimes explicitly, like in the "Who Am I?" sequence.

CMK: Is there anything else you'd like to say, especially given the news about *Sense8* getting this last-minute finale from Netflix?

LW: This is what I would say: *Do not listen* to anything I have said here. Resist any fixed ideas of myself or my work. When I pause for a moment and consider I have been making films for over twenty years, I'm completely gobsmacked. When I look at the films I've been allowed to make, it's really unbelievable. It's nuts. When I look at my career and I look at other people's careers, I *love* my career. The films are so different from anything else and from each other, which seems to me an absolute freaking miracle. All I try to do is constantly say, "Thank you." I have nothing but mad gratitude to the people who have allowed us such creative freedom and given us their trust.

At the same time I'm making all this art, usually with people who are my best friends, including my wife, Karin, who is the person that saved my life. She is also the reason there was a season two of *Sense8*: it was her favorite piece of art we have made. But with all of that, I also get to be an out trans person in an industry where there wasn't an out trans person before me, which is another gobsmacking, crazy miracle. *And* I get to live in Chicago, which is a city I have been in love with my whole life.

Which is not to say, "My life is perfect." Far from it. I suffer with serious depression, but I am conscious of the extraordinary fact that an out trans woman has been able to make a lot of very original work. When people got mad at Netflix, I was like "Look, they gave me *a lot* of money to make two seasons of a show that is super complicated." Nothing is like it. It's full of sex!

That's another thing. What director has shot as much sex as me?

CMK: Good question. It's hard to say, especially now that you're also working in TV. *Sense8* is some of the most sensual, sexy, gorgeous television ever shot. I feel like people are just starting to figure that out now.

LW: Combining the two of them, I've shot sex for every single thing I've done except for *Speed Racer*. And in *Speed Racer*, I have kissing!

CMK: (Laughs) And some of those cars are pretty sexy too. The car and Speed, that relationship is pretty romantic.

LW: There's something that is so strange about a culture in which we reflect ourselves in movies, in these mirrors—which is what all this art is—but we want to see mirrors that reflect something that almost no one experiences: violence. You can make a case that you'll experience *some* type of violence, but the idea that you'll have to get a gun and shoot somebody, or you'll be in a huge fight, or bombs will be blowing up around you . . . We have this super-obsession with something that does not affect almost any of us. And yet the thing that probably affects us the most is sex. As Sun states, as clearly as possible, "We exist because of sex." Everyone has a relationship to sex. Sex, one way or another, will affect your life—and we almost *never* see it. That is bizarre to me in a way that is almost incomprehensible. If I were to imagine a fantasy land where the most essential part of one's existence (you could not be reading this if your parents had not had sex) was constantly hidden, I would tell myself as a writer, "It's not possible. No one would believe this!"

CMK: I feel like trans people are especially attuned to that kind of relationship between visibility and invisibility—these paradoxes we live inside. There's this thing—*sex*—and it's everywhere, but we also don't look at it, *ever*.

LW: We have never looked at it.

CMK: We have no sense of what it *could* look like.

LW: Even though we're all completely obsessed with it, we never look at it. That's crazy, isn't it?

CMK: (Laughter) I remember seeing the sex scenes in *Bound* and just being *blown away*. I still am. I'll tell you a story—short, I promise.

LW: Good. Anecdotes are good. I like an anecdote.

CMK: I show *Bound* in some of my classes—my queer theory class but also in a class on LGBTQ identities. In that class I show it in the context of the stereotype that lesbians don't have "real" sex. No one really knows what lesbian sexuality looks like. Everyone is always wondering, "What's that?" They don't have a visual grammar for it. So for my students I say, "Okay, we are going watch this movie, because this film will disabuse you. If you have no image in your head of what lesbian sex is, *here you go*." It's the best popular cinematic representation I can think of, of lesbian sexuality.

I warn them that this is a pretty sexy movie. I tell them to maybe *not* watch it with their parents, for example. But it is never "sexy" in the way they are expecting, and they are constantly caught off guard. One of my students watched it with her straight boyfriend. I would not necessarily have advised this, but okay. And at some point he had to physically disengage. She described how, over the course of the film, he slowly started sliding down the couch . . . and then at some point he just backed *right out of the room*. She realized that he was so used to seeing images of women that invited him in, and this film did the opposite. She had never seen a film do that to someone. In class she said, "That was so amazing, because I could see that the film was affecting him very deeply and he was *not* prepared for it." Talk about assault!

Bound still surprises people in that way, which tells you everything you need to know about queer representation twenty years later. A lot of *Sense8* has this same electric, riveting feeling to it. It's challenging. It's not just this same, flat depiction of sex using the same standard shots. It doesn't cut away. It takes its time and makes you *stay with it*. It's beautiful and organic, and demands something of you. It refuses objectification. You have to be a bodily witness to what's happening.

LW: With *Bound* there was a very deliberate desire to obviously depict and empower female sexuality. I remember I involved Susie Bright, and one of the principal reasons I did was because I wanted to give credit to her for helping me describe where I felt I was. I was trying to express something personal. That was how I engaged in sex—more female than male. She wrote this line in which she said, "We too have stiff, incessant, probing sex organs. We call them *hands*." I thought that was not just hot but incredibly insightful, because so much of noir language is around hardness and penises and guns and this phallic imagery. I wanted to take that and reappropriate it for women.

CMK: (Makes finger-cutting-off motion)

LW: Yeah (laughs), exactly! So castration became a way to assault these sovereign narratives but to also bring in a feeling of danger for the women. I was mixing all of that in a way that I knew would be a cauldron for straight men. It would also be difficult for women, because when you start bringing violence and sexuality together, it's hard for women too. Yet I knew that was where the language of noir could be enlisted to undermine traditional male narratives. The fight over the gun is also fighting over the sex. At the end it all comes back to Violet essentially having the gun—Violet with the penis.

CMK: She reveals her power and dethrones the false king!

LW: Talk about sovereignty! He's so sovereign, he's unconscious of any other agency but male agency.

CMK: Caesar has all these tactics. First he assumes he's got everything under control. That's the story. "I got it all. I got the wife. I got the power. I got it all locked down."

LW: *All* of this.

CMK: One little crack appears, which is his inability to control Violet's desire, her gaze. She's independent from him in ways he can't see. Corky shows up, and then the money disappears. Paranoia sets in. So he starts trying to control the narrative, telling stories, trying to enlist Violet in his version of things. The stories fall apart. So he starts arranging objects in the apartment: "If my story doesn't work, I'm going to physically rearrange the space." That doesn't fix the problem, so then he starts physically moving the women's bodies around. He immobilizes Corky in the closet. He ties Violet up.

LW: They literally become objects, yes! I wanted to speak about the objectification of women.

CMK: Lastly, when Violet kills him, it's because he tries to tell her what her *desire* is—what's on the inside of her.

LW: Yeah, that she doesn't want to escape *him*.

CMK: He's like, "I know what's inside of you, Violet. You don't want to kill me." Well, guess what? That's not what's *happening* in this film. It's such a sustained investigation of that sovereign, grasping . . .

LW: Misogynist.

CMK: . . . misogynist masculinity, and the lengths it will go to to dictate reality.

LW: And it's so unconscious or inoculated against any other kind of agency that I turned it into a joke at the end. Even the guy who she uses to basically wipe Caesar out—what's his name—Mickey. Even Mickey at the end can't possibly imagine her with any agency, and I use that, then, as a plot invisibility for her.

CMK: Her cloak.

LW: Her cloak!

I've been privileged to be given these opportunities to represent the diversity of human sexuality. It was not easy to put sex in the trilogy, but I needed it, because I needed to understand Neo, and Neo and Trinity—we did not want their relationship to be like so many relationships we see today in film, without physical, sexually mature connection. I needed to understand Zion as *bodies*, and if you want to understand bodies, you have to understand *desire*. The condition of identity—if that's your investigation—the human condition, you can't *not* talk about sex. The art, which is to say the mirrors, that I am interested in reflects the things that matter and are important to me—identity, desire, and love.

CMK: Would you describe yourself as a utopian, then?

LW: Obviously, I would resist any label . . . but I think the making of art is inherently optimistic. If you are a true pessimist, then why do anything if you believe there is no point to it? Whereas *making* is an act of creation, and all creation is in the service of hope.

Good?

CMK: Thank you. Yes. Perfect.

Bound (1996)
USA
Production: Dino De Laurentiis Company, Spelling Films
Executive Producers: Lana Wachowski, Lilly Wachowski, Dino De Laurentiis
    (uncredited)
Producers: Stuart Boros and Andrew Lazar
Distribution: Gramercy Pictures
Directors: Lana Wachowski, Lilly Wachowski
Screenplay: Lana Wachowski, Lilly Wachowski
Editor: Zach Staenberg
Cinematography: Bill Pope
Music: Don Davis
Art Direction: Andrea Dopaso, Robert C. Goldstein
Production Design: Teresa Kelly, Pearl A. Lucero
Principal Cast: Jennifer Tilly (Violet), Gina Gershon (Corky), Joe Pantoliano (Caesar), John P. Ryan (Micky Malnato), Christopher Meloni (Johnnie Marzzone)
Format: 35mm, color
108 min.

The Matrix (1999)
USA
Production: Warner Bros., Village Roadshow Pictures, Groucho II Film Partnership, Silver Pictures
Executive Producers: Bruce Berman, Andrew Mason, Barrie M. Osborne, Erwin Stoff, Lana Wachowski, Lilly Wachowski
Producer: Joel Silver
Distribution: Warner Bros.
Directors: Lana Wachowski, Lilly Wachowski
Screenplay: Lana Wachowski, Lilly Wachowski
Editor: Zach Staenberg
Cinematography: Bill Pope
Music: Don Davis

Art Direction: Hugh Bateup, Michelle McGahey
Production Design: Owen Paterson
Principal Cast: Keanu Reeves (Neo), Laurence Fishburne (Morpheus), Carrie-Anne Moss (Trinity), Hugo Weaving (Agent Smith), Gloria Foster (Oracle), Joe Pantoliano (Cypher), Marcus Chong (Tank), Julian Arahanga (Apoc), Matt Doran (Mouse), Belinda McClory (Switch), Anthony Ray Parker (Dozer)
Format: 35mm, color
136 min.

The Animatrix (2003)
USA, Japan
Production: Warner Bros., Warner Bros. Animation, Silver Pictures
Executive Producer: Joel Silver
Producers: Lana Wachowski, Lilly Wachowski, Michael Arias, Spencer Lamm, Phil Oosterhouse, Steve Richards
Screenplay: Lana Wachowski, Lilly Wachowski
Music: Don Davis, Machine Head, Photek
Format: 35mm, color
136 min.

"Matriculated"
Production: DNA Productions
Producer: Soon-Hong Park
Director: Peter Chung
Writer: Peter Chung
Principal Cast: Melinda Clarke (Alexa), Dwight Schultz (Nonaka), Rodney Saulsberry (Chyron), James Arnold Taylor (Raul), Olivia d'Abo (Rox), Jack Fletcher (Sandro)

"Program"
Production: Madhouse
Producers: Masao Maruyama, Yoshimichi Murata
Director: Yoshiaki Kawajiri
Writer: Yoshiaki Kawajiri
Principal Cast: Hedy Burress (Cis), Phil LaMarr (Duo), John DiMaggio (Kaiser)

"World Record"
Production: Madhouse
Director: Takeshi Koike
Writer: Yoshiaki Kawajiri
Principal Cast: Victor Williams (Dan), John Wesley (Dan's dad), Alex Fernandez (Tom), Allison Smith (Reporter), Tara Strong (Nurse), Matt McKenzie

(Agent #1), Kevin Michael Richardson (Agent #2), Julia Fletcher (Narrator)

"Final Flight of the Osiris"
Production: Square USA
Producers: Jun Aida, Spencer Lamm, Gary Mundell, Joel Silver, Cameron Stevning
Director: Andrew R. Jones
Writers: Lana Wachowski, Lilly Wachowski
Principal Cast: Kevin Michael Richardson (Thadeus), Pamela Adlon (Jue), John DiMaggio (Crew Man), Tom Kenny (Operator), Rick Gomez (Pilot), Tara Strong (Crew Woman), Bette Ford (Old Woman)

"The Second Renaissance Part 1"
Production: Studio 4°C
Producer: Eiko Tanaka
Director: Mahiro Maeda
Writers: Lana Wachowski, Lilly Wachowski
Principal Cast: Julia Fletcher (The Instructor), Dane A. Davis (01 Versatran Spokesman), Debi Derryberry (Kid), Jill Talley (Mother), Dwight Schultz, James Arnold Taylor

"The Second Renaissance Part 2"
Production: Studio 4°C
Producer: Eiko Tanaka
Director: Mahiro Maeda
Writers: Lana Wachowski, Lilly Wachowski
Principal Cast: Julia Fletcher (The Instructor), Dane A. Davis (01 Versatran Spokesman), Debi Derryberry (Kid), Jill Talley (Mother), Dwight Schultz, James Arnold Taylor

"Kid's Story"
Production: Studio 4°C
Director: Shinichirô Watanabe
Story by: Lana Wachowski, Lilly Wachowski
Writer: Shinichirô Watanabe
Principal Cast: Clayton Watson (Michael Karl Popper), Keanu Reeves (Neo), Carrie-Anne Moss (Trinity), John DeMita (Teacher), Kevin Michael Richardson (Cop), James Arnold Taylor

"Beyond"
Production: Studio 4°C
Producers: Suguru Sato, Eiko Tanaka, Hiroto Yonemori

Director: Kôji Morimoto
Writer: Kôji Morimoto
Principal Cast: Hedy Burress (Yoko), Tress MacNeille (Housewife/Kenny/
  Agent), Kath Soucie (Pudgy/Masa/Sara), Pamela Adlon (Manabu), Tara
  Strong (Misha), Matt McKenzie (Agent/Ash)

"Detective Story"
Production: Studio 4°C
Director: Shinichirô Watanabe
Writer: Shinichirô Watanabe
Principal Cast: James Arnold Taylor (Ash), Carrie-Anne Moss (Trinity), Ter-
  rence Carson (Clarence), Matt McKenzie (Agent)

The Matrix Reloaded (2003)
USA, Australia
Production: Warner Bros., Village Roadshow Pictures, Groucho II Film Part-
  nership, Silver Pictures
Executive Producers: Bruce Berman, David Forbes, Grant Hill, Andrew Mason,
  Barrie M. Osborne, Erwin Stoff, Lana Wachowski, Lilly Wachowski
Producer: Joel Silver
Distribution: Warner Bros.
Directors: Lana Wachowski, Lilly Wachowski
Screenplay: Lana Wachowski, Lilly Wachowski
Editor: Zach Staenberg
Cinematography: Bill Pope
Music: Don Davis
Art Direction: Hugh Bateup, Nanci Noblett
Production Design: Owen Paterson
Principal Cast: Keanu Reeves (Neo), Laurence Fishburne (Morpheus), Car-
  rie-Anne Moss (Trinity), Hugo Weaving (Agent Smith), Jada Pinkett Smith
  (Niobe), Gloria Foster (Oracle), Harold Perrineau (Link), Lambert Wilson
  (the Merovingian), Monica Bellucci (Persephone), Randall Duk Kim (the
  Keymaker), Harry Lennix (Commander Lock), Nona Gay (Zee)
Format: 35mm, color
138 min.

The Matrix Revolutions (2003)
USA, Australia
Production: Warner Bros., Village Roadshow Pictures, NPV Entertainment,
  Silver Pictures
Executive Producers: Bruce Berman, David Forbes, Grant Hill, Andrew Mason,
  Lana Wachowski, Lilly Wachowski
Producer: Joel Silver
Distribution: Warner Bros. (USA), Roadshow Entertainment (Australia)

Directors: Lana Wachowski, Lilly Wachowski
Screenplay: Lana Wachowski, Lilly Wachowski
Editor: Zach Staenberg
Cinematography: Bill Pope
Music: Don Davis
Art Direction: Hugh Bateup, Jules Cook, Catherine Mansill, Charlie Revai
Production Design: Owen Paterson
Principal Cast: Keanu Reeves (Neo), Laurence Fishburne (Morpheus), Carrie-Anne Moss (Trinity), Hugo Weaving (Agent Smith), Jada Pinkett Smith (Niobe), Mary Alice (Oracle), Harold Perrineau (Link), Lambert Wilson (the Merovingian), Monica Bellucci (Persephone), Harry J. Lennix (Commander Lock), Nona Gay (Zee)
Format: 35mm, color
129 min.

V for Vendetta (2005)
USA, UK, Germany
Production: Warner Bros., Virtual Studios, Silver Pictures, Anarchos Productions, Studio Babelsberg, Medienboard Berlin-Brandenburg, DC Comics
Executive Producer: Benjamin Waisbren
Producers: Grant Hill, Joel Silver, Lana Wachowski, Lilly Wachowski
Distribution: Warner Bros.
Director: James McTeigue
Screenplay: Lana Wachowski, Lilly Wachowski
Editor: Martin Walsh
Cinematography: Adrian Biddle
Music: Dario Marianelli
Art Direction: Marco Bittner Rosser, Stephen Bream, Stephan O. Gessler, Sarah Horton, Sebastian T. Krawinkel, Kevin Phipps
Production Design: Owen Paterson
Principal Cast: Natalie Portman (Evey), Hugo Weaving (V), Stephen Rea (Finch), Stephen Fry (Deitrich), John Hurt (Adam Sutler)
Format: 35mm, color
132 min.

Speed Racer (2008)
USA, Australia
Production: Warner Bros., Village Roadshow Pictures, Groucho II Film Partnership, Silver Pictures
Executive Producers: Bruce Berman, Michael Lambert, David Lane Seltzer
Producers: Grant Hill, Joel Silver, Lana Wachowski, Lilly Wachowski
Distribution: Warner Bros.
Directors: Lana Wachowski, Lilly Wachowski
Screenplay: Lana Wachowski, Lilly Wachowski

Editors: Roger Barton, Zach Staenberg
Cinematography: David Tattersall
Music: Michael Giacchino
Art Direction: Hugh Bateup, Marco Bittner Rosser, Stephan O. Gessler, Sebastian T. Krawinkel, Anja Müller
Production Design: Owen Paterson
Principal Cast: Emile Hirsch (Speed), Christina Ricci (Trixie), Matthew Fox (Racer X), Rain (Taejo Togokahn), John Goodman (Pops), Susan Sarandon (Mom), Scott Porter (Rex Racer), Kick Gurry (Sparky)
Format: Digital, color
135 min.

Cloud Atlas (2012)
USA, Germany, Hong Kong, Singapore
Production: Cloud Atlas Productions, X-Filme Creative Pool, Anarchos Pictures, A Company Filmproduktionsgesellschaft, ARD Degeto Film, Ascension Pictures, Dreams of Dragon Picture, Five Drops, Media Asia Group
Executive Producers: John Chong, Caroline Kwauk, Philip Lee, Wilson Qiu, Uwe Schott, Pearry Reginald Teo, Tony Teo, Ricky Tse
Producers: Stefan Arndt, Alex Boden, Grant Hill, Tom Tykwer, Lana Wachowski, Lilly Wachowski
Distribution: Warner Bros.
Directors: Tom Tykwer, Lana Wachowski, Lilly Wachowski
Screenplay: Tom Tykwer, Lana Wachowski, Lilly Wachowski
Editors: Alexander Berner, Claus Wehlisch
Cinematography: Frank Griebe, John Toll
Music: Reinhold Heil, Johnny Klimek, Tom Tykwer
Art Direction: Daniel Chour, Sabine Engelberg, Stephan O. Gessler, Kai Koch, Nicki McCallum, Charlie Revai, Thorsten Sabel, David Scheunemann, Steve Summersgill
Production Design: Hugh Bateup, Uli Hanisch
Principal Cast: Tom Hanks, Halle Berry, Jim Broadbent, Hugo Weaving, Jim Sturgess, Doona Bae, Ben Whishaw, Keith David, James D'Arcy, Xun Zhou, David Gyasi, Susan Sarandon, Hugh Grant, Robert Fyfe, Martin Wuttke, Brody Nicholas Lee
Format: Digital, color
172 min.

Jupiter Ascending (2015)
USA, Australia
Production: Warner Bros., Village Roadshow Pictures, RatPac-Dune Entertainment, Anarchos Productions
Executive Producers: Bruce Berman, Roberto Malerba
Producers: Grant Hill, Lana Wachowski, Lilly Wachowski

Distribution: Warner Bros., Roadshow Entertainment
Directors: Lana Wachowski, Lilly Wachowski (as The Wachowskis)
Screenplay: Lana Wachowski, Lilly Wachowski (as The Wachowskis)
Editor: Alexander Berner
Cinematography: John Toll
Music: Michael Giacchino
Art Direction: David Allday, Dominic Hyman, Peter James, David W. Krummel, Charlie Revai, Mark Scruton, Merje Veski, Su Whitaker
Production Design: Hugh Bateup
Principal Cast: Mila Kunis (Jupiter Jones), Channing Tatum (Caine Wise), Sean Bean (Stinger Apini), Eddie Redmayne (Balem Abrasax), Douglas Booth (Titus Abrasax), Tuppence Middleton (Kalique Abrasax), Nikki Amuka-Bird (Diomika Tsing)
Format: Digital, color
127 min.

Sense8 (2015–2018)
USA
Production: Anarchos Productions, Georgeville Television, Javelin Productions, Motion Picture Capital, Studio JMS, Unpronounceable Productions
Executive Producers: Leon Clarance, Tara Duncan, Peter Friedlander, Cindy Holland, J. Michael Straczynski, Lana Wachowski, Lilly Wachowski, Grant Hill, Deepak Nayar, Marc Rosen, John Toll
Producers: Alex Boden, Marcus Loges, L. Dean Jones Jr., Roberto Malerba, Terry Needham
Distribution: Netflix
Directors: Lana Wachowski, Lilly Wachowski, James McTeigue, Tom Tykwer, Dan Glass
Writers: J. Michael Straczynski, Lana Wachowski, Lilly Wachowski
Editors: Joseph Jett Sally, Joe Hobeck, Fiona Colbeck
Cinematography: John Toll
Music: Johnny Klimek, Tom Tykwer
Art Direction: Stephan O. Gessler, Thorsten Klein, Jami Primmer, Peter Walpole, Chris Cleek, Damien Drew, Eggert Ketilsson, Tim Black, Nanci Noblett, Jessie Haddad, Dominic Hyman, Stephanie Rass
Production Design: Hugh Bateup
Principal Cast: Terrence Mann (Mr. Whispers), Doona Bae (Sun Bak), Jamie Clayton (Nomi Marks), Tina Desai (Kala Dandekar), Tuppence Middleton (Riley Blue), Max Riemelt (Wolfgang Bogdanow), Miguel Ángel Silvestre (Lito Rodriguez), Brian J. Smith (Will Gorski), Freema Agyeman (Amanita Caplan), Daryl Hannah (Angelica Turing)
Format: Digital, color
60 min.

What follows includes works cited in the text as well as sources that proved essential to my argument, even if not cited directly. Scripts, storyboards, models, and other original archival materials accessed at Ravenswood Kinowerks in Chicago, Illinois, are cited in the endnotes and do not appear here.

"5 Questions à . . . David Mitchell, l'auteur de 'Cloud Atlas'!" *Allociné*, 6 March 2013. http://www.allocine.fr/article/fichearticle_gen_carticle=18622230 .html.

"20th Anniversary San Francisco International Lesbian & Gay Film Festival Program Guide (1996)." *issuu*, 28 August 2012. http://issuu.com/frameline/ docs/20th-sanfrancisco-international-lgbt-film-festival.

Aaron, Michelle. "Pass/Fail." *Screen* 42.1 (2001): 92–96.

Abrams, Simon. "Starship Wachowski: The Cloud Atlas Team Dares You to Leave Your Pod." *Village Voice*, 24 October 2012.

Ahmed, Sara. *Queer Phenomenology: Orientations, Objects, Others.* Durham, NC: Duke University Press, 2006.

Aizura, Aren, and Susan Stryker, eds. *The Transgender Studies Reader 2.* London: Routledge, 2013.

Alter, Ethan. "V *for Vendetta." Film Journal* 109.4 (2006): 3.

Amin, Kadji. "Temporality." *TSQ: Transgender Studies Quarterly* 1.1–2 (2014): 219–22.

Baccolini, Rafaella. "Utopia in Dystopia: *Cloud Atlas." Utopia Anniversary Symposium, Science Fiction Film and Television* 9.1 (2016): 73–76.

Bahng, Aimee. "Queering *The Matrix*: Hacking the Digital Divide and Slashing into the Future." *The Matrix in Theory.* Edited by Myriam Diocaretz and Stefan Herbrechter. Amsterdam: Rodopi, 2006. 167–92.

Bailey, Moya, micha cárdenas, Laura Horak, Lokeilani Kaimana, Cáel M. Keegan, Genevieve Newman, Roxanne Samer, and Raffi Sarkissian. "*Sense8* Roundtable." *Spectator* 37.2 (2017): 74–88.

Baim, Tracy. "Second Wachowski Filmmaker Sibling Comes Out as Trans." *Windy City Times*, 8 March 2016. http://www.windycitymediagroup.com/lgbt/Second-Wachowski-filmmaker-sibling-comes-out-as-trans-/54509.html.

Barker, Jennifer M. *The Tactile Eye: Touch and the Cinematic Experience*. Berkeley: University of California Press, 2009.

Baudrillard, Jean. *Simulacra and Simulation*. Translated by Sheila Faria Glaser. Ann Arbor: University of Michigan Press, 1994.

Beckham, Karen. "The Tortoise, the Hare, and the Constitutive Outsiders: Reframing Fast and Slow Cinemas." *Cinema Journal* 55.2 (2016): 125–30.

Benjamin, Walter. "The Work of Art in the Age of Mechanical Reproduction." *Modern Art and Modernism: A Critical Anthology*. Edited by Francis Frascina and Charles Harrison. London: Sage Publications, 1982. 217–20.

Berenstein, Rhona J. "Where the Girls Are: Riding the New Wave of Lesbian Feature Films." *GLQ* 3.1 (1996): 125–37.

Bhabha, Homi K. *The Location of Culture*. London: Routledge, 2004.

Bird, James, and Maxim Fleury. "*Jupiter Ascending*: Constructing Large Scale Environments." ACM Siggraph 2015 (conference proceedings, no. 4), 9 August 2014. http://dl.acm.org/citation.cfm?id=2792579&CFID=949596202&CFTOKEN=86270137.

Blas, Zach, and micha cárdenas. *The Transreal: Political Aesthetics of Crossing Realities*. New York: Atropos Press, 2012.

Blazer, Alex E. "*The Matrix* Trilogy and the Revolutionary Drive through the Desert of the Real." *Literature/Film Quarterly* 35.4 (2007): 265–73.

Boucher, Michel J. "'You Look Very Authentic': Transgender Representation and the Politics of the 'Real' in Contemporary United States Culture." Dissertation. University of Massachusetts Amherst, 2010.

Brinkema, Eugenie. *The Forms of the Affects*. Durham, NC: Duke University Press, 2014.

Brown, Michael P. *Closet Space: Geographies of Metaphor from the Closet to the Globe*. New York: Routledge, 2000.

Brubaker, Rogers. *Trans: Gender and Race in an Age of Unsettled Identities*. Princeton, NJ: Princeton University Press, 2016.

Bukatman, Scott. *Terminal Identity: The Virtual Subject in Postmodern Science Fiction*. Durham, NC: Duke University Press, 1993.

Bulloch, Douglas. "V is For Vendetta: P is for Power: A Film Reading of V for Vendetta." *Millennium: Journal of International Studies* 35.2 (2007): 431–34.

Butler, Judith. *Excitable Speech: A Politics of the Performative*. London: Routledge, 1997.

———. "Imitation and Gender Insubordination." *The Lesbian and Gay Studies Reader*. Edited by Henry Abelove, Michèle Aina Barale, and David M. Halperin. London: Routledge, 1993. 307–320.

Califia, Patrick. *Sex Changes: The Politics of Transgenderism*. San Francisco: Cleis Press, 1997.

Call, Lewis. "A is for Anarchy, V is for Vendetta: Images of Guy Fawkes and the Creation of Postmodern Anarchism." *Anarchist Studies* 16.2 (2008): 154–72.

cárdenas, micha. "Shifting Futures: Digital Trans of Color Praxis." *Ada: A Journal of Gender, New Media, and Technology* 6 (January 2015).

Carrington, André M. *Speculative Blackness: The Future of Race in Science Fiction*. Minneapolis: University of Minnesota Press, 2016.

Carter, Julian. "Embracing Transition, or Dancing in the Folds of Time." Aizura and Stryker, 130–43.

Césaire, Aimé. *Discourse on Colonialism*. New York: Monthly Review Press, 2000.

Chen, Mel. *Animacies: Biopolitics, Racial Mattering, and Queer Affect*. Durham, NC: Duke University Press, 2012.

Chu, Andrea Long. "The Wrong Wrong Body: Notes on Trans Phenomenology." *TSQ: Transgender Studies Quarterly* 4.1 (2017): 141–52.

Clover, Carol J. *Men, Women, and Chainsaws: Gender in the Modern Horror Film*. Princeton, NJ: Princeton University Press, 1992.

Clover, Joshua. *The Matrix*. London: British Film Institute, 2004.

Colombe, Audrey. "White Hollywood's New Black Boogeyman." *Jump Cut: A Review of Contemporary Media* 45 (Fall 2002). https://www.ejumpcut.org/archive/jc45.2002/colombe.

Constable, Catherine. *Adapting Philosophy: Jean Baudrillard and the Matrix Trilogy*. Manchester: Manchester University Press, 2009.

———. "Baudrillardian Revolutions: Repetition and Radical Intervention in *The Matrix* Trilogy." Gillis, 151–61.

Cranny-Francis, Anne. "Moving *The Matrix*: Kinesic Excess and Post-Industrial Being." Gillis, 101–113.

Crawford, Lucas. *Transgender Architectonics: The Shape of Change in Modernist Space*. New York: Routledge, 2016.

Cromwell, Jason. *Transmen and FTMs: Identities, Bodies, Genders, and Sexualities*. Urbana: University of Illinois Press, 1999.

Dargis, Manhola. "Mila Kunis's Dizzying Orbit in *Jupiter Ascending*." *New York Times*, 5 February 2015. https://www.nytimes.com/2015/02/06/movies/mila-kuniss-dizzying-orbit-in-jupiter-ascending.html?_r=0.

Debruge, Peter. "Review: *Cloud Atlas*." *Variety*, 8 September 2012.

De Lauretis, Theresa. "Sexual Indifference and Lesbian Representation." *Theatre Journal* 40.2 (1988): 155–77.

———. *Technologies of Gender: Essays on Theory, Film, and Fiction*. Bloomington: Indiana University Press, 1987.

Doane, Mary Ann. "Film and the Masquerade: Theorising the Female Spectator." *Screen* 23.3–4 (1982): 74–88.

"DP/30: Cloud Atlas, Screenwriter/Directors Lana Wachowski, Tom Tykwer, Lilly Wachowski." *YouTube*, uploaded by DP/30 The Oral History of Hollywood, 13 October 2012. http://www.youtube.com/watch?v=3MXR4MCuAoo.

Dyer, Richard. *The Culture of Queers*. London: Routledge, 2001.

Ellison, Treva, Kai M. Green, Matt Richardson, and C. Riley Snorton. "We Got Issues: Toward a Black Trans/Studies." *Transgender Studies Quarterly* 4.2 (2017): 162–69.

Emig, Ranier. "Sexing *The Matrix*: Gender and Sexuality in/as Cyberfiction." *The Matrix in Theory*. Edited by Myriam Diocaretz and Stefan Herbrechter. Amsterdam: Rodopi, 2006. 193–208.

"Enter the Matrix," *Nintendo Power* 170 (July 2003): 142.

"Equality Illinois 2014 Gala—Lana Wachowski Accepts Freedom Award." *YouTube*, uploaded by eqilgala1, 21 February 2014. http://www.youtube.com/watch?v=xpqeXgPEo3Q.

Eve, Martin Paul. "'You have to keep track of your changes': The Version Variants and Publishing History of David Mitchell's *Cloud Atlas*." *Open Library of Humanities* 2.2 (2016): 1–34.

Failes, Ian. "Shoot and Stitch: Making *Jupiter Ascending's* Chicago Chase." *FXGuide*, 9 February 2015.

Fay, Jennifer, and Justus Nieland. *Film Noir: Hard-Boiled Modernity and the Cultures of Globalization*. London: Routledge, 2010.

Feinberg, Leslie. *Trans Liberation: Beyond Pink or Blue*. Boston: Beacon Press, 1998.

Felperin, Leslie. "*V for Vendetta*." *Daily Variety* 290.32, 14 February 2006.

Feng, Peter X. "False and Double Consciousness: Race, Virtual Reality, and the Assimilation of Hong Kong Action Cinema in *The Matrix*." *Aliens R Us: The Other in Science Fiction Cinema*. Edited by Sean Cubitt and Ziauddin Sardar. London: Pluto Press, 2002. 149–63.

Fisher, Mark. *Capitalist Realism: Is There No Alternative?* Washington, DC: Zero Books, 2009.

Flood, Alison. "*Cloud Atlas* Astonishingly Different in US and UK Editions, Study Finds." *The Guardian*, 10 August 2016. https://www.theguardian.com/books/2016/aug/10/cloud-atlas-astonishingly-different-in-us-and-uk-editions-study-finds.

Foucault, Michel. *The History of Sexuality*, vol. 1. New York: Vintage Books, 1978.

Fournier, Matt. "Lines of Flight." *TSQ: Transgender Studies Quarterly* 1.1–2 (2014): 121–22.

Freeland, Cynthia. "Penetrating Keanu: New Holes but the Same Old Shit." *The Matrix and Philosophy: Welcome to the Desert of the Real*. Edited by William Irwin. Chicago: Open Court, 2002. 205–215.

Freeman, Elizabeth. *Time Binds: Queer Temporalities, Queer Histories*. Durham, NC: Duke University Press, 2010.

Friedman, Michael D. "Shakespeare and the Catholic Revenger: *V for Vendetta*." *Literature/Film Quarterly* 38.2 (2010): 117–33.

Fukuyama, Francis. *The End of History and the Last Man*. New York: Avon Books, 1992.

Garret, Diane. "Roles All Over the Map in This *Atlas*." *Variety*, 17 November 2012.

Geller, Theresa L. "Queerying Hollywood's Tough Chick: The Subversions of Sex, Race, and Nation in *The Long Kiss Goodnight* and *The Matrix*." *Frontiers: A Journal of Women Studies* 25.3 (2004): 8–34.

Gillis, Stacy, ed. *The Matrix Trilogy: Cyberpunk Reloaded*. London: Wallflower Press, 2005.

———. Introduction. Gillis, 1–22.

Gunning, Tom. "The Cinema of Attraction: Early Film, Its Spectator and the Avant-Garde." *Wide Angle* 8.3–4 (1986): 63–70.

———. "What's the Point of an Index? Or, Faking Photographs." *Nordicom Review* 25.1–2 (2004): 39–49.

Halberstam, Judith. "Automating Gender: Postmodern Feminism in the Age of the Intelligent Machine." *Feminist Studies* 17.3 (1991): 439–60.

———. *In a Queer Time and Place: Transgender Bodies, Subcultural Lives*. New York: New York University Press, 2005.

———. *Skin Shows: Gothic Horror and the Technology of Monsters*. Durham, NC: Duke University Press, 1995.

Halley, Janet. *Split Decisions: How and Why to Take a Break from Feminism*. Princeton, NJ: Princeton University Press, 2006.

Hanson, Ellis. Introduction to *Out Takes: Essays on Queer Theory and Film*. Edited by Ellis Hanson. Durham, NC: Duke University Press, 1999. 1–19.

Harry Benjamin International Gender Dysphoria Association. "Standards of Care for Gender Identity Disorders," 6th version (February 2001). http://www.cpath.ca/wp-content/uploads/2009/12/WPATHsocv6.pdf.

Hartman, Saidiya V. *Scenes of Subjection: Terror, Slavery, and Self-Making in Nineteenth-Century America*. Oxford: Oxford University Press, 1997.

Harvey, David. *The Condition of Postmodernity: An Enquiry into the Origins of Cultural Change*. Oxford: Basil Blackwell, 1989.

Haslam, Jason. *Gender, Race, and American Science Fiction: Reflections on Fantastic Identities*. London: Routledge, 2015.

Hassler-Forest, Dan. *Science Fiction, Fantasy, and Politics: Transmedia World-Building beyond Capitalism*. Lanham, MD: Rowman and Littlefield, 2016.

Hayward, Eva, and Jami Weinstein. "Introduction: Tranimalities in the Age of Trans° Life." *TSQ: Transgender Studies Quarterly* 2.2 (2015): 195–208.

Hemon, Aleksandar. "Beyond the Matrix: The Wachowskis Travel to Even More Mind-Bending Realms." *New Yorker*, 10 September 2012. http://www.newyorker.com/magazine/2012/09/10/beyond-the-matrix.

Hill, Logan. "The Influences and Techniques behind the 'Poptimistic Photo-Anime' of *Speed Racer*." *New York Magazine*, 21 April 2008.

Hoad, Phil. "*Cloud Atlas*: How Hollywood Failed to Put It on the Map." *The Guardian*, 20 February 2013. https://www.theguardian.com/film/filmblog/2013/feb/20/cloud-atlas-warner-bros.

Hobson, Janell. *Body as Evidence: Mediating Race, Globalizing Gender*. Albany: SUNY Press, 2012.

Horak, Laura. *Girls Will Be Boys: Cross-Dressed Women, Lesbians, and American Cinema*. New Brunswick, NJ: Rutgers University Press, 2016.

———. "Trans Studies." *Feminist Media Histories* 4.2 (2018). 201–206.

Horton-Stallings, LaMonda. *Funk the Erotic: Transaesthetics and Black Sexual Cultures*. Urbana: University of Illinois Press, 2015.

Hughey, Matthew W. "Cinethetic Racism: White Redemption and Black Stereotypes in 'Magical Negro' Films." *Social Problems* 56 (2009): 543–77.

Hulk, Film Crit. "Film Crit Hulk Smash: *Speed Racer* as Artist." *Birth.Movies.Death*, 27 March 2015. http://birthmoviesdeath.com/2015/03/27/film-crit-hulk-smash-speed-racer-as-artist.

———. "Hulk's Favorite Movies: *Speed Racer*." *Birth.Movies.Death*, 20 November 2013. http://birthmoviesdeath.com/2013/11/20/hulks-favorite-movies-speed-racer-2008.

Huston, Shawn. "Fascism and the Text: Alan Moore, the Wachowskis, and *V for Vendetta*." *Popmatters*, 26 March 2006. http://www.popmatters.com/feature/060526-vforvendetta.

Hyman, Nick. "15 Movies the Critics Got Wrong." *Metacritic*, 14 June 2010. http://www.metacritic.com/feature/15-movies-the-critics-got-wrong.

Idato, Michael. "Netflix Officially Goes Global as Non-US Subscriptions Take Platform Majority." *Sydney Morning Herald*, 19 July 2017. https://www.smh.com.au/entertainment/tv-and-radio/netflix-officially-goes-global-as-nonus-subscriptions-take-platform-majority-20170719-gxdy2h.html.

"In Movie Experience." *The Ultimate Matrix Collection*. Warner Bros., 2008. DVD.

Jackson, John L., Jr. *Real Black: Adventures in Racial Sincerity*. Chicago: University of Chicago Press, 2005.

Jenkins, Henry. *Convergence Culture: Where Old and New Media Collide*. New York: New York University Press, 2004.

———. *Spreadable Media: Creating Value and Meaning in a Networked Culture*. New York: New York University Press, 2013.

Jones, Kaylin. "Netflix Cancels Two Beautifully Diverse Shows, and We're Not Happy about It." *Vox*, 7 June 2017. http://www.voxmagazine.com/arts/tv/netflix-cancels-two-beautifully-diverse-shows-and-we-re-not/article_c9316eee-4bb9-11e7-9ec1-73c316fc45b9.html.

Kalin, Tom, Derek Jarman, Isaac Julien, Pratibha Parmar, B. Ruby Rich, and Amy Taubin. "New Queer Cinema." *Sight and Sound; London* 2.5 (1992): 30–39.

Kaulingfreks, Ruud, and Femke Kaulingfreks. "In Praise of Anti-Capitalist Consumption: How the *V for Vendetta* Mask Blows Up Hollywood Marketing." *Ephemera: Theory and Politics in Organization* 13.2 (2013): 453–57.

Keegan, Cáel M. "Moving Bodies: Sympathetic Migrations in Transgender Narrativity." *Genders* 57 (Spring 2013). http://www.colorado.edu/genders

archive1998-2013/2013/06/01/moving-bodies-sympathetic-migrations-trans
gender-narrativity.

———. "Revisitation: A Trans Phenomenology of the Media Image." *Medie-Kultur* 61 (Fall 2016): 26–41.

———. "Tongues without Bodies: The Wachowskis' *Sense8*." *TSQ: Transgender Studies Quarterly* 3.3–4 (2016): 605–610.

Keeling, Kara. "Looking for M—: Queer Temporality, Black Political Possibility, and Poetry from the Future." *GLQ* 15.4 (2009): 565–82.

———. "Queer OS." *Cinema Journal* 53.2 (2014): 152–57.

———. *The Witch's Flight: The Cinematic, the Black Femme, and the Image of Common Sense*. Durham, NC: Duke University Press, 2007.

Keller, James R. *V for Vendetta as Cultural Pastiche: A Critical Study of the Graphic Novel and Film*. Jefferson, NC: McFarland, 2008.

Kessler, Kelly. "Bound Together." *Film Quarterly* 56.4 (2003): 13–22.

Kessler, Sarah. "Eleven TV Shows Professors Are Watching This Summer." *Public Books*, 19 June 2017. http://www.publicbooks.org/11-tv-shows-colleagues
-watching-summer.

King, Richard C., and David J. Leonard. "Racing the Matrix: Variations on White Supremacy in Responses to the Film Trilogy." *Cultural Studies ↔ Critical Methodologies* 6.3 (2006): 354–69.

Knepper, Wendy. "Toward a Theory of Experimental World Epic: David Mitchell's *Cloud Atlas*." *Ariel* 47.1–2 (2016): 93–126.

Krishna, Rachael. "Inside the Totally Insane and Sort of Effective Fan Campaign to Bring Back *Sense8*." *BuzzFeed*, 29 June 2017. https://www.buzzfeed.com/
krishrach/how-fans-brought-sense-8-back.

Lachenal, Jessica. "*Wonder Woman* First Live-Action Film with Female Director to Receive $100 Million Budget." *The Mary Sue*, 25 May 2016.

"Lana Wachowski Receives the HRC Visibility Award." *YouTube*, uploaded by Human Rights Campaign, 24 October 2012. http://www.youtube.com/
watch?v=crHHycz7T_c.

Lawrence, Matt. *Like a Splinter in Your Mind: The Philosophy behind the Matrix Trilogy*. Malden, MA: Wiley-Blackwell, 2004.

Lessard, John. "*A Sense of the World: Sense8*, Transmedia Storytelling, and the Erotics of Distraction." 24th Annual Interdisciplinary German Studies Conference, Focus in Distraction. February 2016, UC Berkeley, Berkeley, California.

Leung, Helen Hok-Sze. "Trans on Screen." *Transgender China*. Edited by Howard Chiang. New York: Palgrave Macmillan, 2012. 183–98.

Levesley, David. "Here's the Best Queer Scene in *Sense8*." *Slate*, 22 June 2017. http://
www.slate.com/blogs/outward/2015/06/22/in_sense8_netflix_has_created_a
_queer_masterpiece.html.

Lewis, Thomas, Fari Amini, and Richard Lannon. *A General Theory of Love*. New York: Random House, 2000.

Li, Sijia. "Netflix by Netflix: On 'Sense8.'" *Los Angeles Review of Books*, 16 May 2017. https://lareviewofbooks.org/article/netflix-by-netflix-on-sense8.

Liddle, Henry George, and Robert Scott. *An Intermediate Greek-English Lexicon*. Oxford: Oxford University Press, 2002.

Light, Claire. "*Sense8* and the Failure of Global Imagination." *The Nerds of Color*, 10 June 2015. http://thenerdsofcolor.org/2015/06/10/sense8-and-the -failure-of-global-imagination.

"Lilly Wachowski and Lana Wachowski." *YouTube*, uploaded by DePaul Visiting Artists Series, 2 May 2014. http://www.youtube.com/watch?v=ARoKJoocEZ8.

"Lilly Wachowski Shares Her Serendipitous Coming Out Story | GLAAD Media Awards 2016." *YouTube*, uploaded by Logo, 3 April 2016. http://www.youtube .com/watch?v=bHBq_PF7va4.

Longino, Bob. "Movie Talk: Does *Speed Racer* Have Enough Velocity?" *Atlanta Journal-Constitution*, 6 May 2008.

Lothian, Alexis. "*Sense8* and Utopian Connectivity." Utopia Anniversary Symposium, *Science Fiction Film and Television* 9.1 (2016): 93–95.

Lyall, Sarah. "From the Wachowski Brothers, an Ingénue Who Blows Up Parliament." *New York Times*, 19 June 2005. http://www.nytimes.com/2005/06/19/ movies/from-the-wachowski-brothers-an-ingenue-who-blows-up-parliament .html.

"Making the Matrix." *The Ultimate Matrix Collection*. Warner Bros., 2008. DVD.

Manovich, Lev. *Software Takes Command*. New York: Bloomsbury Academic, 2013.

Marks, Laura U. *The Skin of the Film: Intercultural Cinema, Embodiment, and the Senses*. Durham, NC: Duke University Press, 2000.

———. *Touch: Sensuous Theory and Multisensory Media*. Minneapolis: University of Minnesota Press, 2002.

Martin, Kevin H. "Jacking into the Matrix." *Cinefex* 79 (October 1999): 66–89.

Massumi, Brian. *Parables for the Virtual: Movement, Affect, Sensation*. Durham, NC: Duke University Press, 2002.

The Matrix Trilogy: A Bibliography of Materials in the UC Berkeley Library. Media Resources Center, Moffitt Library, UC Berkeley, 20 June 2012. http:// www.lib.berkeley.edu/MRC/matrix.html.

McCarthy, Todd. "*Speed Racer*." *Variety*, 2 May 2008.

McDowell, John C. *The Politics of Big Fantasy: Ideologies of Star Wars, The Matrix, and Avengers*. Jefferson, NC: McFarland, 2014.

McGrath, Charles. "Bending Time, Bending Minds: *Cloud Atlas* as Rendered by Tom Tykwer and the Wachowskis." *New York Times*, 9 October 2012. http://www.nytimes.com/2012/10/14/movies/cloud-atlas-as-rendered-by-tom -tykwer-and-the-wachowskis.html.

McWeeny, Drew. "An Epic Interview with the Wachowskis and Tom Tykwer: From *Cloud Atlas* to *Jupiter Ascending*." *Hitfix*, 10 October 2012. http://

uproxx.com/hitfix/an-epic-interview-with-the-wachowskis-and-tom-tykwer
-from-cloud-atlas-to-jupiter-ascending.

———. "*Jupiter Ascending* Directors Wachowskis on 9/11 and Modern Blockbuster Culture." *Hitfix*, 5 February 2015.

———. "Our Wachowskis Interview Continues on Blockbuster Culture and
9/11." *Hitfix*, 5 February 2015.

———. "Part One of a Major Interview with the Wachowskis—'Jupiter Ascending' Secrets." *Hitfix*, 4 February 2015. http://uproxx.com/hitfix/part-one-of
-a-major-interview-with-the-wachowskis-jupiter-ascending-secrets.

Miller, Lucy J. "Fear and the Cisgender Audience: Transgender Representation
and Audience Identification in *Sleepaway Camp*." *Spectator* 37.2 (2017): 40–47.

Mills, Brett. "What Does It Mean to Call Television 'Cinematic'?" *Television
Aesthetics and Style*. Edited by Jason Jacobs and Steven Peacock. New York:
Bloomsbury Academic, 2013. 57–66.

Mitchell, David. "Translating *Cloud Atlas* into the Language of Film." *Wall
Street Journal*, 19 October 2012. https://www.wsj.com/articles/SB10000872
396390443675404578060870111158076.

Mittell, Jason. *Complex TV: The Poetics of Contemporary Television Storytelling*.
New York: New York University Press, 2015.

———. "The Qualities of Complexity: Vast versus Dense Seriality in Contemporary Television." *Television Aesthetics and Style*. Edited by Jason Jacobs
and Steven Peacock. New York: Bloomsbury Academic, 2013. 45–56.

Moore, Alan, and David Lloyd. "Behind the Painted Smile." *V for Vendetta*.
New York: Vertigo/DC Comics, 2005. 267–78.

Morris, Jan. *Conundrum*. New York: Harcourt Brace Jovanovich, 1974.

Mulvey, Laura. "Afterthoughts on 'Visual Pleasure and Narrative Cinema' In-
spired by Duel in the Sun." *Film Theory: Critical Concepts in Media and
Cultural Studies*, vol. 3. Edited by Philip Simpson, Andrew Utterson, and K.
J. Shepherdson. London: Routledge, 2004. 68–77.

———. *Visual and Other Pleasures*. New York: Palgrave Macmillan, 2009.

Muñoz, José Esteban. *Cruising Utopia: The Then and There of Queer Futurity*.
New York: New York University Press, 2009.

———. *Disidentifications: Queers of Color and the Performance of Politics*.
Minneapolis: University of Minnesota Press, 1999.

Musto, Michael. "*Cloud Atlas* under Attack from Asian Group." *Village Voice*,
26 October 2012.

Nakamura, Lisa. *Cybertypes: Race, Ethnicity, and Identity on the Internet*.
London: Routledge, 2002.

———. "Race in the Construct, or the Construction of Race: New Media and
Old Identities in *The Matrix*." *Domain Errors! Cyberfeminist Practices*. Ed-
ited by Maria Fernandez, Faith Wilding, and Michelle M. Wright. New York:
Autonomedia, 2003. 63–78.

Nama, Adilifu. *Black Space: Imagining Race in Science Fiction Film*. Austin: University of Texas Press, 2008.

Ndalianis, Angela. "The Frenzy of the Visible: Spectacle and Motion in the Era of the Digital." *Senses of Cinema* 3, February 2000. http://sensesofcinema .com/2000/feature-articles/matrix-2.

Newitz, Annalee. "10 Reasons Why *Speed Racer* Is an Unsung Masterpiece." *io9*, 24 October 2012. http://io9.gizmodo.com/5954595/10-reasons-why-speed -racer-is-an-unsung-masterpiece.

Nishime, LeiLani. "*The Matrix* Trilogy, Keanu Reeves, and Multiraciality at the End of Time." *Mixed Race Hollywood*. Edited by Mary Beltrán and Camilla Fojas. New York: New York University Press, 2008. 290–312.

———. "Whitewashing Yellow Futures in *Ex Machina, Cloud Atlas*, and *Advantageous*: Gender, Labor, and Technology in Sci-fi Film." *Journal of Asian American Studies* 20.1 (2017): 29–49.

Noble, Jean. "Lesbian Desires: Bound and Invested." *CineAction* 45 (February 1998): 30–40.

North, Dan. "Virtual Actors, Spectacle and Special Effects: Kung Fu Meets 'All that CGI Bullshit.'" Gillis, 48–61.

Nyong'o, Tavia. *The Amalgamation Waltz: Race, Performance, and the Ruses of Memory*. Minneapolis: University of Minnesota Press, 2009.

O'Hara, Mary Emily. "*Matrix* Director Lana Wachowski on Trump and the 'Power of a Crisis.'" *NBCNews.com*, 21 April 2017. http://www.nbcnews.com/ feature/nbc-out/matrix-director-lana-wachowski-trump-power-crisis-n749476.

Oliver, Kelly, and Benigno Trigo. *Noir Anxiety*. Minneapolis: University of Minnesota Press, 2002.

"Open Letter to *Hypatia*." 2 May 2017. Retrieved from *GoogleDocs*. https:// docs.google.com/forms/d/1efp9CoMHch_6KfgtlmoPZ76nirWtcEsqWHcvg idl2mU/viewform?ts=59066d20&edit_requested=true.

O'Riordan, Kate. "Changing Cyberspaces: Dystopia and Technological Excess." *The Matrix Trilogy: Cyberpunk Reloaded*. Gillis, 138–50.

Ott, Brian L. "The Visceral Politics of *V for Vendetta*: On Political Affect in Cinema." *Critical Studies in Media and Communication* 27 (2010): 39–54.

Palmer, Dexter. "*Speed Racer*: Misunderstood Art Film?" *Tor.com*, 31 March 2010.

Park, Jane Chi Hyun. "Virtual Race: The Racially Ambiguous Action Hero in *Pitch Black* and *The Matrix*." *Mixed Race Hollywood*. Edited by Mary Beltrán and Camilla Fojas. New York: New York University Press, 2008. 182–202.

———. *Yellow Future: Oriental Style in Hollywood Cinema*. Minneapolis: University of Minnesota Press, 2010.

Peberdy, Donna. "Narrative Trans-actions: *Cloud Atlas* (2012) and Multi-Role Performance in the Global Ensemble." *Transnational Cinemas* 5.2 (2014): 167–80.

Petri, Alexandra. "Why Are You Not Watching *Jupiter Ascending* Right Now?" *Washington Post*, 5 March 2015. http://www.washingtonpost.com/blogs/

compost/wp/2015/03/05/why-are-you-not-watching-jupiter-ascending-right
-now/?utm_term=.6af78c639105.

Phillips, John. *Transgender on Screen*. New York: Palgrave Macmillan, 2006.

Prosser, Jay. *Second Skins: The Body Narratives of Transsexuality*. New York: Columbia University Press, 1998.

Puar, Jasbir. "Bodies with New Organs: Becoming Trans, Becoming Disabled." *Social Text* 33.3 (2015): 45–73.

Rai, Amit S. "Race Racing: Four Theses on Race and Intensity." *Women's Studies Quarterly* 40.1–2 (2012): 64–75.

Rawson, K. J., and Cristan Williams. "Transgender°: The Rhetorical Landscape of a Term." *Present Tense* 3.2 (2014): 1–9.

Raymond, Janice. *The Transsexual Empire: The Making of the She-Male*. Boston: Beacon Press, 1979.

Rehak, Bob. "The Migration of Forms: Bullet Time as Microgenre." *Film Criticism* 32.1 (2007): 26–48.

Rich, B. Ruby. *New Queer Cinema: The Director's Cut*. Durham, NC: Duke University Press, 2013.

Richmond, Scott C. *Cinema's Bodily Illusions: Flying, Floating, and Hallucinating*. Minneapolis: University of Minnesota Press, 2016.

Rogin, Michael. *Blackface, White Noise: Jewish Immigrants in the Hollywood Melting Pot*. Berkeley: University of California Press, 1996.

Rose, Steve. "Lilly Wachowski: Putting Gender on the Agenda in Life and Film." *The Guardian*, 11 March 2016. https://www.theguardian.com/film/2016/mar/11/lilly-wachowski-profile-gender-sense8-matrix.

Rothman, Joshua. "Sympathetic Sci-Fi." *New Yorker*, 14 July 2015. http://www.newyorker.com/culture/cultural-comment/sympathetic-sci-fi.

Russ, Joanna. *To Write Like a Woman: Essays in Feminism and Science Fiction*. Bloomington: Indiana University Press, 1995.

Ryan, Maureen. "A Troubling Trend in Cancellations: Are Inclusive Shows in Danger?" *Variety*, 1 June 2017. http://variety.com/2017/tv/opinion/canceled-shows-2017-sense8-get-down-underground-sweet-vicious-1202450885.

Salamon, Gayle. *Assuming a Body: Transgender and Rhetorics of Materiality*. New York: Columbia University Press, 2010.

Sears, Clare. "All That Glitters: Trans-ing California's Gold Rush Migration." *GLQ* 14.2–3 (2008): 383–402.

Sedgwick, Eve Kosofky. *Epistemology of the Closet*. 2nd ed. Berkeley: University of California Press, 2008.

Serano, Julia. *Whipping Girl: A Transsexual Woman on Sexism and the Scapegoating of Femininity*. Berkeley, CA: Seal Press, 2016.

Sharpe, Christina. *In the Wake: On Blackness and Being*. Durham, NC: Duke University Press, 2016.

———. *Monstrous Intimacies: Making Post-Slavery Subjects*. Durham, NC: Duke University Press, 2010.

Shaviro, Steven. *The Cinematic Body*. Minneapolis: University of Minnesota Press, 1993.

———. *No Speed Limit: Three Essays on Accelerationism*. Minneapolis: University of Minnesota Press, 2015.

Shaw, Deborah. "Sense8 and Sensibility: How a TV Series Is Transcending Geographical and Gender Borders." *The Conversation*, 25 May 2017. http://theconversation.com/sense8-and-sensibility-how-a-tv-series-is-transcending-geographical-and-gender-borders-77377.

Shimizu, Celine Parreñas. *The Hypersexuality of Race: Performing Asian/American Women on Screen and Scene*. Durham, NC: Duke University Press, 2007.

Silberman, Steve. "Matrix2." *Wired*, 1 May 2003.

Simpkins, Rebekah. "Visualizing Jean Baudrillard's *Simulacra and Simulation* through *The Matrix*." *Notes on Contemporary Literature* 30.4 (2000): 6–9.

simpkins, reese. "Temporal Flesh, Material Becomings." *Somatechnics* 7.1 (2017): 124–41.

Snorton, C. Riley. *Black on Both Sides: A Racial History of Trans Identity*. Minneapolis: University of Minnesota Press, 2017.

Snorton, C. Riley, and Jin Haritaworn. "Trans Necropolitics: A Transnational Reflection on Violence, Death, and the Trans of Color Afterlife." Aizura and Stryker, 66–76.

Sobchak, Vivian. *The Address of the Eye: A Phenomenology of Film Experience*. Princeton, NJ: Princeton University Press, 1991.

———. *Meta-Morphing: Visual Transformation and the Culture of Quick Change*. Minneapolis: University of Minnesota Press, 2000.

Spade, Dean. "Mutilating Gender." Stryker and Whittle, 315–32.

———. *Normal Life: Administrative Violence, Critical Trans Politics, and the Limits of Law*. Durham, NC: Duke University Press, 2015.

Steinbock, Eliza. "Shimmering Images: Trans Cinema, Embodiment, and the Aesthetics of Change." Unpublished manuscript.

———. "Speaking Transsexuality in the Cinematic Tongue." *Somatechnics: Queering the Technologisation of Bodies*. Edited by Samantha Murray and Nikki Sullivan. Farnham, MD: Ashgate Publishing, 2009. 127–52.

———. "Towards Trans Cinema." *The Routledge Companion to Cinema and Gender*. Edited by Kristin Lené Hole, Dijana Jelača, E. Ann Kaplan, and Patrice Petro. New York: Routledge Press, 2017. 395–406.

———. "The Violence of the Cut: Transgender Homeopathy and Cinematic Aesthetics." *Violence and Agency: Queer and Feminist Perspectives* (Gewalt und Handlungsmacht: queer_feministiche Perspektiven). Edited by Gender Initiativkolleg Wein. Frankfurt: Campus Publications, 2012. 154–71.

Steinmetz, Katy. "The Transgender Tipping Point." *Time*, 29 May 2014.

Stone, Alluquère Roseanne. *The War of Desire and Technology at the Close of the Mechanical Age*. Cambridge: MIT Press, 1995.

Stone, Sandy. "The *Empire* Strikes Back: A Posttranssexual Manifesto"(1992). Stryker and Whittle, 221–35.

Straayer, Chris. *Deviant Eyes, Deviant Bodies*. New York: Columbia University Press, 1996.

———. "*Femme Fatale* or Lesbian Femme: *Bound* in Sexual Différance." *Women in Film Noir*, 2nd ed. Edited by E. Ann Kaplan. London: British Film Institute, 1998. 153–61.

Straube, Wibke. "Trans Cinema and Its Exit Scapes: A Transfeminist Reading of Utopian Sensibility and Gender Dissidence in Contemporary Film." Dissertation. Linköping University, 2014.

Stryker, Susan. "Caitlyn Jenner and Rachel Dolezal: Identification, Embodiment, and Bodily Transformation." *AHA Today*, 13 July 2015.

———. "(De)Subjugated Knowledges: An Introduction to Transgender Studies." Stryker and Whittle, 1–17.

———. Foreword. *Out of the Ordinary: A Life of Gender and Spiritual Transitions*. Edited by Jacob Lau and Cameron Partridge. New York: Fordham University Press, 2017. vii-x.

———. "My Words to Victor Frankenstein above the Village of Chamounix." *GLQ* 1.1 (1994): 237–54.

———. *Transgender History*. Berkeley CA: Seal Press, 2008.

———. "Transsexuality: The Postmodern Body and/as Technology." *The Cybercultures Reader*. Edited by David Bell and Barbara M. Kennedy. London: Routledge Press, 2000. 588–97.

Stryker, Susan, Paisley Currah, and Lisa Jean Moore. "Trans, Trans-, or Transgender?" *Women's Studies Quarterly* 36.3–4 (2008): 11–22.

Stryker, Susan, and Monica Nolan. "Christine in the Cutting Room: A Multimodal Way of Interacting Differently with Queer Media." *YouTube*, uploaded by Confluencenter for Creative Inquiry, 28 January 2013. http://www.youtube.com/watch?v=erNy3Mh41gQ.

Stryker, Susan, and Stephen Whittle. *The Transgender Studies Reader*. London: Routledge, 2006.

Sullivan, Nikki. "Somatechnics." *TSQ: Transgender Studies Quarterly* 1.1–2 (2014): 187–90.

Swale, Alistair D. *Anime Aesthetics: Japanese Animation and the "Post-Cinematic" Imagination*. New York: Palgrave Macmillan, 2015.

Tourjee, Diana. "The Real Red Pill: What Men Still Don't Get about *The Matrix* and *Sense8*." *Broadly*, 6 June 2017. http://broadly.vice.com/en_us/article/7xpbgg/the-real-red-pill-what-men-still-get-wrong-about-the-matrix-and-sense8.

Traub, Valerie. "The Ambiguities of 'Lesbian' Viewing Pleasure: The (Dis)Articulations of *Black Widow*." *Out in Culture: Gay, Lesbian, and Queer Essays on Popular Culture*. Edited by Corey K. Creekmur and Alexander Doty. Durham, NC: Duke University Press, 1995. 115–36.

Turnock, Julie. *Plastic Reality: Special Effects, Technology, and the Emergence of 1970s Blockbuster Aesthetics*. New York: Columbia University Press, 2015.

Tuvel, Rebecca. "In Defense of Transracialism." *Hypatia* 32.2 (2017): 263–78.

Vaid, Urvashi. *Virtual Equality: The Mainstreaming of Gay and Lesbian Liberation*. New York: Anchor Books, 1995.

Valentine, David. *Imagining Transgender: An Ethnography of a Category*. Durham, NC: Duke University Press, 2007.

VanDerWerff, Todd. "I Watched Netflix's *Sense8* and I Don't Know If It's a Travesty or a Whacked-Out Masterpiece." *Vox*, 10 June 2015. https://www.vox.com/2015/6/10/8756283/sense8-review-netflix.

Vary, Adam B. "The Wachowskis Refuse to Take No for an Answer." *BuzzFeed*, 5 February 2015. http://www.buzzfeed.com/adambvary/the-wachowskis-jupiter-ascending-the-matrix-cloud-atlas?utm_term=.ieoG1m8KR#.ow4PLwkop.

Virilio, Paul. *The Art of the Motor*. Minneapolis: University of Minnesota, 1995.

Wachowski, Lana. "Closets." *Clive Barker's Hellraiser* Book 9. New York: Epic Comics, 1991.

Wachowski, Lana, and Lilly Wachowski. "An Introduction from the Wachowski Brothers." *The Ultimate Matrix Collection*, 2008.

———. Audio Commentary. *Bound*. Dino De Laurentiis Company, 1997. Laserdisc. Deluxe Widescreen Edition.

———. "Bits and Pieces of Information." *The Matrix Comics*, vol. 1. Edited by Lana and Lilly Wachowski. Brooklyn: Burlyman Entertainment, 2003. 5–16.

Wade, Chris. "*Speed Racer*, the Wachowskis' Masterpiece." *Slate*, 25 October 2012. http://www.slate.com/blogs/browbeat/2012/10/25/speed_racer_the_wachowskis_ masterpiece_is_underrated.html.

Waites, Rose. "*V for Vendetta* Masks: Who's Behind Them?" *BBC*, 20 October 2011. http://www.bbc.com/news/magazine-15359735.

Wallace, Lee. "Continuous Sex: The Editing of Homosexuality in *Bound* and *Rope*." *Screen* 41.4 (2000): 369–87.

Warner, Michael. *The Trouble with Normal: Sex, Politics, and the Ethics of Queer Life*. Cambridge: Harvard University Press, 1999.

Wegner, Philip E. "Romantic and Dialectical Utopianism in *Cloud Atlas*." Utopia Anniversary Symposium, *Science Fiction Film and Television* 9.1 (2016): 114–18.

Weintraub, Steve. "The Wachowskis Talk *Jupiter Ascending*, Creating the Chicago Sequence, *Sense8*, and More." *Collider*, 4 February 2015.

Weiss, Andrea. *Vampires and Violets: Lesbians in Film*. New York: Penguin Books, 1993.

Whilk, Nat, and Jason Whitehead. "Glory Bound: An Interview with Larry and Andy Wachowski." *Gadfly Online*, January 1998. http://www.gadflyonline.com/home/archive-wachowski.html.

Whissel, Kristen. *Spectacular Digital Effects: CGI and Contemporary Cinema*. Durham, NC: Duke University Press, 2014.

White, Patricia. *Uninvited: Classical Hollywood Cinema and Lesbian Represent-ability*. Bloomington: Indiana University Press, 1999.

Williams, Tony. "Assessing *V for Vendetta*." *CineAction* 70 (2006): 17–23.

Woerner, Meredith. "How the Wachowskis Tried to Shoot 'The Most Beautiful Chase Ever Filmed'." *io9*, 4 February 2015. http://io9.gizmodo.com/how-the -wachowskis-imagined-the-most-beautiful-chase-e-1683796063.

Wood, Aylish. "Vectorial Dynamics: Transtextuality and Complexity in *The Ma-trix*." Gillis, 11–22.

Xiao, An. "Celebrating Intersectionality in the Futuristic Netflix Series 'Sense8.'" *Hyperallergic*, 20 February 2017. http://hyperallergic.com/349182/celebrating -intersectionality-in-the-futuristic-netflix-series-sense8.

Žižek, Slavoj. "The Matrix: Or, The Two Sides of Perversion." *The Matrix and Philosophy: Welcome to the Desert of the Real*. Edited by William Irwin. Chicago: Open Court, 2002. 240–66.

———. *Welcome to the Desert of the Real: Five Essays on September and Related Dates*. London: Verso, 2002.

aesthetics, 59, 102; anarchist, 66, 68; black, 45; cinematic and televisual, 128–29n80; cubist, 79; dissent and, 47, 75–76; miscegenated, 50; postracial, 91; queer, 13; of sensuality, 135; serial graphic, 66–67; trans°, 13, 17, 24, 27, 39, 49, 82, 113, 116, 127n65; transsexual, 36–37, 74, 123n37; utopian, 81
affect: bullet time and, 43; cinema and, 3–4; dissent and, 75–76, 96; gender identity and, 129n81; of greed, 88; injury and, 82; networked, 108, 111; others and, 12; queer desire and, 73; sincerity and, 78; of space opera, 100; speed and, 81–83, 87; time and, 7; trans°, 3–4, 6, 15–17, 19, 34, 104, 113–15; transmisogynistic, 52; vertigo as, 103
agency, 61–62, 134, 136, 151–52
alienation, 40–41, 62, 74, 80, 83–85, 104
Animatrix, The (2003), 48–55
Anonymous, 66
Assassins (1995), 8, 120n13
assault, 76, 144

Baccolini, Rafaella, 127n68
Baudrillard, Jean, 37, 57, 65, 125n49
biopolitics, 30, 57–58, 60
Bound (1996), 7–23, 26, 30–31, 120–21nn14–20, 121n23, 121–22nn25–26, 132–34, 138–39, 150–52
Boys Don't Cry (1999), 24–26
Bright, Susie, 8, 10
Brubaker, Rogers, 127n70
bullet time, 26, 31, 42–44, 59, 62, 124n40

Call, Lewis, 126n57
capitalism: cannibalism and, 96; commodification of time, 103; imagination and, 37; neoliberal, 65, 128n76; racial, 89–90, 92–94, 99; speed and, 84; temporality, 81; verticality of, 105. See also Jupiter Ascending (2015)
Chung, Peter, 54
cinema: "cinematic reality," 3–6, 26, 42–44, 59, 76, 79–80, 102, 109, 119n6; digital, 27–28, 122n31; gender and, 6, 34; phenomenology and, 3; as "social art," 67; subjunctivity of, 137; televisual media and, 128–29n80; temporality of, 4 (see also bullet time); transsexuality and, 27, 71–72; voyeurism and, 71. See also New Queer Cinema; transgender, cinema
cissexism, 25, 97
closet, 12–14, 16, 120n17
Cloud Atlas (2012), 52, 87–100, 139, 145–46, 148
common sense, 3, 6, 47–48, 75–76, 108, 113, 119n5
Constable, Catherine, 125n49
control, 10, 14, 19, 30, 57, 65, 67, 81, 142, 151

Daly, Mary, 128n74
dissent, 45, 47–48, 65, 68–69, 72–76, 90, 93–94, 96, 118
Dolezal, Rachel, 91
dystopia, 29, 67–68, 89, 94, 106

English: as universal language, 116–17, 129n83

Enter the Matrix (2003), 48, 124n43

false consciousness, 31, 67, 77, 94
Fawkes, Guy, 66–67, 73–74
Film Crit Hulk, 78
Fournier, Matt, 121n24

gaze: cissexist, 25; lesbian spectatorship, 16–17; male, 16, 121n21; transgender look, 19, 24–25
gender: administrative violence and, 104; Asian Americans and, 121n25; binary, 119n7; cinema as, 6; cisgender, 125n47; closet and, 13; cross-dressing, 127n69; cross-gender, 90–91; dysphoria, 13–14, 19, 25, 29, 33–35, 121n24, 122n28; identity, 114; Orientalism and, 96–97; passing, 123n34; post-gender, 38; sexual orientation and, 17. *See also* trans°; transgender
genre: counternarratives and, 138; fantasy, 2, 137; identity and, 134; as language, 136; noir, 8, 10, 12, 18–19, 54, 138, 151 (see also *Bound*); science-fiction, 2–3, 137, 147; trans as, 3
governmentality, 58, 63

Halberstam, J. Jack, 25, 122n28, 128n74
Hayward, Eva, 104
heteronormativity, 13, 72, 136–39
Horak, Laura, 127n69

identity: biopolitics and, 30, 57; closet and, 16; desire and, 18; gender, 55, 70, 104, 114, 118–19n3; genre and construction of, 134; as guise, 48–49; heroic, 56; identical, 61; identity wars, 11; LGBQ, 11–12; narrative and, 137; perception and, 139; politics, 58; provisionality of, 140, 148; relativity of, 24; sex and, 152; sexual orientation and gender, 17; sovereign, 56–57; transgender, 6, 13, 26, 29–30, 111, 139; transracial, 91; transsexual, 3, 82; whiteness and, 20, 91
ideology: capitalist, 77–78; dissent and, 69; violence of, 96; white supremacist, 93

Jenkins, Henry, 125n
Jenner, Caitlyn, 91
Jupiter Ascending (2015), 100–106, 138, 147–48

Kaimana, Lokeilani, 129n81
Kawajiri, Yoshiaki, 53
Keeling, Kara, 119n5, 119n6, 120n11
Koike, Takeshi, 54

labor: alienated, 80; commodification of, 37, 62; feminized, 95, 103–4, 128n72; heterosexual, 13–14
Leung, Helen Hok-sze, 120n10
lesbian, 9; sex, 150; spectatorship theory, 16–17. *See also Bound* (1996)
limbic resonance, 112, 129n82
lines of flight, 20, 121n24. *See also* trans°, phenomenology

Matrix, The (1999), 7, 23–50, 57, 60, 122n27, 122–23nn33–35, 123–24n39, 125n45, 138, 143
Matrix Reloaded, The (2003), 30, 55–65, 125n48, 138
Matrix Revolutions, The (2003), 55–65, 125n48, 138
McGrath, Charles, 127n67
McTeigue, James, 65, 67–68, 74–75
Media Action Network for Asian Americans, 91–92
Mills, Brett, 128–29n80
Mitchell, David, 88, 90, 145
modernity, 6, 38, 74, 85, 89–90, 93, 98, 103, 111–12
Moore, Alan, 66–69, 74–75
morph, 26, 59, 62, 125n53
Morris, Jan, 97
Mulvey, Laura, 121n21
Muñoz, José Esteban, 121n22

Nakazawa, Kazuto, 54
New Queer Cinema, 8, 25, 133–34, 138
Nishime, LeiLani, 128n72
Noble, Jean, 120n16

Orientalism, 96–97
Orlando Pulse massacre, 1–2, 118n1

Phillips, John, 119n9

postmodernity, 23–24, 27, 29, 34, 50, 55, 66, 68, 136

proprioception, 36, 44, 75–77, 103, 111, 113

Prosser, Jay, 2–3

queer: aesthetics, 13; auditory effect, 69; *Bound* and/as, 8–11, 145, 150; dissent, 73; experience, 136; film studies, 25, 133–34 (*see also* New Queer Cinema); genderqueer, 41; identity, 24; illegibility of, 121n25; kinship, 106, 110; lesbian erotics, 17–19; oppression, 14; *Sense8* and, 108–10; space, 112, 135; as speculative, 137; theory, 12, 142; trans° and, 9–11, 13; transgender and, 118n3; utopia, 22, 72

race: Asian, 84–85, 91–92; Asian-ness, 85, 92, 97; Asian women, 95, 97, 128n72 (see also *Cloud Atlas*; labor, feminized); blackness, 23, 37–42, 46–47, 52, 54, 82, 84, 89, 91–93, 98–99; cross-race, 90–91, 99, 115; fixity of, 85; hybridity, 40–43, 63, 90–91, 99; passing and, 90–91; post/racial, 38–40, 46, 58, 61, 65, 88–90, 94, 99, 111, 113–14; postracial, 38–41, 56–58, 65, 82–85, 87, 90–91, 95, 99, 111, 113; race war, 37; trans° and, 41; in Wachowskis' cinema, 37–38; whiteface, 42; whiteness, 19–21, 23, 32–33, 37, 40–41, 62, 82, 84–85, 87, 90–93, 97–98, 105, 116, 136

racialization, 21, 38, 83–85, 87, 93

Rai, Amit S., 84

Raymond, Janice, 91, 127n64

realism, 28, 101, 111, 144–45

red pill, 29, 32–35, 48–49, 53, 55, 124n42

redpill, 47–50, 56, 62, 65, 74–75. *See also* dissent

revisitation, 5

Rich, B. Ruby, 8

Russ, Joanna, 118n2

Samer, Roxanne, 118n2

Sedgwick, Eve Kosofsky, 142

Sense8 (2015–2018), 106–18, 128–29n80, 131–32, 139, 148–50

sensuality, 58, 135–36, 149

sex, 149–52

Simpkins, Rebekah, 65

Sobchak, Vivian, 125n53

social media, 108

somatechnics, 80, 84, 126n61

sovereignty, 137–38, 151

special effects, 30, 58–59, 128–29n80. *See also* bullet time

Speed Racer (2008), 76–87, 126n59, 143, 149

Stone, Sandy, 3–4, 114, 127n65

Stonewall, 23

Straayer, Chris, 121n26

Straczynski, J. Michael, 108

Stryker, Susan, 4, 26–27, 33, 124–25n44, 127n70

subjunctive, 2–4, 6, 20, 108, 111, 118

Sullivan, Nikki, 126n61

Swale, Alistair D., 126n59

temporality: analog, 40; capitalist, 62, 85, 93, 103; carceral, 60, 63; chrononormativity, 63; cinematic, 4, 13, 26, 146; of the closet, 13–14; colonial, 38, 85, 111; cubist, 79; digital, 26; disjunctive, 42–43; dysphoric, 64, 86; ecstatic time, 111; juxtaposed, 102; looped, 62–63; ludic, 81; mirror and, 36–37; modernity and, 90, 112; patriarchal time, 15; race and, 82–85, 87, 92, 99; serial, 100; speed, 80 (see also *Speed Racer*); of the state, 74; temporal drag, 73, 83; trans°, 3–4, 40, 63, 72, 79–81, 83, 90, 98; white, 20, 87; "yellow future," 94. *See also* bullet time

terrorist drag, 73

Thatcher, Margaret, 67, 128n76

Tourjee, Diana, 124n42

trans°, 118–19n3: aesthetics, 6, 13, 17, 25–28, 32, 34–36, 39, 44–45, 49–50, 73, 82, 85, 87, 90, 92, 98, 110, 113, 116, 127n65; affect, 16–17, 34; as anti-hierarchy, 104–6; asterisk, 5; awareness, 112–13; biopolitical assimilation and, 58; body, 27, 63–65, 81–82, 92–93;

trans° (*continued*): cinema studies, 119–20n9; cyborg phenomenologies and, 55; as deconstructive, 24, 123n38, 127n70; as event, 118; feminism, 23; as "futurist force," 79–80; historical consciousness, 99; ideation, 4, 17, 22, 28, 92; as intra/intersubjective, 110, 113; lesbian film theory and, 16–17; as paratactic, 3, 113; phenomenology, 7, 44, 110, 118–19n3, 121n24; race and, 38–39, 41–42, 45–46, 84, 89, 91–92, 113, 116, 127n70; sensorium, 24, 34, 37, 47, 60, 110, 113; transition and, 114, 119n7; as transversal, 105; utopianism, 98, 111; virality, 70–71
transgender, 118–19n3; cinema, 3–7, 28, 119n9; cultural production, 5, 9, 24, 49; digital technologies and, 26–27, 32; feminism and, 127n64; narratology, 30; Orientalism and, 96–97; phenomenology, 2–5, 44–45, 47; race and, 90–91; "red pill" and, 33–34; representation, 5–6, 25, 110, 119n9, 138; sensing, 6; "transgender look," 19, 25; transgender studies, 3–4, 124–25n44, 127n65; transition, 4, 13–14, 29, 33–34, 36, 44, 53, 55, 86, 91, 96–97, 119n7, 122n30; transmisogyny, 52–53, 125n46; transracial and, 123n38
transmedia, 23, 48–50, 66, 125n45. See also *The Matrix* (1999)
transpecies, 104
transracial, 91, 123n38, 127n70
transreal, 27, 32, 44, 49–50, 53–54, 59, 81
transsexual, 2, 26, 28, 82, 118–19n3: aesthetics, 36–37, 74, 114, 123n37; body, 4, 27, 62, 82–83, 87; feminism and, 127n64; medical model, 3, 54; mirror scene, 35–36, 70, 123n36; Orientalism and, 96; racialized, 82; representation, 27, 71–73; temporality and, 86–87; transition and, 4, 26; *V for Vendetta* and, 68–74, 126n57
Tuvel, Rebecca, 123n38
Tykwer, Tom, 87–88, 111

utopia: aesthetics, 81; in *Cloud Atlas*, 88–90, 92, 94, 98–99; desire, 16, 19, 72;

dissent and, 65, 67; as horizon, 105–106, 111; lesbian, queer, trans° and, 11–12, 19–20, 22–23; multicultural, 24; popular art and, 59; post/racial, 113; optimism and, 2, 152; in *Sense8*, 111, 113, 118; speculation and, 102; trans°, 15, 98

vertigo, 103
V for Vendetta (2005), 65–76, 126n55, 126n57

Wachowski, Lana: on aesthetics, 76, 79, 135; on art, 134–37, 141, 143–44; on *Bound*, 8, 15–16, 120nn14–15, 121n19, 132–34, 138–39, 151–52; on bullet time, 43, 124n41; on categorization, 126n62; on cinematic cuts, 78; on *Cloud Atlas*, 145–46, 148; coming out, 5, 9; Epic Comics, 16, 66; on genre, 136, 138; on ideas and affect, 44; influence of comics on, 43, 66–67; on in/visibility, 127–28n71; on *Jupiter Ascending*, 147–48; on love as empathy, 141; on materiality of knowledge, 28; on *The Matrix* (trilogy), 24, 125n52, 152; on mirrors, 123n36; on originality, 122n32; on post-9/11 entertainment, 125n50; on queer cinema, 136, 138; on queerness, 134–36; on relationship to cinema, 139–40, 143–44; on relationship to gender, 139; on science fiction and fantasy, 2, 137; on sex, 149–52; on *Sense8*, 107, 131–32, 148–49; on sociopolitical science fiction, 147; on sovereignty, 137–38, 151; on structures of power, 142; on survival and imagination, 144; on time, 102; on Wilde, 135
Wachowski, Lilly, 5, 7, 15–16, 24, 119n7
Wachowski Brothers, The, 8–9
Wallace, Lee, 121–22n26
Watanabe, Shinichiro, 54
Weinstein, Jami, 104
Whissel, Kristen, 122n31
Wilde, Oscar, 135
Williams, Tony, 126n58
Wizard of Oz (1939), 64, 77–78

Žižek, Slavoj, 122n27

Cáel M. Keegan is an assistant professor of women, gender, and sexuality studies and liberal studies at Grand Valley State University.

Books in the series Contemporary
Film Directors

Nelson Pereira dos Santos
  Darlene J. Sadlier

Abbas Kiarostami
  Mehrnaz Saeed-Vafa and Jonathan
  Rosenbaum

Joel and Ethan Coen
  R. Barton Palmer

Claire Denis
  Judith Mayne

Wong Kar-wai
  Peter Brunette

Edward Yang
  John Anderson

Pedro Almodóvar
  Marvin D'Lugo

Chris Marker
  Nora Alter

Abel Ferrara
  Nicole Brenez, translated by
  Adrian Martin

Jane Campion
  Kathleen McHugh

Jim Jarmusch
  Juan Suárez

Roman Polanski
  James Morrison

Manoel de Oliveira
  John Randal Johnson

Neil Jordan
  Maria Pramaggiore

Paul Schrader
  George Kouvaros

Jean-Pierre Jeunet
  Elizabeth Ezra

Terrence Malick
  Lloyd Michaels

Sally Potter
  Catherine Fowler

Atom Egoyan
  Emma Wilson

Albert Maysles
  Joe McElhaney

Jerry Lewis
  Chris Fujiwara

Jean-Pierre and Luc Dardenne
  Joseph Mai

Michael Haneke
  Peter Brunette

Alejandro González Iñárritu
  Celestino Deleyto and Maria del
  Mar Azcona

Lars von Trier
  Linda Badley

Hal Hartley
  Mark L. Berrettini

François Ozon
  Thibaut Schilt

Steven Soderbergh
  Aaron Baker

Mike Leigh
  Sean O'Sullivan

D.A. Pennebaker
  Keith Beattie

Jacques Rivette
  Mary M. Wiles

Kim Ki-duk
  Hye Seung Chung

Philip Kaufman
  Annette Insdorf

Richard Linklater
David T. Johnson

David Lynch
Justus Nieland

John Sayles
David R. Shumway

Dario Argento
L. Andrew Cooper

Todd Haynes
Rob White

Christian Petzold
Jaimey Fisher

Spike Lee
Todd McGowan

Terence Davies
Michael Koresky

Francis Ford Coppola
Jeff Menne

Emir Kusturica
Giorgio Bertellini

Agnès Varda
Kelley Conway

John Lasseter
Richard Neupert

Paul Thomas Anderson
George Toles

Cristi Puiu
Monica Filimon

Wes Anderson
Donna Kornhaber

Jan Švankmajer
Keith Leslie Johnson

Kelly Reichardt
Katherine Fusco and Nicole Seymour

Michael Bay
Lutz Koepnick

Abbas Kiarostami, Expanded Second Edition
Mehrnaz Saeed-Vafa and Jonathan Rosenbaum

Lana and Lilly Wachowski
Cáel M. Keegan

107 549

The University of Illinois Press
is a founding member of the
Association of American University Presses.

University of Illinois Press
1325 South Oak Street
Champaign, IL 61820-6903
www.press.uillinois.edu